Lucky in Love

52 Fabulous, Foolproof Strategies

for Every Week of the Year

SUSAN RABIN

WITH BARBARA LAGOWSKI

A PLUME BOOK

PLUME
Published by Penguin Group
Penguin Group (USA) Inc., 375 Hudson Street, New York, New York 10014, U.S.A.
Penguin Group (Canada), 90 Eglinton Avenue East, Suite 700,
Toronto, Ontario, Canada M4P 2Y3 (a division of Pearson Penguin Canada Inc.)
Penguin Books Ltd., 80 Strand, London WC2R 0RL, England
Penguin Ireland, 25 St. Stephen's Green, Dublin 2, Ireland (a division of Penguin
Books Ltd.)
Penguin Group (Australia), 250 Camberwell Road, Camberwell, Victoria 3124,
Australia (a division of Pearson Australia Group Pty. Ltd.)
Penguin Books India Pvt. Ltd., 11 Community Centre, Panchsheel Park,
New Delhi – 110 017, India
Penguin Books (NZ), cnr Airborne and Rosedale Roads,
Albany, Auckland 1310, New Zealand (a division of Pearson New Zealand Ltd.)
Penguin Books (South Africa) (Pty.) Ltd., 24 Sturdee Avenue, Rosebank,
Johannesburg 2196, South Africa

Penguin Books Ltd., Registered Offices: 80 Strand, London WC2R 0RL, England

First published by Plume, a member of Penguin Group (USA) Inc.

First Printing, November 2005
10 9 8 7 6 5 4 3 2 1

 REGISTERED TRADEMARK—MARCA REGISTRADA

LIBRARY OF CONGRESS CATALOGING-IN-PUBLICATION DATA
Rabin, Susan.
     Lucky in love : 52 fabulous, foolproof flirting strategies for every week of the
year / by Susan Rabin with Barbara Lagowski.
         p. cm.
     ISBN 0-452-28609-3 (pbk.)
     1. Flirting.   2. Man–woman relationships.   I. Lagowski, Barbara J.
II. Title.
     HQ801.R143 2005
     306.7—dc22   2005014954

Printed in the United States of America
Set in New Baskerville
Designed by Eve L. Kirch

PUBLISHER'S NOTE
The scanning, uploading, and distribution of this book via the Internet or via any
other means without the permission of the publisher is illegal and punishable by
law. Please purchase only authorized electronic editions, and do not participate in
or encourage electronic piracy of copyrighted materials. Your support of the author's rights is appreciated.

BOOKS ARE AVAILABLE AT QUANTITY DISCOUNTS WHEN USED TO PROMOTE PRODUCTS OR
SERVICES. FOR INFORMATION PLEASE WRITE TO PREMIUM MARKETING DIVISION, PENGUIN
GROUP (USA) INC., 375 HUDSON STREET, NEW YORK, NEW YORK 10014.

To my children, my family, and
close friends, may you always
feel my love.

I thank my loyal readers for all their insightful
stories, and wish everyone picking up this
book luck and love!

I especially wish readers unfamiliar with the "art of
flirting" to relish in the happiness and possibilities
flirting will bring into your life.

I hope you will all be

LUCKY IN LOVE.

Acknowledgments

I want to thank my readers, clients and School of Flirting attendees for sharing their flirting stories with me. It was gratifying to hear how much fun, spontaneity and success flirting has brought into their lives.

I want my family and friends to know how much they make me feel "Lucky in Love."

A special thanks to my daughter, Frannie, for her expertise, love and patience in skillfully organizing *Lucky in Love* on the computer.

Thanks to my editors, Julie Saltman and Hilary Redmon, for their skill, patience and hard work. It was very much appreciated, and it was a pleasure to work with them both. I want to thank Brant Janeway, once again, for all the expert and enduring publicity.

Thanks to the people who have supported me from the beginning of my flirting career: Rich Gosse, chairman of American Singles Education, Inc., the world's largest nonprofit singles organization and sponsor of my School of Flirting events. Also Frederic Bien, friend and founder of flirt.com. (Flirt.com and the School of Flirting were some of the first sites on the Internet. Flirt.com continues to be an exceptional singles site.) Dan Bender, friend, entrepreneur and troubleshooter for www.schoolofflirting.com.

And last, but not least, to the gentlemen in my life I have flirted with and who have flirted with me. Isn't it fun?!

Contents

Part Three. Approach

Part Four.   Action

Introduction

As she climbed the steps of the Museum of Natural History, Cynthia thought eagerly of the lecture on "The Role of Pair Bonding in Primitive Society," she was headed for, but perhaps even more eagerly about her real project for the evening: meeting Mr. Right. Since she'd read Susan Rabin's book on flirting, *101 Ways to Flirt*, she knew that *anyplace* could harbor flirting opportunities— dances, bars and singles parties were no longer her only options.

The auditorium was packed with like-minded people, which made it a perfect place to make a connection, but how would she know who was single? She watched for the signs of an eligible gentlemen: searching for a single seat—though, of course, that was no guarantee of his singledom—and not wearing a wedding ring.

She lingered at the entrance until the lights went dim, and then made her decision. A tall blond man with spectacles, dressed in a Harris Tweed suit, seemed like a good candidate. If she was wrong, there was always intermission. After all, there was no law against changing your seat or sidling up to some other gentleman in the lobby.

Cynthia's exquisitely carved African elephant necklace and bright-turquoise blouse were carefully selected to attract attention. But to improve her odds, she also carried a prop: *National Geographic.* Armed with her magazine, she edged down the aisle. She tripped getting into her seat, dropped her magazine, and when she brushed against the blond stranger's arm, he reached out a hand to steady her.

"Thank you so much," she said, smiling.

"Of course. Are you OK?"

"Yes, thanks. I shouldn't have been in such a rush." She gave him a small smile, indicating her awkwardness.

"You dropped your magazine," he said, handing it to her. "My favorite."

"What did you think about that volcano piece? I liked it, but why does it always seem as though . . ."

Just then the house lights went down.

"Later," she said.

"Later," he smiled.

I was really proud of Cynthia. What had she done? Not only had she chosen a fascinating place to flirt, she'd arrived ahead of time to case the joint, so to speak, and make a flirting plan. She plotted her moves with pleasure instead of desperation, and took fate into her own hands. She had a prop, and even took action, gently tripping in the hope that the handsome gentleman would notice. She smiled easily, made eye contact and nodded. Cynthia was polite, thanking him for his help. She made small talk and closed the encounter with a promised future meeting at intermission. Cynthia made it known that she wanted to get to know this special stranger. Some might call Cynthia manipulative; I call her smart. She wasn't always, but today Cynthia is a Master Flirt!

During intermission, Mr. Harris Tweed asked if he could buy Cynthia a drink. She followed him to the refreshment bar in the outer lobby, where conversation came easily. They had much in common beyond their shared interest in the magazine and lecture. Deftly asking open-ended questions, Cynthia had encouraged him to talk and had listened attentively.

Her skills were well honed. I don't know how their romance turned out, but I do know that Cynthia flirted with style. Would he be a new friend or a romantic partner? The answer doesn't matter, because the choice was now hers. Cynthia's newfound flirting skills gave her an opportunity that many never have.

I wrote this book to share with my readers the possibilities that flirting opens for all of us. Many of you have sent in your stories and I thank you for that. All the stories in this book are true (names have been changed, of course) and each illustrates a different flirting situation and style. These hints and lessons are guaranteed to help you become the best flirt you can be.

I have given you fifty-one stories to ponder and enjoy. *Fifty-one stories,* one for each week of the year, minus one. The fifty-second story is yours! I purposely left the last page free for you to write your own flirting story. I hope it will be a good one and that you will share it with me. Please e-mail your story to SRabin7128@aol.com and title it *Lucky in Love* so it will make it through the spam protector ☺. Or send it snail mail to PO Box 37, New York, NY 10128. Good Luck! Happy Flirting!

—Susan

Part One

Quiz

The Three Keys to Flirting Success

Contrary to what your mother may have told you, "flirt" is not a five-letter synonym for all those four-letter words that mean "tease." Flirting is a charming and honest expression of interest in another person—it is never manipulative or insincere. It is a skill that enables you to communicate your feelings and understand the signals others send your way. Most important, flirting is the art of interacting with others without serious intent, and that's what makes it so much fun.

But aren't the most successful flirts born, not made? Absolutely not! Since 1985, I have shown tens of thousands of single men and women how to make that all-important first move, how to turn that first move into a first date and how to use their untapped flirting skills to add all sorts of people—fascinating friends, casual companions, professional contacts and, yes, life-long lovers—to their date books and their lives. These men and women have adopted my belief that the secret to becoming "Lucky in Love" lies in attaining the right balance of Attitude, Approach and Action. A number of them have since taken themselves out of the singles' market completely.

Attitude without Approach will get you nowhere. And Action without Attitude is definitely in need of adjustment! Which of these three tenets is working for you? Which is working against you? The following short quiz will help you discover which As you've already earned and which of my strategies will help you most. Enjoy!

1. You are in a ski-lift line. You hear the lift operator yell, "Single? Is there a single in the line?" You look toward the load-

ing zone. The single in question, though swaddled in Gore-Tex, is definitely a member of the opposite sex. You

a. stay right where you are. Someone you know is sure to come *schussing* up soon. You can wait.
b. think it over. Is he cute? Does she/he look ready for love? Whoops. Too late. The chair is gone.
c. get on the chair, but sit quietly. Just because you're sharing space doesn't mean you have anything to talk about.

2. At a party, you strike up a conversation with a fabulous hottie. He/she seems to have no interest in you. You

a. must be dreaming. Strike up a conversation with a complete stranger? *You?* Not in this lifetime.
b. wonder how you will ever extract yourself from this awkward situation gracefully. Maybe if you stare at the guacamole stain on the carpet long enough she/he will get the hint and wander off.
c. tell him or her off. If this clown can't see that you're wonderful, who needs him/her?

3. You know you've met this intriguing person somewhere before, but you can't remember his/her name! You

a. ask a friend. If he/she knows you, you must have a mutual friend. Someone you know will fill in the details.
b. grab Mr./Ms. X's arm, look into his/her eyes and purr, "Don't I know you from somewhere? You seem so *familiar*."
c. do nothing. He/she was not interested enough to follow up the first time you met. Why would he/she be interested in you now?

4. The conversation you are having with a new acquaintance is starting to lag. You

a. tell a dirty joke. You know a million of them!

b. say nothing. It doesn't do much for the conversation but it sure beats saying the wrong thing!

c. excuse yourself. If this person can't think of anything to ask you about, how interested can he/she be?

5. You think flirting is

a. a nerve-racking experience. How do you ever know if you're doing or saying the right thing?

b. easy to do if you just tell people what they want to hear.

c. something you have to do if you ever want to get married or have sex.

6. It's 8:15 p.m. You've just left your method-acting class and you're ravenous! That attractive thespian you've been role-playing with looks like he/she could use a snack, too. You turn to this promising prospect and

a. whisk him or her into the closest romantic bistro. Why not sate two appetites at once?

b. invite that special someone and all the other after-class stragglers to the local greasy spoon. There's safety in numbers.

c. say good night. It's been a long class and you've all been doing animal studies so long, you want to hibernate. He/she is very cute, but probably wants to get some sleep.

7. You have just joined a new political organization and you are suddenly energized! The old, apathetic you has been replaced by a firebrand who lives, eats and breathes your beliefs. Naturally, when you meet a new person you

a. walk right up and suggest he or she join you at a meeting! This group changed your life! It could do the same for him/her.

b. expound on your opinions. What could be more rousing or attractive than someone who is active and involved?

    c. find out which side he/she is on. There will be no sleeping with the enemy as far as you're concerned.

8. At the organic farmers' market, you notice an attractive shopper squeezing the tomatoes. You also notice that he/she is not wearing a ring. You

    a. inform him/her that the best way to judge ripeness is by aroma. Maybe that will keep him/her from reducing the entire bin to pulp.

    b. smile, select a few ripe tomatoes and put them into his/her basket. Then wait for thanks.

    c. walk on by. If this person doesn't know anything about choosing produce, he or she will never fit into your healthy lifestyle.

SCORING:

A Matter of Approach

(Mostly As)

    If you chose the A answer most frequently, your approach may be keeping you from being the adventurous, accessible flirt you truly are! Whether your tendency is to come on too strong or not at all, you will find just the right strategies in the Approach section of this book. Stop waiting for opportunity—and that knockout!—to tap on your door. Reach out with the right approach and you'll make your own romantic luck!

Action and Reaction

(Mostly Bs)

    For every action there is an equal and opposite reaction. If you're not getting a reaction from the intriguing guys or gals you meet, and answered B most of the time, you may need to make some waves in the ocean of love. Flirting should be spontaneous! Stop planning and live in the moment! Not sure how to begin? Check out the no-fail conversation starters, nifty nonverbal techniques and easy action strategies in the Action section of this book. You'll soon be out of the doldrums and on your way to happiness!

Attitude Alignment

(Mostly Cs)

Negative thinking never leads to positive action! If you enter each new experience with a black cloud over your head, or if you tend to put yourself down before anyone else can do it for you, an attitude adjustment is in order. To change your luck, you need to change your mind! How? By using the hundreds of tips and techniques you'll find in the Attitude section of this book, you'll go from bashful to belle of the ball.

No matter what type of flirt you are, this book is sure to make you a more attractive, successful one. Based on the same techniques drawn from a lifetime flirting experience that have worked for thousands of my workshop graduates, *Lucky in Love is* a sourcebook of secrets you can use to attract anyone you want, anywhere you happen to be, every week of the year! Ready to get started? Go!

Part Two

Attitude

To Arrive at a Different Destination, Take a Different Route

Russ was like so many of the single men I see at my seminars. Ambitious and accomplished at thirty-something, he was trying hard to hang on to the playful side that had made him so popular in college. As Russ and I tried to figure out why such an active, interesting guy was having such a hard time meeting available women, I wondered whether he was getting out enough.

Russ was incredulous. "Are you kidding? I'm never home! In fact, let me give you a rundown of my typical week. Monday and Wednesday nights, I go to the gym. There's a spin class I like to take at the beginning of the week and then, on Wednesday, I do a strength class with a personal trainer."

I looked at Russ. He was obviously just getting warmed up. I was fatigued just listening to him.

"Every Tuesday night, I play 'Texas Hold 'Em' with a group of guys I've known since college. It's a traveling game so each week we meet at someone else's place. On Thursdays I like to catch up on any unfinished business lying around on my desk so I tend to work late. Then I grab some Thai takeout on the way home. On Friday, a group of us meet after work at an Irish pub near the office. We have a few beers, maybe watch a soccer game, eat some greasy corned beef and head home. And Saturday is date night. Or laundry! One way or the other, I clean up." Russ laughed heartily.

But was Russ "cleaning up" in the date department? Apparently not.

"To tell you the truth, Susan, I haven't had a date in six weeks," he confessed. "Why? I have no idea! I'm totally stumped!" Russ shrugged his shoulders. "You always say that I should make 'anyplace work for me,'" Russ summed up. "Well, I'm not just 'anyplace,' Susan—I'm nearly every place! And guess what? It's not working for me! So now what?"

It may be our traditional three-mile Sunday morning bike ride to the best bagel place in town. Perhaps it's the Tuesday pasta dinner with "the girls" we've dutifully penciled into every date book we've bought for the last three years. Maybe it's the time-honored, post–staff meeting gripe session and debriefing at the midtown wine bar, or the every-other-Friday book club meeting with "every-other" friend we have—in particular, those who can't make the pasta dinner. Whatever our routines and however we must shoehorn them into our tight schedules, they are still a comfort to us: a little oasis of predictability in a world that can seem erratic and off-kilter. But what do we give up when we opt for the humdrum? That's something many compulsively busy singles, like Russ, need to consider. Running from commitment to commitment may seem frenetic but, in fact, this kind of activity requires little of us. Old friends don't need to be impressed or entertained the way a date might. These social events may get you off the couch, but they aren't likely to add much to your flirting skills.

And there's more. Long-established routines give us somewhere to go even when there is nowhere to go. They also provide us with a group of people to keep us company while we wait for Mr./Ms. Right to appear. That's a good thing, right? Not necessarily! We may end up like Russ: busy bodies whose engagement calendars are bulging—yet who feel emotionally disengaged. Sure, that once-a-week poker game is a safe bet socially, but what are the odds of you finding yourself across the table from someone who could win your heart? And what about the gym? If you're gasping your way through spin class, trying to catch your next breath, are you likely to use that breath to make conversation with the woman sweating next to you? Would she want you to? Even a Friday night pub-crawl like Russ's is of limited value to a fledgling flirt. Of course, it's fun to hoist a few as a group, but a gang of people who work, play or hang together can seem impenetrable. It would take a very confident outsider to breach those borders.

Flirting is about making someone *else* feel comfortable in your presence. It's about being open and approachable—even if you think the person who has approached you is not your type. It is about setting off on a previously unexplored path to an unknown destination with somebody you don't yet know.

Unless we venture from the path, try a different route, plot a new course, can we really expect to arrive anywhere but at the same destination? Certainly not! That's why this week I am asking you to break your routine, to cast off the same-old-same-old and try two new things—or an old favorite activity two new ways—every single day. Why two? Because one can be too easy. I'm trying to get you to look outside the box for ideas, stimulation and, hopefully, companionship. Why not three? Because flirting—the fine art of noticing and being noticed by others—doesn't take effort, it takes awareness. Become aware of the ways your companions, your activities and your routines may be isolating you from potential friends and lovers. The smallest changes in your daily routine can make a world of difference.

Here are a few suggestions:

♡ *Dare to detour!* Whether you're walking the pooch, picking up the dry cleaning or moseying to work, don't take the path of least resistance! All this time you've gone the same old way. Where has it taken you other than to your destination?

There is likely a whole new world—populated by people whose faces you haven't memorized—just a block or two over. You'll still get where you're going and you may pick up a charming walking buddy en route.

♡ *Stop and smell the coffee.* New cafés, unexplored bookstores, funky coffee shops, overstuffed secondhand stores and no less than three pizzerias (one of them Portuguese) all claiming to be the best in the city: These are the delights that might await you in just a few blocks of unexplored turf. So what are you supposed to do about it? What any creative single would do! Stop! Savor! Put on your best smile and browse the wares. Who knows what surprises you'll bring home?

♡ *Make being the new guy work for you.* Now that you've gathered the courage to stop for lunch at Piotr's Pierogi Pagoda, what the heck should you order? Expanding into new territory can make you feel like a stranger in a strange land. Why not make it work for you? Wondering what Piotr's specialties are? Why not ask that dashing cossack in the takeout line? Where did that delicious woman get that flaky chocolate croissant? (Or was that a flaky woman and a . . . oh, never mind.) She'll certainly share her secret if you ask. People don't just "need people"—they need to feel needed! Ask for advice and you've opened the door to conversation. At the very least, you'll get a delicious snack. With practice, you'll get someone to share your table.

♡ *Break out of situations that isolate you.* Others relish chatting at the hot dog stand; you eat lunch at your desk. Some can't stand ankle-deep in grass without getting up an impromptu Frisbee game; when you head to the park, you park behind a book. We all need a little peace and quiet; some solitude keeps us sane. But too much alone time can keep you single! This week, focus on the habits that isolate you from the people around you. Make the changes you need to improve your approachability quotient. By the way, cars are rolling isolation chambers. Get out on the streets! Walk, ride a bike, Rollerblade . . . do anything that puts you in contact with something warmer and more animated than a Cordovan leather interior.

♡ *Stop overscheduling yourself!* The problem with schedules like Russ's is that they allow one to fill every available moment without allowing time to *be* available to the people who share the world with you. I suggest that you put a couple of nights with absolutely no agenda on your calendar. Ask yourself what you want to do rather than what you have to do. Force yourself out the door if you have to. Then just go with your whims. Drop into the new sculpture studio in the neighborhood and see what's going on in there. Wander into the local bar on "Open-Mike Poetry Night." Volunteer to walk dogs at the local animal shelter. Follow your interests and interesting people will materialize. That's one piece of flirting advice I've never seen fail.

Week 3

Fix Up Your Love Life

They care about you. They want you to be happy. And wouldn't you know it, they just happen to know somebody who, coincidentally, is the second cousin (once removed) of somebody else who—would you believe it?—is *just right for you!* Your friends, your coworkers, your foot reflexologist . . . clients who think you are just too good to be true . . . these are just a sampling of the people who consider it their mission not only to celebrate your happy commitment but to arrange it.

But should you let them? A man at one of my recent talks summed up his feelings about being fixed up this way: "A couple of weeks ago, I was getting ready for yet another blind date. I had already gooped my hair, polished my teeth and picked the green sweater over the blue one. I was looking in the mirror trying to decide whether to shave my goatee or assume that my date had no strong opinions about facial hair when it occurred to me: Why am I stressing over a total stranger? Why do I care whether someone I may or may not like likes my beard? Why do I find it necessary to rehearse my answers to entry-level questions? And most of all, why do I consider the people who do this to me my *friends?*"

Some people think about sitting across a table from a total stranger and say, "Why?" Freewheeling, open-minded, adventurous flirts say, "Why not?" No doubt about it, blind dates can be unnerving. Hearsay isn't admitted as legal evidence; but it's all you've got to go on when you're standing in a cocktail lounge doorway, searching for the anonymous companion who nevertheless seems "totally made for you." Then, of course, there's the question of interpretation. According to your pal, the woman you're looking for in the bar is "athletic." So how come she looks like she's been power-lifting doughnuts? As for the man your boss recommended as "well turned out," is it *you* or do his eyes seem to turn *in?* And do you dare show up unarmed when a date has been described as "worldly"?

No two ways about it, fix-ups can have their glitches. But, as smart flirts know, when it comes to finding love, it isn't always what you know but who you know that counts! Here's a case in point:

My friend Patti loved blind dates. How could that be? Hadn't she had any clunkers? "Absolutely!" Patti laughed. "But I love to meet new people. I always learn something new. It's fun. Besides, what can I say? I enjoy the company of men!"

When Patti wasn't mingling herself, she mixed and matched her friends like one-of-a-kind pieces of rare, thrift-shop china. One weekend, Patti decided to put her neighbor, Ellen, together with Stan, an old friend, and see what came of the pairing. She wasn't optimistic. Ellen was notoriously picky when it came to men. She had been widowed two years earlier and hadn't dated much since. Stan was the classic older man who had replaced his fifty-year-old wife with two twenty-fives. And that was just for starters. Stan rarely drove anywhere without a much younger woman in the passenger's seat of his Boxster. Patti doubted he and Ellen would hit it off, she was simply rounding out the male-to-female ratio at the dinner table. At least that's what she told Ellen and Stan.

Maybe it was the absence of pressure. Maybe it was a case of late-onset maturity. Whatever the reason, Stan was attracted to Ellen the minute she walked in the door.

"You're friend is a stunner," he whispered. "Is she smart, too?"

Patti assured him that Ellen had beauty *and* brains. Then she elbowed him gently in the ribs. "I thought you only went for young women?"

"Well maybe it is time to act my age," Stan said.

Over pâté and French bread, Stan discovered that Ellen was every bit as smart as advertised. But Ellen felt a little uncomfortable with Stan. In fact, she made an abrupt exit after the cordials. Stan was disappointed that she had left so early.

Later that evening, he shared his feelings with Patti. "I'm sorry Ellen had to go. I think I should have offered to walk her home."

Now Patti was excited! Stan not only liked Ellen, he liked her too much to let her go! She told Stan that Ellen lived right across the street and didn't need an escort.

"It would have been the gentlemanly thing to do," Stan insisted. "Do you think I could go over and apologize tomorrow morning?"

"I don't see why not," Patti urged.

The next morning, Stan went over to Ellen's—and Patti paced the porch wondering whether they were hitting it off. Ellen was not amused by Stan's romantic track record. He hardly seemed like the stand-up guy Ellen was looking for. Yet they chatted amiably for two hours that morning, and soon began dating exclusively.

Six months later, Stan has matured into an unabashed ro-

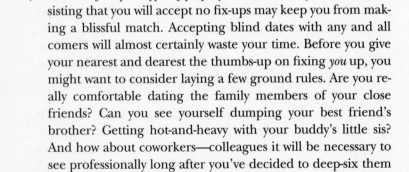

mantic. He celebrates his very grown-up romance every chance he gets. He constantly surprises Ellen with gifts large and small—chocolates . . . roses . . . a Volvo sedan roomy enough for both of them, to replace the Boxster. Though they feel no need to marry, they are planning a life together. Neither of them could be more surprised or delighted.

Some of us refuse to dabble in blind dates. Others welcome an opportunity to get out of the house and into the social swim. Is it possible you could benefit by resetting *your* attitude toward set-ups?

Think about it. If you wouldn't hesitate to hook up with an Internet match, why would you refuse to meet someone who has been handpicked by someone who knows you, who likes you and who can edit out those who don't share your values, your interests or your twisted sense of humor?

There are lots of fish in the sea. Some we catch. Others catch us by surprise. If our networking friends cast a wide net, why shouldn't we singles enjoy a part of the haul? And the process will be easier if you bear these important guidelines in mind:

♡ *Limit the fix-ups to types of people you would be comfortable with.* Insisting that you will accept no fix-ups may keep you from making a blissful match. Accepting blind dates with any and all comers will almost certainly waste your time. Before you give your nearest and dearest the thumbs-up on fixing *you* up, you might want to consider laying a few ground rules. Are you really comfortable dating the family members of your close friends? Can you see yourself dumping your best friend's brother? Getting hot-and-heavy with your buddy's little sis? And how about coworkers—colleagues it will be necessary to see professionally long after you've decided to deep-six them socially? Accepting fix-ups should broaden your horizons without complicating your life. Think about those you'd rather not see and make your feelings well known.

♡ *Ask for fix-ups from people who really do know you best.* Ask and you shall receive. Ask the intimates who know you inside and out, warts and all, and you might receive a fabulous encounter with Mr./Ms. Right! Need proof that networking works? Check this out: On the eve of his very amicable divorce, one man I know e-mailed an Internet postcard to all of his closest friends. The card featured a photo of him in tennis whites, standing on an empty court, holding two tennis rackets. On the bottom of the photo he had inserted this message: "I need a match!" Who was the first to set him up? His very gracious ex! The resulting relationship didn't last forever (you've got to watch those rebounds!) but he did find someone to play with for the next six months.

♡ *Don't obsess over what it's not—appreciate it for what it is!* You were looking for love but you've found a friend or a business contact or just a fun date instead? Lucky you! A good friend is hard to find! And isn't it possible that he or she might know someone who might be right for you?

♡ *Realize that certain fix-ups require your best behavior.* A questionable movie? A comedian whose rap is limited to four-letter words? Sex on the first date? Not when you're out with your office manager's niece or a dear friend's brother! Activities that stretch the limits of polite behavior may strain your friendship with the friend who brought you and your date together. There are very few casual acquaintances who justify the loss of a lifelong pal.

♡ *The match is not for you? Don't just "pass." Pass it on!* You flattened her toe while learning to Texas Two-Step; she managed to laugh it off. Sometimes the men and women we're fixed up with are truly wonderful people—they're just not right for *us*. In that case, why not share the wealth? If you've got a friend who might be a better match, introduce them! You never know when someone might return the favor.

Remember: Every fix-up is an opportunity to practice your flirting skills! So what if that monosyllabic hand model isn't date material? Don't wave him off! Hone your flirting skills on him and you'll be prepared for meeting someone who is.

Week 4

When It Isn't Love at First Sight . . . Take a Second Look

Tara disliked cats. Consequently, any friend's tabby would abandon a full bowl of food to leap into Tara's lap. She also hated blind dates. Needless to say, hers was the first name on any friend or coworker's lips when they were looking for "a sophisticated companion" for cousin Jarek from Prague, or "someone to fill out the table" when that too-good-to-be-true neighbor would be barbecuing his special ribs. ("Did we mention that he's single? Oh, we *did*? What do you know!")

Tara was thirty-one. She knew what types of men appealed to her. She was looking for a guy who appreciated art but who wasn't "artsy" and stuffy. She was looking for a guy who liked physical activity but wasn't a drill sergeant on the hiking trail. And most of all, she was looking for a man she could talk to who would talk back—not from his vocal chords but from his heart.

Esteban—the history professor Tara had been set up with by her friend Jen—had none of these qualities. Esteban peered at her from behind his dark-framed glasses as though she were a specimen, and said little. Even when Tara sat quietly, hoping that prolonged silence would draw out her reticent date, Esteban did not take the bait. He simply sat back in his chair, waiting for Tara to fill the void. This was not what she had had in mind at all. If she had wanted to talk to herself, she could do that without ever leaving her apartment.

The date, of course, was their last. Although Esteban suggested that they meet again at some upcoming event (Tara was not open to suggestion at this point), all Tara wanted to do was go home. She had no desire to set eyes on the man she called "the Nutty Professor" again.

But a week later Tara did see Esteban again. She was at a street fair in the Spanish neighborhood of her Florida hometown listening to a Latin jazz band when she caught a glimpse of her friend Jen salsa dancing with Esteban! They were terrible dancers but they were giggling and laughing like children. With four left feet between them, they couldn't hope to keep up with the music—but they were obviously in tune with each other.

Tara was shocked at the change in Esteban. She was also more than a bit annoyed. Who was this wild-and-crazy guy? And why had Esteban been such a stick-in-the-mud with her? Jen was blubberingly happy to share the details. Esteban was not much of a conversationalist. He didn't much like talking about himself. But he was a font of information about the history of Spanish-speaking people in America—and a wonderfully enthusiastic dancer! Although the dinner with Tara had been dull, Esteban had come vividly to life at the street fair. He wasn't just erudite . . . he was loads of fun!

And that's not all, Tara thought—Esteban happened to be just the kind of guy she had told Jen was looking for. Why hadn't she seen that when she had a chance?

Love at first sight is the cosmetically enhanced superstar in the emotional pantheon. It is showy; explosively, totally overblown; and it gets all the media. Think of the way it is portrayed: Two hapless people are miraculously drawn into each other's orbits. Their eyes meet. Their hearts open. Moments later, what has been lost is found. What was lacking or deficient is now magically complete. Bells ring, birds sing. These people will never be the same again.

Sometimes that really is the way things happen—like a bolt from the blue. Other times, you need to listen longer and more carefully to hear a nearly imperceptible "click."

Not long ago, I was watching a television show about couples who had been married for fifty years or longer. After a lifetime together, these men and women were holding hands and looking at each other as if they just met. But what did they have to say about that all-important first meeting? Their comments might surprise you as much as they did me:

"To tell you the truth, I didn't really like him when we first met."

"She was annoying. A kid. And she was always hanging around."

"He wasn't my type."

"I looked at her and I thought, 'Maybe if she'd stop talking, I'd like her better.'"

"I didn't hear any bells ringing. That's for sure!"

Clearly, just because bells aren't ringing, doesn't mean there isn't going to be a wedding. Immediate attraction truly is skin-deep. Sometimes it takes a second or even a third look to see all that is truly there. That was what my friend Claudia discovered when she finally connected with her husband-to-be, Ben.

Claudia met Ben on a cross-country airplane flight. It turned out that they had a lot in common. Claudia was engaged to be married—so was Ben. They worked for the same west-coast publishing company, though in different departments. They also both believed that their pleasant but casual acquaintance would end that day, at the baggage claim. They said good-bye and went their separate ways.

Weeks later, they bumped into each other in the halls of the building where they worked. They decided they would meet for coffee. At that meeting, Claudia filled Ben in on the changes that had taken place since their flight together. The wedding and all of the associated planning had put too much stress on her tenuous romance and she had broken her engagement. Her fiancé didn't seem to want the things she wanted. Most of all, his mother had turned into an interfering shrew. It was clear to her that this was the last exit before the highway to oblivion. She took it.

Ben's comments were mild; mostly, he just let Claudia vent. But before going back to work, he made sure to set a date to see her again—this time for lunch. That lunch turned into a series of meetings in which Ben and Claudia forged a real friendship. When at last Ben, too, broke off his engagement, the friendship burgeoned into romance. Their new liaison wasn't about weddings—it was about marriage. They remain blissfully happy today.

It gives us pause when we hear someone say, "I married my best friend." Romances come and go but our friends are truly there for us for better and for worse. Finding both passion and devotion in a single person can seem impossible until we take a closer look—not only at the men and women we see socially but at our attitudes, as well. How many of us believe that love "happens," but friendship develops? That kind of thinking eliminates all of those worthy prospects who capture our hearts day by day. How many of us are so busy listening for bells that we never hear the quiet "click" that signals deep, lasting affection?

So your date was not love at first sight. Is he or she worth a second look? Consider these eye-opening romantic strategies:

♡ *Don't be the typecasting type.* "I like tall, slender blonds," my friend Vicki announced. "Every significant boyfriend I've ever had has been that physical type. I can't explain it . . . but I prefer it!" That's fine. I have an inclination for classical art—but that doesn't keep me from appreciating a cubist sculpture or a seaside scene rendered in tropical colors by a Haitian street artist.

If you feel that you can discern which partner might be right for you on first glance or even from across the room, maybe you need to take a closer look at your own belief system. Does the physical type you prefer reveal something about the image you want to portray? What physical characteristics denote success to you? Sensitivity? Uber-cool?

Your happiness is at stake here. The choosing of a new friend should at least merit the kind of consideration you would put into selecting a new pair of shoes: Style is a factor, but comfort is key. It may take a bit of aimless strolling to know if the fit is right.

♡ *Focus on what's really important.* Some people come to us for a reason; others are important to us for a season. Which type of person is the one you are with? If a fling is in order, then you can afford to throw caution to the wind. But if it's lasting love you're looking for, then friendship and communication must develop—and that takes time. Give a new friendship time to take its course.

♡ *Set to "defrost." Wait.* Even in this age, when confession is considered good for the soul (and great for publishers!), there are still many people who do not spill their guts until they've gotten to know you. If he seems reserved, maybe he's saving himself for someone who'll put in a little effort. If she is the kind of nut you might like, but a tough one to crack, maybe she's looking for the right person to open up to. People don't warm at the same rates. Give your partner a little time to acclimate.

♡ *Are you being too picky?* Think of the last twenty men or women you've dated. Make a list of the ones who were really interested in you. Now that you've got your "hot-for-you" list in order, go through it again, this time checking off the men or women *you* were attracted to. In what percentage of your recent dates was mutual attraction a factor? If you feel attracted to at least half of the men/women you date, you are open to a healthy range of types and personalities. But if you are having a hard time mustering up interest in the people who want to see you, you may have set your sights especially high.

♡ *Know the difference between a harmless habit and a deal-breaker.* Something may be bugging you about a recent date, but is it a permanent or passing issue? This question is worth careful consideration. I can't tell you how many men and women I know who gave a perfectly nice date the boot because he or she was too chubby, couldn't dance, didn't like museums, was a vegetarian or showed some other characteristic that might evolve over time. Meanness or intellectual dullness may be a permanent condition but hair, hips and habits are subject to change. Don't be quick to say good-bye forever to someone who might mellow over time.

♡ *Consider a change of venue.* If he's a dud over dinner, if she's a clod on the tennis court, it is possible that these are not the places where he or she can shine! Set up a second date but allow him or her to choose the location or the activity. Even a jewel loses its luster when it's not in the right setting.

Make Shyness a Thing of the Past

Most of the time, I like to maintain the tone of a controlled riot at my School of Flirting workshops. While my audiences are always respectful when I'm speaking, these aren't lectures, they're casual, social events. Talking, laughing and chatting up the guy at the next table are encouraged, as are all kinds of teacher-student interactions, including singing, role-playing and calling out responses. So when I asked the following question, I wasn't sure what type of answer to expect.

"A hard-body with soft brown eyes slipped you a phone number as you were leaving the gym a few nights ago. The racquetball is definitely in your court. You know you'll have to call or you might miss your turn to serve. What do you do to prepare to make that call to someone you don't know?"

"I rehearse a few times," responded one young woman in the third row.

"How few exactly?" asked a man sitting nearby.

"More than twenty, less than fifty," she admitted with a smile. Rehearsing was a great confidence-builder, I assured her.

"I do just the opposite," announced a young guy in baggy jeans, a funky hat and a neon-green leg cast. "I just pick up the phone and dial it. No stressing. It's the telephone equivalent of holding your nose and taking a running jump off of the high dive. You just take the plunge."

Now there was one guy who didn't need to build confidence! Now the room was abuzz.

A professionally dressed woman in the back seemed dubious.

"You don't stress when you're calling a complete stranger? How in the world do you do that?"

"I just remind myself that I've never had a 'telephone accident,'" the young man said with a smirk. He picked up a crutch from the floor and waved it at the crowd.

The audience laughed. This was definitely a self-assured group. Except for the man in a gray sweater peering up at me from a folding chair on the aisle. He seemed like he had something to say, yet was hesitant to say it.

"And what about you?" I asked him. "Is there anything special you do to prepare for that important first phone contact?"

"Yes," he mumbled, barely audibly.

"What do you do?"

"My face turns red," he murmured, "and my palms sweat. I try to plan what I'm going to say, but sometimes I just hang up without saying anything."

I leaned toward him in an attempt to make eye contact. The man stared resolutely at the floor. Finally he peeked up at me.

"I'm *really* shy," he said.

I patted him on the shoulder. His answer had taken a lot of guts. His condition, I knew, couldn't be covered over with a bright-colored cast, yet it was every bit as debilitating and limiting as a broken bone. I thanked him for bringing up the subject. He may have felt alone in his self-consciousness, but he had introduced a subject that affects every flirt at one time or another.

Many of us think of shyness as a condition that affects a small percentage of stammering, sweaty-palmed people. Yet when we examine the phenomenon more closely, it is easy to see why, in a recent poll, more than 80 percent of the men and women interviewed reported having experienced the effects of shyness at some time in their lives. What may surprise you, however, is this: of the 80 percent of people who acknowledged feeling shy at some point in their lives, 40 percent said that they were working to overcome the effects of shyness at the time the poll was taken. What does that mean for you as a flirt? It means that four out of every ten of those suave, poised, too-too-together people who seem so aloof, so superior or simply too preoccupied to flirt with the likes of you are actually too bashful to make the first move!

What is shyness? Shyness can be defined as an exaggerated fear of rejection or of an indeterminate "negative unknown." In the extreme, the effects of shyness can be much the way the man in the gray sweater described them: They can include a range of disconcerting symptoms such as excessive perspiration, blushing, heart palpitations, stammering, uncontrollable laughter and even the total inability to speak. Yet shyness is not always so easy to pinpoint. Quiet detachment, an air of distraction and other superficially "normal" behaviors can mask social anxiety. What differentiates a person who is truly shy, then, from someone who is simply quiet or introverted? Simply, the feeling of inhibition. If you are a self-contained person who relishes being alone, you aren't necessarily shy. You are simply like my friend Rick, who needs to spend time curled up with a good book in order to "detox" from what he considers a bustling, "overpopulated" work week. If, on the other hand, you have anxiety that is actually preventing you from going where you want to go, doing what you want to do and, most of all, flirting up a storm, it is time to put your shyness in its place.

Yes, you can make the transition from bashful to belle of the ball! Untie your tongue and begin!

♡   *Practice on somebody who doesn't matter.* To a flirt, everybody matters, of course, but not everybody matters enough to press your panic button. Shyness tends to be situational. And the situations most likely to trigger it are one-on-one encounters with people who spark our desire for intimacy.

In flirting, there is no asbestos suit. Even the most experienced flirt goes down in flames now and then. But a flirt with skill is insulated against rejection—and skill is something even the shyest singles can develop. If conversation with people you don't know is a problem, I suggest that you try your moves out on salespeople, waitstaff, taxi drivers . . . anyone who will allow you to improve your repartee without creating anxiety. As you begin to feel comfortable, you can enlarge your conversational circle to include those women or men you find attractive.

♡ *Ask open-ended questions.* Does spontaneous conversation cause your confidence to combust? Does approaching that hottie give you the heebie-jeebies? You can score big points by talking less and listening more! An interested look, a friendly smile and a handful of questions is really all it takes to keep a conversation going. So tune in to an acquaintance's chatter and when you can get a word in edgewise, ask for more info! People like people who are interesting, but they are *really* impressed by people who are interested in *them.* Give the men and women you meet a platform for self-expression and they'll walk away thinking that *you're* a brilliant conversationalist!

♡ *Have something to say.* I like to say that I am a vast storehouse of useless information . . . and that's a good thing! People who know a little about a lot of things are never at a loss for words . . . or opportunities to flirt! If you are shy, you often feel that the focus of an encounter is on you, uncomfortably so. Being able to draw upon a wealth of informational tidbits—on current events, local happenings, hobbies—anything!—keeps the focus off of you (and your discomfort) and on a neutral, non-threatening topic.

♡ *To be at your best, anticipate the worst!* The worst-case scenario, that is. As we have seen, some cases of shyness stem from the fear of the unknown . . . a paralyzing dread of a monumental but unspecified bad result. The idea that "something is going to happen" is a difficult fear to overcome. Because you have no idea what will occur, there is no way to prepare; and because the fear is never delineated, it can build to unlimited proportions. As unlikely as it may sound, imagining the worst *in a detailed, specific way* can help you see how unrealistic your fears really are and limit your imagination to an outcome with which you can cope.

This is how it worked with a very shy man I'll call Jorge, whom I met at a resort in Florida.

Like many shy people, Jorge was a very pleasant personality who had no difficulty making and keeping friends. Making the acquaintance of a beautiful stranger, however, was his undoing.

Jorge had seen the object of his flirtation—a lushly built Latin woman in a fuschia skirt—at dinner the previous evening. Twenty-four hours later, he was breathless at the sight of her, but he had yet to speak with her. Fate was not dropping this woman into Jorge's lap; wasn't it time he made his own luck?

"You mean, just walk up and speak to her? I couldn't possibly!" Jorge argued. "What could I say to impress her? And what would happen if I tried?"

Good question! "I don't know. What *would* happen if you tried?" I urged.

"Who knows?" Jorge shrugged, never taking his eyes off the woman as she chatted happily with a group of people across the patio. "She might ignore me."

"And what if she did? What would happen then?" I asked him.

Now Jorge turned to me and locked his eyes on mine. "I'll tell you what would happen. I'd be embarrassed. My cheeks would turn red. Ever since I was a kid, my cheeks have turned bright red when I am embarrassed."

"When I'm embarrassed, mine do, too," I reassured him with a smile. "But let's say your cheeks turned the color of a . . .

strawberry daiquiri." I lifted my drink in his direction. "What then?"

Jorge stared at me. Somehow the script had never been fleshed out beyond this point. I could see that imagining the reality of what might happen next was unexplored territory for him. He thought for a long while before answering.

"I guess I would have to figure out how to make my escape! I have learned from experience that the ground will probably not open and swallow me whole . . ."

We shared a knowing smile. "So what would you do?" I prompted.

"I suppose I'd walk away."

"And then?"

Now Jorge laughed. "I'd probably go for a swim in the ocean. I mean, it's right here!"

"So you would survive," I commented.

"Just barely!"

"But you would."

"I would." He looked at the woman. She was full of life, comfortable in her own skin . . . she was beautiful. Was she also *possible?*

The lesson here is clear: The unknown is only unknown until we begin to explore it. Shy or bold, diffident or definite, your actions can incite only a finite number of reactions. Can you live with those? Of course you can! Everybody on the planet has been rejected. You've been there and done that!

A final reality check: For every woman hoping that some significant other will break the silence barrier, there is a man who is hoping the same. Most attractive people will respond warmly to a greeting from a stranger. They've been in your position and will appreciate the courage it took for you to speak up. Take the bonus points and go for it! You have only your shyness to lose and the possibility of a very rewarding friendship to gain!

I cannot tell you the number of times I arrive at a talk, look out over the audience and see a sea of the grimmest faces this side of an IRS tax audit. Why? If I've said it once, I've said it a thousand times: Flirting is *never* serious. It is a playful proposition, as quirky as a grin, as spontaneous as a belly laugh. So why do some flirts face the prospect of meeting and greeting others with grim resolve?

I know finding love can seem like serious business—particularly if you've been single a lot longer than your mattress's ten-year guarantee—but there is something you should know: There is lots of evidence that the way to a person's heart is through the funny bone!

For our purposes as flirts, a moment of shared laughter is a moment of connection between two people. One spirit touches another and our psyches are quite literally "tickled." That's just what happened to me one recent morning—and the results will live in my top-ten one-liners list forever.

I was out and about doing errands in the neighborhood when I ran into a man who lived in an adjoining building. We had seen each other many times but we had never spoken. On this particular day, he stopped to chat. He asked me what I did for a living. I told him that I was a therapist and a flirt.

"Now, there's a unique job," he commented. "Do you find it difficult?"

"Not me!" I quipped. "I can flirt with a lamppost!"

The man smiled wryly. "But can you turn it *on*?"

I laughed then and there and I have been laughing at that witty remark ever since.

And that is what is so beautiful about shared laughter: The initial encounter may have lasted only a few seconds but its charm lingers. Is there a more enjoyable way to make yourself unforgettable?

As for *your* sense of humor, can *you* turn it on? Absolutely! Just use these tips and you're sure to leave them rolling:

♡ *Wink, wink, nudge, nudge.* Joking is easy when you're among those who know the nuances of your sense of humor, but someone who doesn't know you well may mistake your dry or deadpan delivery for sarcasm or even anger. To make sure people realize you're joshing, make sure your facial expression reflects your intention. A wink, an eyebrow raise or just a wry smile will reassure your audience that it's OK to laugh.

♡ *Laugh at yourself.* We look down and realize we are wearing two different shoes. We look up just in time to see we're on a collision course with a bird's digestive schedule . . . some days it seems that wherever we look, we're seeing ourselves at our silliest. Great! Our foibles are not life's annoyances; they are the pratfalls that make us human and approachable to others! They are instant icebreakers.

♡ *Use your "prop"!* The large foam finger you find on your hand long after the playoff has been played. A sled being dragged along the sidewalk in the dog days of August. The discarded banana peel on the library steps. These aren't just random bits of life's flotsam . . . they are punch lines waiting to happen! Use them! (A friend recently told me about a man she encountered at the laundrette. He opened a dryer he thought was his and began piling the clothes into his basket. He was totally oblivious to his mistake until he pulled out a very large bra. Instead of blushing and shoving the item back into the dryer, he held it to his chest and said, "I knew I should have handwashed this. Now it will never look right under my knits!")

♡ *Look around you.* The headlines may be ominous, the fate of the world may be in the hands of people who don't have opposable thumbs, but life in all of its comical beauty is happening all around you. Quip the light fantastic! Did that gorgeous girl traipsing past you in the airport stumble? Tell her, "I had always hoped someone like you would fall for me!" What have you got to lose? Your inhibitions? Your own doldrums?

♡ *And if he or she doesn't get the joke?* It isn't that you aren't funny . . . he or she is humorless! Why would you want such a stick-in-the-mud? Laugh it off and move on! Make it a rule: The person who "gets it" is the person who deserves it. Don't settle for less.

Week 6

Say Something Nice and Mean It

My close friends know what I do for a living. But when they're out with me, do you think it's easy to get them to take my advice? They can be as untrainable as earthworms. Consider my good friend Christian.

Christian is a fun-loving, good-looking, "I'll try anything once" type with whom I had the good fortune to work. While the rest of us would spend our vacations installing a backyard water fountain or lying on some beach, Christian was off hot air ballooning over the Arizona desert or climbing an icy crag in Nepal. You would think an adventurer who collected hair-raising tales the way less-intrepid travelers collected postcards would find it easy to cross the borders of an appealing woman's personal space. But Christian just couldn't get his visa stamped.

The bar where Christian and I agreed to meet was loud, the crowd warming up. I had just begun to recount the grim details of a recent disastrous date (yes, I have them, too!) when I noticed that Christian's attention had contracted a case of wanderlust. Although he was smiling and nodding politely at me, his eyes were following a woman who had just worked her way through the crowd to a table near the bar.

"She looks like your type," I noted. "Why don't you go over and introduce yourself?"

Christian looked at me in horror. "You must be kidding! Why, I don't even know her!" my otherwise courageous friend cried. "And besides, don't you think there's something that's just so . . . *obvious* about an unsolicited introduction? It's like knocking on a total stranger's door and inviting yourself to dinner."

I sat back in my chair. I had to admit I knew what he meant. Strolling over to someone you've handpicked from a roomful of people was a little like stamping "I am interested in *you*!" on your forehead. Still, Christian was a man who celebrated his last birthday by parachuting out of an airplane.

I looked the woman over. Pleasant looking and dressed down in jeans and a fleece vest, she hardly seemed like the type who would take exception to a simple, well-intentioned introduction. Still, the direct approach was obviously too direct for Christian. I would suggest another tack.

I tapped my empty glass with my finger. "OK then. If introducing yourself seems too bold a move, then why don't you compliment her? Go over to the bar, order a drink and, while you're there, casually say something nice. Then if she doesn't speak to you or seems like a dud you can just pick up your drink and walk away. But if it works, you can stay."

Now Christian was laughing at his own timidity. "Susan, she's an unknown quantity! It's not easy saying something complimentary to someone you know nothing about."

"Yes, it is," I soothed. "Something about this woman attracted your attention. Maybe it was her smile. Or her manner. Or her hair. Maybe it was the way she squeezed through the crowd like somebody swimming without making a ripple. Whatever it was, just remember what first impressed you and mention it to her."

"That sounds reasonable," Christian said, more to himself than to me. He rose from his chair and fidgeted for his wallet.

"And don't forget to smile," I hissed after him.

That was the last I saw of Christian for nearly an hour. Finally, he dropped by my table to let me know that he and his new friend, Davita, were heading out to the local Indian joint for samosas and tea. Before he left, I wanted the details. Did he compliment his pretty acquaintance?

Christian blushed. "I never got the chance. *She* complimented *me*! As I reached across the bar, she noticed the thick callouses I have on my fingers and said, 'Oh! Your hands are a mess! This may seem like a strange question, but do you rappel?' "

Thick callouses? *This* was a compliment? Apparently in Christian's world it was. And what in the world did "rappel" mean? I've had some experience with people who repel. Presumably this was not the same activity.

"OK. So what did you say?"

Christian was clearly excited now. He handed Davita her coat then whispered the rest of his tale in my ear. "I told her I've been taking ice-climbing lessons on weekends and my hands got blistered from the handle of the pick. Then she showed me her hands. They were totally torn up! She's been rappelling . . . in Central Park, of all places."

I couldn't help but laugh out loud. What a touching exchange! One only a sports physician could love. And as for the complimenting? Was that technique perilous enough to engage Christian?

"It's not bad—but I prefer to let the females go first." He laughed. "Better to be safe than sorry!"

He joined Davita at the door. Then they walked contentedly off into the night.

Maybe insincere compliments will "get you nowhere," but an accolade that comes from the heart will get even first-time flirts to dinner and beyond! Validating and playful, always mutually satisfying, a compliment is a surprise gift we bestow on someone who has presented *us* with his or her uniqueness.

Compliments are not "lines"—they are one of the trade secrets of people who are "Lucky in Love." That's why I recommend you use them liberally, but with care. If she's impressed you with her vast knowledge of Tuscan wine varieties, if he has a voice that wraps itself around you like a soft, cool fog, say so! Most of us put a great deal of time and effort into our appearance, intellect and abilities. Knowing that those efforts are appreciated gives us a sense of validation—and we, in turn, give big brownie points to those special people who make us feel good.

Of course, that doesn't mean you should spread on the sweet stuff with a trowel. While compliments can be great conversation starters, most people have taken a very clear inventory of their strengths and weaknesses. Hearing you expound on qualities they feel they haven't got—or worse, showering them with flattery that seems over the top—will make others doubt your sincerity and suspect that your interest is insincere.

There is nothing more satisfying than a kind word from someone whose opinion we trust. They make us feel truly appreciated. That's why I am suggesting that this week you share your admiration with the special individuals you encounter. To make sure your compliments are received in the spirit with which they were given, here are a few factors to consider:

 Overlook the obvious. Frank is a public-relations copywriter who lives in Los Angeles. His line of work puts him in constant contact with a number of stunningly beautiful actresses and models who work as spokespersons for the products Frank promotes. Now Frank is generally a terrific "schmoozer": He's a genial guy who can banter with the best of them, but when it comes to complimenting these gorgeous women, he's at a loss.

"Just last week, I was with a very well-known model for a line of cosmetics. It was a situation any man would envy. The only thing I could think to say to this woman was, 'You are even more beautiful in person than you are in your photographs!' Lame, right?" Frank laughed. "But it was really true! She was a hundred times more attractive to me without the airbrushing and the goofy pose. But I felt like my comment was something she must have heard so many times it would just sound like a line. And really, it isn't."

It doesn't matter if the object of your flirtation has a face that's launched a dozen ad campaigns or whether she/he is merely the star of the family's photo album. Rather than run the risk of repeating someone else's compliment, it's always best to focus on something that is unique to the person you're complimenting. Does her smile light up the room? When he's in the park, does he seem to attract children? Are her cheeks the exact hue of the coral rosebud on her lapel? These compliments don't just focus on the physical—they are a celebration of inner beauty, as well! I guarantee that your distinctive comment will be cherished long after the other skin-deep compliments are forgotten. And so will you. You had the sensitivity and aplomb to make mention of the subtle qualities less sensitive admirers could not see. And that makes you a memorable flirt!

♡   *Sound sincere.* If your tone of voice doesn't match up with the sentiment you're delivering, your compliment will fall flat. Even the most effusive praise, delivered in a dull tone, can sound like a line you've practiced too many times. If his smile warms you, he should hear the happiness in your voice. If her tendency to read medieval French poetry on the subway intrigues you, your voice should reflect your excitement and curiosity.

♡   *Comment on what she/he is, not what she/he has.* "Nice car, Ed!" "Great dress, Kat!" These may pass for compliments in some circles but think about it: Aren't you really complimenting the car, the dress or maybe the designer of the car or dress? Feel free to compliment Ed on his decision to buy the car or to praise Kat's taste in clothes, but save your acclaim for people, not their possessions. (Note: Complimenting a man's very expensive car can be dangerous territory for a woman! You may look as though you are sizing the driver up financially, and that's never attractive. To avoid all of the gender-sensitive subjects, see the complete list in week 29.)

 Last but not least, be careful what you say in public. You may be dying to pant out your paean to his bedroom eyes, but is the company picnic (within earshot of his entire astonished department) really the best forum? And while you may be certain she'll appreciate your tribute to her perfect accent in conversational Italian class, is it possible she might be a tad embarrassed by the *attenzione?* Public praise makes your private feelings known to those around you. It can also focus a great deal of attention on its recipient. If the object of your admiration tends to shyness or would rather not be the focus of other people's attention, you may have jinxed your chances with that person forever. Remember, compliments should make the recipient feel self-confident; never self-conscious. If you have any doubt about whether your message might be suitable for broadcast, save it for a more private moment. After all, there is no compliment that doesn't sound just a bit more convincing when it is whispered in that appreciative someone's ear.

Week 7

Practice Random (But Not Anonymous) Acts of Kindness

Chances are your mother told you, "Be nice. You never know who's watching!" Indeed. As a flirt you never know who's on the lookout for a thoughtful, considerate companion like you!

Erik had worked as a guidance counselor in a private high school for many years. Although most kids at the school weren't wealthy, their families were solidly middle-income. To turn the teenagers' attention to their less fortunate neighbors, Erik created a program called "Sweet Dreams," a volunteer project in which teens would read bedtime stories to the critically ill children in nearby hospitals.

The program was a lovely idea, to be sure—but it wasn't always convenient for Erik. He had just broken up with a long-term girlfriend and was looking forward to dating again. Nevertheless, there he was on most Friday and Saturday nights in the pediatrics wing, passing out copies of *Good Night Moon* to readers with cracking voices.

It took Erik several months, but he had finally gotten Sweet Dreams running well enough that one of the teens associated with the group had been able to step in to take over the organizational duties. Erik was free to move on to a new project: re-invigorating his sleepy social life. He arranged to meet his friends at a dance club one night, then went home to wash off the scent of the high-school cafeteria. That's when the phone rang. Two of the boys who were supposed to read that night hadn't shown up. Those who were present couldn't possibly read to all of the sick children in the hour before the wing was closed to visitors. The group leader was in a panic. Erik put his plans aside and filled in for the missing boys. He would meet his friends at the club later on.

At first, Erik wasn't happy about the abrupt change in plans. Yet by the time he had finished reading to the second patient, an adolescent girl who was recovering from spinal surgery, he was feeling relaxed and happy. He was even happier when the very attractive young woman who'd also been at the patient's bedside followed him into the hall.

"I just wanted to tell you what a lovely program I think this is," she commented. "My niece is only ten and she's had a difficult time recovering emotionally. The nurses have been great, but I think it's really helped her to spend some time with another kid. Even if the visit is only the length of a story."

Erik chatted with this amiable young woman for about twenty minutes. She was just his type—dark, petite and energetic. But when he caught sight of the large clock behind the nurses' station, he suddenly remembered his friends and his plans for that evening. He thanked the woman for her kind words and rushed off into the night.

It wasn't until Erik was in his car and on his way that he realized what he had done. He was going to the club in the hopes of meeting someone cute, kind and sincere. He had just abandoned exactly that kind of person—and possibly his senses— back at the hospital!

Unexpected acts of kindness stand out. Some are simple— fetching supplies from a high grocery store shelf for someone unable to reach . . . picking up an item that has been dropped by a passerby . . . or simply offering a kind word or compliment to someone you don't know. Other acts of kindness are definitely above and beyond. I am thinking now of a day my car stopped running and started spewing clouds of black, acrid smoke in the middle of a busy intersection. The two men who pushed it to a nearby gas station risked black lung to do so. Their willingness to aid a panic-stricken automaphobe will live forever in my heart. Isn't it a shame that their names never made it into my little black book?

Most people don't do good deeds hoping for credit or compensation. In fact, many of these humanitarians are so altruistic they don't even share their names. Consequently, you may read about their exploits in the newspaper ("I want to thank the guy with the uninflated ego who stopped to fix my flat . . .") but never in the engagement section! It's a wonderful thing to turn in that missing wallet to the lost and found—but do you have to lose an opportunity to get to know the owner in the bargain? If you don't want a reward, fine. But don't you want a date?

Being kind to others lets the rest of the world see you in the best possible light, and opens the door to the pleasure of someone else's company. It builds a bridge between you and people you might not otherwise socialize with. It's good for you as a human being, but it's also good for your social life—sometimes in unexpectedly delightful ways.

Kyle was the seventeen-year-old son of a single mother, Marianne, who had recently moved to a new town. She and Kyle had just finished shoveling out after a nor'easter that had dumped nearly a foot of snow on the region when Marianne noticed that the elderly couple up the street was still totally snowed in. She had to cajole and even ply her son with money, but she finally got Kyle to agree to shovel the frail, ancient pair out.

It wasn't easy. The snow was heavy and wet. It took Kyle more than three hours to finish the job. Marianne noticed that he stopped now and then to shoot a withering glance her way. But in the end, the aged couple won him over. The woman invited Kyle in for a snack and pressed two dollars into his hand—a lot of money when she was seventeen. The man of the house asked him whether he had a girlfriend. If not, he suggested that Kyle might like to drop by for a plate of his wife's famous baccala on Sunday. The old man said he knew a young woman who was just right for him.

Kyle was skeptical. These people were so old, they remembered when the Dead Sea was alive. How old might this "young woman" be? Middle age looked sprightly to them! Still, when Sunday came, Kyle's curiosity had the best of him. At the very least, he'd find out what baccala—and the girl—was like.

Of course, baccala turned out to be salted codfish and there was no ketchup to be found anywhere on the table—still, Kyle was pleasantly surprised. The girl, Kayla, was the old couple's great-granddaughter. Kyle had always admired Kayla in school but had never spoken to her. They dated throughout the spring and summer until Kayla left for college. Since they parted as friends, there is every possibility the relationship will continue. And so will Kyle's acts of kindness. He learned that helping others is one way to help yourself to a more fully realized life.

The good you share with others comes back to you. But what goes around cannot possibly come around if you have left no forwarding address! How can you get credit where credit is due without seeming like an approval-seeking love sponge? Here are some suggestions for random acts of kindness. Each begins with a heart that is open to the possibility of pleasing others. Each ends, reasonably, with a "close:"

♡ *Have a card and use it.* People act as though humanitarianism only counts when it is anonymous. Is the good deed any less laudable because you hope to get to know the person whose day you've brightened?

♡ *Treat city workers, your favorite librarians or others whose jobs go largely overlooked to cookies or another "happy food" you've concocted.* Put your telephone number on the bottom of the serving container. Say you'll be back to pick up the platter when your sweet treat is gone.

♡ *If you work in a public place, bring in flowers*—then share them with special clients or patrons.

♡ *Share your valuable talents and abilities with others.* As I write this, my local public library is teeming with volunteer tax-preparers. These people are professionals who are willing to share their knowledge with those for whom complex forms just don't seem to add up! No matter what your unique skill might be, the grateful recipients aren't likely to forget someone who has provided them with a service they would otherwise have to pay for or that will bring them on-going pleasure.

♡ *When you're volunteering with a group, be sure to sign in.* And by all means, wear that dorky name tag!

♡ *To spread goodwill as well as your your name and telephone number, become part of a car pool.*

♡ *Become a tutor in a school or, if you can, teach a class.* Offering an ongoing service, such as lessons, enables you to establish an ongoing presence. You'll get to know your cohorts in the teachers' lounge—and they'll get to know you.

♡ *If the company you work for sponsors a toy drive or holiday food collection, offer to be the one who works the drop-off point.* You'll get to know everyone in your office building in no time flat.

♡ *Keep a stash of fresh fruit or another healthy snack and encourage others to help themselves.*

♡ *Spread sunshine.* Almost every large organization has a sunshine group whose job it is to offer congratulations or condolences and spread congeniality in general. You'll hear everyone's news and become everyone's favorite coworker.

♡ *Be a good neighbor.* Hey, it worked for Kyle!

♡ *Become a dog-walker for the local animal rescue group.* This random act of kindness not only provides you with a chance to meet like-minded people and get some exercise, it even comes with a cute, cuddly flirting prop!

♡ *Sponsor a special program or speaker at a nearby library or bookstore.* This idea need not break the bank; budding artists and local authors are happy for any opportunity to share their thoughts and talents.

♡ *Offer to answer the phone for a busy school or church secretary.* You'll be in the thick of the action.

♡ *Write notes of appreciation* to teachers or other significant people whose care and compassion in the past transformed your future. You never know where a reestablished contact can lead.

♡ *Invite new coworkers or classmates over for dinner.*

♡ *Wherever you are in the early morning hours, bring enough coffee to share.*

♡ *Join in a neighborhood effort.* Help to build the new jungle gym; dig into a tree-planting effort. My coauthor got to know everyone within a three-block radius by joining forces with nearby homeowners when a large business threatened to move in.

♡ *If there is a reward for what you do, share it!* Provide lunch or some other treat for the other "good-deed-doers." The way to that significant other's heart may not be through his or her stomach, but feeding someone generally puts you in the right vicinity.

Lighten Up!

I had just boarded a plane in New York en route to California. It would be a long trip and I wanted to make sure I had plenty to keep me busy. I also wanted to be comfortable. Considering that a passenger has about as much chance of getting comfy in an airplane seat as she does getting dressed for a coronation in a phone booth, this was going to take some effort.

I slid into my row and said hello to my seatmate, a businessman in a blue suit who smiled up at me from behind his doorstop-sized hardcover. Then I set about settling in. I opened the overhead compartment and checked out the remaining space. There were few people in the rows surrounding mine, yet the compartment was about three-quarters full. Obviously, there were poachers in the area. I folded my jacket into a compact rectangle and slid it between a carry-on bag and the ceiling. I then took out my own carry-on and removed a handful of my favorite distractions—moisturizer, gum, a bottle of water, the novel of the moment—and stuffed them into the pocket behind the seat in front of mine. I stashed the bag overhead and took my seat.

I had only been sitting long enough to leaf through the in-flight magazine when it occurred to me that I might want my laptop during the flight. I got to my feet, opened the bin, removed my computer and put it under my seat. That's when I felt the cold blast from the air spigot above the seat. I remembered that I had seen blankets in the overhead. Once again, I got to my feet, extracted a blanket and a pillow (just in case) and reclaimed my seat. I fastened my seat belt.

About that time, I noticed my seatmate. He was trying to catch my eye. I turned to him and smiled. He put his book aside, winked in my direction and quipped, "I can just imagine how long it takes you to get ready for bed at night." Then he re-opened his book.

I laughed for a very long time. The ice between us wasn't just broken, it was liquefied! We spent the next several hours chatting happily and, although we didn't make a romantic connection, we had a wonderful time. I never used the laptop once.

Lighten Up

♥ A good sense of humor is one of the best flirtation skills.
♥ It's OK to tease, but make sure your humor is gentle and not sarcastic. Sarcasm is clever, but a deal breaker.
♥ Be able to laugh at yourself.
♥ None of us is perfect. Humor levels the playing field. It makes us human, vulnerable and fun.

Week 9

Embarrassing Moments Every Flirt Would Like to Forget

A usually impeccably put-together woman, Marissa walked from the restroom of the theater all the way to her seat before a nearby patron told her what her date could not: The hem of her skirt was tucked into her waistband. In the last few minutes, hundreds of people had seen her behind.

Ray had waited months for Nita to get over a former love. At last, she was ready to start dating! Ray took her to a restaurant in Baltimore's Little Italy. Halfway through the meal, he noticed that his fly was partially open. Congratulating himself on a crisis averted, he discreetly zipped. Until he stood up, he had no idea that he had zipped the edge of the tablecloth into his fly. He took one step and upended Nita's *pasta a la vongole* right into her lap. He still remembers the sound of the clamshells clattering to the tile floor and the shocked look on Nita's face. Did she forgive him? He'll never know. He never called her again.

Judy had always wanted to go to the GreenWater Café, partly because the restaurant had gotten such stellar reviews and partly because it was not a place she would ever be able to afford on her salary as an administrative assistant. She was thrilled, then, when Jeff chose this very upscale restaurant for their first date.

"Do your want to sit upstairs where it's quiet or downstairs where the jazz combo plays?" he asked her.

"The jazz would be nice as long as it isn't too loud."

"I'll make sure we can talk," Jeff assured her. He asked the hostess for a table just far enough from the band so they could hear each other and the jazz as well.

When the waiter came to take their drink orders, they independently ordered a pair of dirty martinis. Judy took that as a good sign. She wanted to like Jeff. Not only was he a real gentleman, he was very good looking—and affluent enough to afford great food served in beautiful surroundings. She had suffered through some rotten dates lately. Jeff was the prize in her Cracker Jack box.

Conversation flowed at the GreenWater Café. Jeff and Judy were a fix-up but, as they had learned on the telephone, they were both in banking. They talked profits, losses, mergers and acquisitions until the waiter handed them the menu and described the specials.

After sharing a dozen oysters, which were superb, they decided on a fish course. He ordered salmon and she, seared tuna, rare. The tuna was delicious, but after two bites, Judy laid down her fork. Suddenly, inexplicably, she was overcome with nausea. She looked at Jeff eating happily across the table. Judy felt her eyes begin to water. Her throat clenched. She was sure she was going to throw up now—and she wasn't going to make it to the ladies' room, either. She pressed her napkin to her lips and waited for the inevitable.

Now Jeff noticed Judy's distress. "What's the matter? Are you OK?"

"I feel very sick," Judy gasped. Then she upchucked into the white cloth napkin. "Will you ask the waiter for more napkins, please?"

She didn't have to ask twice. A stack of napkins arrived, and before she was through, Judy had vomited into every one of them. When she had collected herself again, Jeff wrapped his arm around her, steered her out of the restaurant and into his car.

At first, Judy was reluctant to get in. Jeff was driving an impeccable—and expensive—Mercedes. The last thing she wanted to do was spew in that car! But Jeff was insistent—he would deliver her to her door in the best shape possible.

Once her stomach seemed settled, Judy couldn't help but laugh. "I'm sorry—I really am! I can't believe I threw up on our very first date! If this were *The Bachelorette* I don't think I'd be getting a rose."

Jeff smiled. "It's OK, really. I have two young children. They've thrown up many times. On me! I'm used to it!"

Judy giggled and burped and relaxed in the heated leather seat. The rest of the ride was uneventful. She didn't get sick again. And although she expressed her regret continuously—for causing such a commotion . . . for the waiter's inconvenience . . . even for the condition of the napkins . . . she was sure she'd never see Jeff again. She had truly been the date from hell.

Much to her surprise, Jeff did call Judy again—the very next day. He also arranged to see her again as soon as she felt she was back on her feet. Unfortunately, that date didn't go well. Judy's ego was still smarting from her debut performance. She kept her wits—and her meal—about her but somehow she was so nervous that she said all the wrong things. Jeff didn't call again after that.

Even now, months later, Judy still regrets losing her composure—and, most of all, Jeff. He was one of the kindest men she had ever met. Should she call and tell him the way she feels? Sometimes she thinks so, but her embarrassment has been hard to digest.

We flirts are fascinating, we're entertaining and we're as hot as the law and nature permits. Nevertheless, we're only human. And therein lies the possibility for profound embarrassment as we explore the bumpy terrain of love.

A date, particularly a first date, is an especially exciting event. It's an opportunity for us to break some new ground, to get to know that mysterious stranger who's captured our fancy. It's hard to be blasé about the promise that situation holds. But a first date is also our only chance to make a good first impression—and that can pack some additional pressure into an already charged situation.

Consider the painstaking process Martha laughingly calls "the prep." Martha is a genuine Southern belle, born and bred in Savannah. She takes her pre-date primping as seriously as she does her mother's recipe for cheese grits. And so do most of us. By the time the appointed hour arrives, our teeth are polished, our skin is buffed and every hair is as meticulously groomed as the putting green at Pebble Beach. The image we want to convey, however temporarily, is that we are people who, incredibly, are totally

free of bad hair days or klutziness or inconvenient natural emis-
sions. Deep inside we know that our dates will eventually see us—
and maybe even love us—in our imperfection. Nevertheless, we
attempt to delay the delivery of the bad news that we are only human, with bodies that we can't always control.

One thing I know for sure: There are as many ways to flirt with
disaster as there are flirts! What do I mean? I mean common date-
night blunders like these:

♥ You've had a wonderful evening. You'd like to move on to
somewhere more private. You reach into your wallet to
pay the check. If not for a slip of paper containing someone else's telephone number, it would be totally empty.

♥ You regale your date with a hilariously funny story about
that jerk of a boss of yours. Who would have suspected
that jerk was your date's sister?

What is there to learn from foibles like these? *Plenty*.

Every flirt has experienced embarrassment. Big deal! Who
wouldn't risk an occasional red face for red-hot romance? And
where is it written that an embarrassing boo-boo (or two) necessarily means the end of an otherwise beautiful friendship? Nobody
really wants to hang out with someone who considers a hint of humanity a deal breaker. If your date has a sense of humor and/or
empathy, the two of you can laugh off almost any embarrassing
situation—even if there is spinach in your teeth!

But if you do inadvertently commit an unfortunate gaffe, it's
important that you get off on the right foot. (Hint: Ignore the
streamer of toilet paper stuck to the bottom of it.) These goof-
proof guidelines will help.

♡ *Apologize.* Whatever you've done, whatever you've failed to
do, acknowledge it and move on. Remind yourself that you
cannot be responsible for anyone else's reaction. Be your
most considerate self, be accountable for your error and let
the chips fall where they may.

♡ *Repair any damage.* That's what dry-cleaners, Superglue, emergency rooms and charm are for.

♡ *Know what really happened.* Sure it was awful—but was it terminal? Did he leave burning rubber, or burning with desire for more of your haphazard hijinks? Vulnerability may be occasionally embarrassing, but to many singles who are tired of "bulletproof" partners, it is also refreshing.

♡ *Don't go to the replay.* Why dwell on one moment of clumsiness when there are so many more pleasant things to think about? Tomorrow is another day. Plan to begin anew.

♡ *Laugh at yourself* . . . and invite your date to do the same. The difference between a romance-ending cataclysm and a great "you'll never believe how we met" story is attitude! Show a sense of humor about the hot water you're in and don't be surprised if someone joins you!

Week 10

Be a Little Vulnerable

Charles was a television executive who worked for a morning news show. He was also trying to adjust to a recent job transfer from L.A. to New York City and sort through the emotional fallout from a messy divorce. One evening, in therapy, Charles announced that he had just signed on with a very exclusive matchmaking service in the city. "I feel good about it," he gushed. "The woman who runs the company seemed genuinely happy to see me."

I looked Charles over. If I ran a matchmaking company that specialized in six-figure clients, I'd be elated to see Charles, too! Charles was a behind-the-scenes guy at the television network where he worked, but he was blessed with "let's go for the tight shot" dazzling good looks. And whatever "it" was, Charles had it. "It" spilled from the pockets of his pristinely tailored suits like alms. What had moved this very special man to join a matchmaking service? Did the matchmaker who composed his profile use a thesaurus to find adjectives to adequately describe him?

Charles laughed. "It's easy to describe me. I'm a guy who can't seem to get a second date. To tell you the truth, I'm not exactly up to my ears in first dates, either."

While that breaking news might surprise a lot of people, I had some suspicions about what might be causing Charles's problem. Since that was not the topic that brought him to therapy, we moved on to other issues.

Several weeks later, I asked Charles how the matchmaking service was working out. He smiled broadly. "I'm seeing someone," he announced. "But it isn't someone I met through the service. I don't suppose that entitles me to a refund . . ."

No chance of that—but I was entitled to ask for details!

"Her name is Beate. She's Norwegian. And we met in the strangest way," Charles reported. It was a Friday and Charles had just wrapped up the programming meeting that would set the morning show schedule for the upcoming week. He was walking though the park to an outdoor café where he would meet a woman who had been matched with him by the agency. He had just passed the statue of Columbus at Columbus Circle when he felt something warm and moist dripping from the side of his perfectly coifed hair. He reached for his head reflexively. The evidence was now in hand. He had been christened by a passing pigeon.

It was then that he heard the laughter . . . spontaneous, loud and totally unapologetic. "Isn't nature beautiful?" the young woman called to him. As she walked toward him, she pulled a wad of tissues from the pocket of her suede jacket. "I know I shouldn't be laughing and I really am sorry, but I have to tell you, just last week, I got a souvenir from one of these carriage horses. And I was wearing sandals at the time!"

They both laughed at that. And as Charles cleaned himself up, they had a chat. He asked about Beate's accent. She identified it. She asked about the studio ID hanging around his neck. He described his job. She said she worked for an agency that matched university students with host families all over the world. *Agency. Match.* Hmmmm . . . That reminded Charles! He checked his watch. Sure enough, he was late for lunch. He called the woman's cell to cancel—but he did not cancel his reservation. He had lunch with Beate instead. And they've been together ever since.

I asked Charles if he thought Beate would have approached had he not met with disaster. She seemed like a very confident, comfortable-in-her-skin kind of girl, so perhaps she would have—but, then again, maybe not. According to Charles, Beate is a back-to-nature, earthy type who believes that makeup "clogs the pores." He, on the other hand, appears to be as vulnerable as a moving tank. He is nice looking, to be sure . . . but his hair is impervious to the breeze. He looks buttoned-down even when he's wearing sweats. On the whole, he is so dazzlingly together that he doesn't seem to need anything from anybody . . . not admiration . . . not conversation. Not even affection.

The lesson is clear: We, as flirts, spend so much time making ourselves appear invulnerable. But if there's no chink in your armor, how can you be nicked by Cupid's arrow?

Of course, exposing our vulnerable emotional "underbelly" doesn't always work in our favor. The message—that we tempest-tossed flirts who already feel bruised and a little beaten up need to open ourselves to more of the same—isn't always easy to accept. As one chum, Marcia, chided, "Oh, yes, Susan. I know just what I'll say. I'll say, 'Hello, my name is Marcia. Here is my open wound. Please pass the salt.'" But hasn't every lover been wounded? And how could it be otherwise? Without vulnerability, no intimacy is possible!

So what is vulnerability? It's a show of trust. A unilateral dismantling of defenses. It is an unveiling of the authentic self, in all of its perfect imperfection, in the hopes that the viewer will respond with equal honesty and authenticity. I am pleased to report that most flirts are perceptive, empathetic people who are delighted to respond in kind.

Much of this book is devoted to guiding the inexperienced flirt to the right thing to say, the most compelling thing to do to attract a date or a mate, but the truth is sometimes saying the wrong thing or doing something goofy and human is most compelling. Sometimes, even in a world of practiced patter, a sincere stammer wins the day. Why? Because nobody wants to be a door prize for the confident and glib. Because when we glimpse someone at their most awkward or embarrassed, we see their humanity—and therefore, our own. What's not to love?

The human brain is our first line of defense. It never fails to alert us to impending dangers, looming consequences and dire outcomes. If, upon meeting a new man or woman, we accessed the catalog of possible bad outcomes, lousy twists, breaks and disappointments, we would run screaming from the encounter. What I am advocating instead is that you put your two left feet forward and use your natural, lovable vulnerability to your advantage. This week, try these strategies:

 Remember: Nobody has ever died from humiliation. Nobody. Like Beate, I say what's on my mind—and, if I'm in the mood, I'll chat up anyone who crosses my path (if they appear to be unarmed and *compos mentis*). Am I rebuffed? Sometimes. Am I ignored? Occasionally. But people are social animals, and most of the time my fellow human beings are happy to hear from me—and that's what makes exposing my vulnerability worth it. Do your social life a favor: Let your guard down.

♡ *Be perfectly imperfect.* Ask for directions. Request assistance. Ask for help. *Need somebody!* Those in need get responses, indeed! If you're feeling insecure, ask yourself: When was the last time someone asked you for help and you refused? If you are like most people, probably never.

What do people get from helping others? According to researcher Cheryl Keen, they get to know someone who they previously thought was very different from them. That is great flirting! But that isn't the only benefit of altruism. *Psychology Today* reports that the sense of belonging and mattering that comes from helping others has a measurable impact on people's health. The bottom line? When you see a likely prospect, don't hesitate to reach out! They want to meet you halfway.

♡ *Men, if you want to get in touch with your vulnerability, get out of the testosterone zone.* Go to a place where women go. Hit the nail salon and get a nail buff, visit a spa and ask about a hot rock massage or drop in on a lecture on love. Admit you are a little shy, not terribly successful with women. Women like to be consulted and valued for their opinions. And don't be afraid to show that "little boy" appeal. Just grow up fast enough to ask if you can buy her a cappuccino.

♡ *If you are a woman, know this: Men like to feel that you are depending on them for something.* (Note: Being totally dependent is something else entirely so don't bet your life on his benevolence.) Even if you are totally self-sustaining, give him an opportunity to take care of you *in some way.* (And if that makes you bristle, think about this: Don't you and your friends take care of each other? In most relationships, doesn't one hand wash the other? Is it really so terrible that someone attractive and sexually interested might want *in?*) Ask him to show you how to set the "lat" machine at the gym so that it accommodates your height (or lack of it). Allow him to give you directions to that totally authentic Tuscan bakery across town. Ask what that clunking noise when you put your car in reverse might be. Asking for help doesn't mean you're inviting him to take over; it means you are asking him to take *part*.

♡ *Don't assume shyness is a detriment.* A sincere stammer, a hesitant approach, a blush or any other sign of visible vulnerability can be charming. It can also be mysterious. Your reticence might be due to the many secrets you hide or it might hint at the depth of your character. As they say, "Still water runs deep." Who knows who might want to go fishing?

♡ *Signal that you're a softie.* Show that you're willing to put your heart on the line without saying a single word! Animals use nonverbal signs of vulnerability to demonstrate their acceptance of a potential mate and ensure the survival of their species. So how can you show your vulnerability and survive? Try the shoulder shrug. Ethnologists believe it derives from an ancient vertebrate posture of helplessness. Tilt your head, or try an upswept hairdo that exposes your neck to your partner. Showing the neck—an extremely physically vulnerable area—sends the message that you trust a partner with your life. To make sure the feeling is mutual, watch for the vulnerability signs your partner is sending. Has she asked to wear your coat to ward off the chill? Is she using self-deprecating humor to poke fun at her weaknesses? The auguries are good! As any naturalist knows, the couple that displays together stays together!

♡ *See that "less is more."* Bumbling or feeling awkward may force you to become a good listener—and that's an invaluable skill! Connect with a man or woman who has something to say and the conversation will flow. Best of all, he or she will think you're totally understanding! Two talkers never get a word in edgewise, and two listeners will find themselves surrounded by endless silence. Connect with a partner who appreciates your vulnerability and your personality will shine.

♡ *Be sensitive to the vulnerability of others!* Although Beate had a laugh at Charles's expense, she also showed compassion by cleaning him up and sharing an equally embarrassing story. But not every flirt cleans up as perfectly as Charles does. The shy guy who stammers out an awkward hello . . . the klutzy woman who falls all over herself as she's falling for you . . . these are people who are wearing their vulnerability on their sleeves. Be kind. Better yet, be kind of interested! Perfect love doesn't always come in a perfect package.

Week 11

Stop Beating Yourself Up!

"Don't know what to say when a compelling cutie catches your eye? Say anything!" I have given that advice to literally thousands of tongue-tied flirts who are having trouble breaking the ice. That simple strategy has always worked for them and for me. But there is an exception to every rule—in this case, that exception was Robert.

Robert was middle-aged, a professional and the owner of a brand new black Harley-Davidson touring bike. The bike, according to Robert, was not meant to become a "chick magnet" but rather a weekend escape from his full-throttle lifestyle. Since he didn't think of his freewheeling hobby as a social thing, the last place Robert thought he would ever meet a young woman he found interesting was at a motorcycle rally.

Nevertheless, there she was—a petite young woman with long dark hair, watching a painter airbrush a gas tank.

Robert was generally a very together guy but there was something about this girl—and this place—that made him feel as though he had been totally caught off guard. He knew he had to say something to her there and then or she would roar off into oblivion forever . . . but what could he say? That's when he remembered my advice and the acronym QCC—Question, Comment, Compliment. He brushed the road dust off of his jacket and went straight over to where the girl was standing.

"Have you been to this rally before?" he asked her. Apparently, she was just as nonplussed by Robert's sudden appearance as he had been by hers. Her cheeks turned scarlet and she stared resolutely at the ground.

"No," she mumbled finally.

Strike one, Robert tallied silently. How could he have crammed so many mistakes into the space of a single sentence? He had never introduced himself or even eased into the conversation in any way. He had ambushed the young woman from behind like a common thief. And as for the question, it wasn't open-ended! No wonder communication had shut down.

Robert knew he had goofed on the Q but he was willing to move on to his second strategy—the C. He quickly rechecked his target. She was wearing a T-shirt that read: "Imagine if there were no hypothetical situations." Around her neck hung a gold nameplate that Robert was unable to read. This young woman seemed to want to send a message. That was a good sign!

Steeling his resolve, Robert took a half step toward the girl. Then he put on his friendliest smile and said, "I'm sorry if I seem a little forward, but I didn't expect to meet someone like you here."

Now the girl turned to face him squarely. "Someone like me? I don't know what you mean," she said. "What were you expecting?"

Now Robert was truly in hot water. Was there a right answer to that question? He thought not. He also thought about gunning his engines and hitting the road but there was one more C up his sleeve. Compliment. At this point, what did he have to lose?

"Look, it's just that you seemed so . . . above it all." He stretched out his arm to indicate the sprawling array of vendors, food kiosks and bikes.

"That's funny. You seem like a jerk," she said.

Months later, Robert was still mulling over that particular connection failure. From what polluted stream of consciousness had he dredged those inane comments? How could he have been so dense? So awkward? And why, many weeks later, was he still beating himself up?

Robert is not alone. There is an old saying that goes something like this: "We never regret what we do; only what we don't do." As flirts, we tend to blow off our successes. At the end of the day, we don't lie awake reliving the things we did right, thinking about the strangers who did smile back . . . the conversations we successfully opened and closed. It's the one who got away who lives on in our memories, undermining our confidence and foiling our flirting efforts.

When does all this self-punishment start? It starts the instant we assume responsibility for someone else's behavior. It goes like this:

Mark has had two dates with Cee. While their time together has been pleasant enough, it is obvious to Mark that this is not a love connection. He plans to reveal his feelings—or lack of them—to Cee as soon as the time seems right.

Mark is happy, then, when Cee suggests that they meet for lunch a few days later in a busy diner between her office and his. It is a casual setting—and a very public one. It is a perfect place to deliver the "I hope we can be friends" speech. Before Mark can begin, Cee tells him that she has something to say. She explains that, although she likes Mark very much, she feels no chemistry between them. She's met someone else—someone she'd like to date—but she wanted to be sure that she and Mark had reached an understanding before she moved on. Oh, and she is also hoping they can still be friends.

On his way back to the office, Mark mulls over all that happened over two spinach knishes and two cups of vegetable barley soup. He isn't thinking about how easy Cee made it for him to stop dillydallying and start flirting. He's thinking, "Cee didn't like me! I must not have been exciting enough or funny enough or good looking enough to hang on to her. I must have done something wrong or Cee would have found me to be more appealing. And as for this other guy, what's he got that I do not?"

No tendency to self-flagellate, possibly? After all, what did Cee really say to Mark? She said that she didn't feel chemistry between them. He had arrived at that conclusion himself! So why was he taking responsibility for her reaction to what both of them agree was a stalled relationship?

"I'm not worthy." "I'm not valuable." "I must have done something wrong." We send irrational and destructive messages like these to ourselves all the time. So why do we notice them so seldom? Unfortunately, we've gotten used to them. Self-deprecation is like a dysfunctional parent. It nags at you until you believe that you must expect less because you are less. The problem is that obsessing about a moment in the past can jeopardize future happiness. Isn't it time to give yourself a break?

Every minute you spend pondering another person's secret thoughts and hidden motives is a minute you aren't using to find someone more compatible. Ready to become a kinder, gentler flirt—to yourself? These tips will help you to stop worrying about what went wrong so you can start looking for Mr./Ms. Right!

 Always have a business card or personal card on you. They are easy enough to have printed or to print yourself on a computer.

♡ *If you miss a person the first time around, walk away too soon or get distracted, it is never too late to seek that person out again!* Tell him/her again how nice it was to meet. Say you're sorry you didn't have time to chat, then arrange to meet another time. Be sure to "close" by giving him or her your card.

♡ *Before you blame yourself, get a reality check.* You may not always be aware that there's a lot right with you, but your friends are! Rather than take responsibility for a rebuff, ask your buddies what *they* saw happen. What might have felt like it was entirely your fault might have looked entirely the opposite to them. Maybe the object of your flirtation was too snooty, too picky, too high-falutin' or just too clueless to pick up on your invitation. Did you ever think of that? Your friends did!

♡ *Stop the flow of the negative messages you send yourself.* Sure, you can think of a million reasons you were rejection bait. Can you come up with just a few pieces of evidence that it wasn't you? We bet you can! Fill in the blanks:

She/he turned me down because of his or her own_____. If only she/he weren't so_____, she/he would have noticed that I am_____.

I'm too good for him/her because_____.

♡ *Most important, let it go.* Bygones are bygones; don't berate yourself. Nobody is perfect. Try not to repeat history, but don't beat yourself up if you do. Be kinder and gentler to yourself. Let go of self-blame. It's the only way to keep negativity out of your head—and your social interactions.

Be Ready to Flirt Back!

I'd love to tell you that I've never let a promising prospect go undiscovered, but I have. That's because sometimes we singles are in such a rush to get where we are going, we forget to notice the interesting men and women we leave in the dust along the way. And often we spend so much time focusing on how to flirt and where to flirt, we zip right past the fun, attractive singles who are trying desperately to flirt with *us*! My footloose friend Laura is a perfect illustration. And her story is a real eye opener for everyone who is "looking" but not *seeing* the chances to connect that come their way daily, weekly or even right this minute.

Laura discovered her yen for physical fitness at age thirty-eight—not long after her divorce. It took her a while to get back into the swing physically—and just as long to find a form of exercise that seemed right for her. She joined a gym and worked out on the weight machines until she finally admitted to herself how much they bored her. It wasn't until Laura gave up on the gym and tried in-line skating that she found her place in the sun. Before long, she was hitting the trails every day the weather allowed. Within a few weeks, she was racking up eight miles per outing. She looked better than she had in years. She lost the twenty-two pounds she had gained immediately after her divorce, a time she described as her "ménage à trois with Ben & Jerry." But she nearly lost a wonderful opportunity to flirt, as well.

As anyone who has ever hit the asphalt can tell you, outdoor fitness trails are usually friendly places. Whether they're walking, running, biking or skating, the people who congregate there can assume they have something in common with each other: their interest in fitness. Moreover, since most of them have jobs, they tend to exercise at the same time each day. Consequently, it doesn't take long before the morning and evening "regulars" get to know each other by sight. By late summer, Laura had begun to catalog the men and women she frequently passed on the course. There was the guy in the Orioles cap who ran alongside his golden Lab. The two older ladies who power-walked exactly one mile every other day. The good-looking runner who chatted constantly on his cell phone while jogging. And the in-line skater Laura secretly dubbed "Mr. Equipment." He raced around the park in aerodynamic spandex skating tights and a matching hoodie. He had all the requisite pads, a streamlined helmet and even carried a water tank on his back. But beyond that, Laura had little opportunity to commune with her fellow fitness friends. She had begun to skate at a blistering pace, often topping ten miles per hour. She never felt better. And she never looked more unapproachable.

Laura finally hit the skids shortly after the first cool breezes of autumn blew in. Suddenly, the trails that had always been clear sailing were drifted with leaves, dotted with seed pods and littered with fallen sticks. Early one morning, as Laura came zooming down a hill, a piece of foliage jammed in the wheels of her right skate. The skate stopped dead. Laura skidded off the trail and landed in a heap on the dewy grass. She was still trying to peel her dignity off the ground when "Mr. Equipment" glided to a stop beside her. He extended his hand.

"I wanted to warn you about this spot but you didn't look up when you skated past," he said, pulling Laura to her feet. "You're pretty intent on your skating."

Laura took a sip of the water he offered from his Camelback tank—then she took a good look at her new friend. He had obviously noticed her. He knew when she skated and how she skated. And his smile told her that he liked what he had no-ticed. So why hadn't she ever noticed how attractive this man was? And most of all, how had she failed to see how interested he was in her?

Laura and Ed (yes, he had a name!) spent the next few min-utes chatting about the merits of off-road in-line skates. (After all, who would be more likely to know all about skates with eight-inch high-pressure tires and hydraulic drum brakes than "Mr. Equipment" himself?) She borrowed the handsome run-ner's cell phone to call work and let her boss know she'd be a bit late. Then, after accepting a Band-Aid for her scraped elbow from one of the two older ladies, she headed for home—but only after agreeing to meet Ed the next day at what he believed would be a safer, better-maintained trail.

Did Laura skate head-on into a love connection? Maybe yes—maybe no. But she did trip over the true meaning—and potential—of flirting. Flirting, as I explain it—and as Laura has come to understand it—is the art of acting and interacting with-out serious intent, to successfully meet and relate to others. It begins when you take note of someone else's special qualities, whether they are as subtle as a kind smile or as compelling as a velvety "hello." It develops when you share your own uniqueness with those intriguing men and women you encounter, even in the course of your everyday activities. Laura didn't just come to know Ed and the others who shared her love of outdoor activity. She also came to understand how much social mileage she might have covered, on wheels and off, if only she had taken no-tice of the interesting, attractive people who were trying to flirt with *her*!

Not every flirt is as fast on her feet as Laura. Many of us still slip when it comes to making the most of our opportunities to connect with others. We overlook the flirting opportunities in-herent in everyday places or, like Laura, become so obsessed with getting from point A to point B, we leave our most promising prospects in the dust.

The only thing that's more fun than flirting is flirting back! So this week, why not cut those interested parties some slack? These tips can help:

♡ *Flirting should be spontaneous.* Whether you're in a supermarket checkout line or the betting window at Saratoga or the sunblock aisle of the drug store (a friend of mine spent a very refreshing fifteen minutes making up new words for the acronyms SPF with a man who asked her what those initials meant). Live in the moment! Really see who's around you. If someone is making eye contact, smile. If he or she smiles back, you're halfway there!

♡ *Remember: Conversations you have in your head tend to stay there.* If you see someone you're interested in, don't just stand there: *Say* something! Feeling tongue-tied? See week 23 for some foolproof conversation openers.

♡ *Be open to advances.* You're becoming more conscious of others; is it really so impossible to believe that others are becoming more aware of you? The handsome passerby who shot you a playful glance, the fellow dog-walker with the inviting body language, or the wry commentator at the crosswalk who can't help but share her funny observations are all using different techniques but they're sending the same message: "You look like my kind of person!" What is the likelihood that you and that captivating stranger are really simpatico? You'll never know unless you stay open, approachable and ready to respond!

♡ *Play the numbers game to win!* Meeting Mr. or Ms. Right is like playing the lottery—you've got to be in the game to win it! This week, improve your odds. Resolve to make contact with at least one appealing new person every day. How to begin?

Don't travel in herds. Separate from your old friends so new friends can approach you. Take notice of men and women around you. Most of all, send a positive message to anyone and everyone who seems to be flirting with *you*! At the very least, you'll make a few new friends. And who knows? You may even meet your match!

Week 13

Make Breaking Up a Little Easier to Do

As Bernice turned the corner toward her favorite lounge, she caught a glimpse of herself in a building window. I look pretty good for a fifty-year-old, she thought. Anyway, in his profile he gave his age as sixty. He thinks I am forty-eight. He isn't expecting a teenager. (And who tells the truth about their age on the Internet anyway?) Forty-eight is close enough. Besides, he didn't ask for a thirty-year-old in his profile.

When Bernice approached the bar, she noticed a nice-enough-looking man with gray hair (full head!) sitting there, nursing a sparkling water. Bernice noted when he stood up that he wasn't tall, but he wasn't conspicuously short, either. His shirt and pants were casual, but in good taste. His shoes, however, were in terrible shape. They were scuffed, worn at the heels . . . and if they were made of the hide of any sort of animal, Bernice guessed, that animal would be the free-range Nauga. They smiled, shook hands and introduced themselves. It seemed to Bernice, in retrospect, that might have been the best part of the evening. Things deteriorated rapidly from that point on.

His name was Ray—and he had the waiter ready and waiting for Bernice's arrival. They were immediately shown to a table for two beside a window. They exchanged pleasantries—then Bernice excused herself.

"I need to use the ladies' room; I will be right back," she said. She'd do a quick inventory, make sure she was at her best, and then rejoin her date.

She spent a few minutes primping, then walked back to her table. It was exactly as she had left it except for one thing: There was no one there. No one. For a moment, Bernice thought she would find her date back at the bar, but a quick glance in that direction assured her that he was not there. She assumed, then, that he must have gone to the men's room. She settled in at the table to wait. She waited ten minutes. Then fifteen. Then, absurdly, twenty. Obviously, Ray was gone.

Bernice was perplexed. Why would he leave? They hadn't even exchanged fifteen minutes of conversation! Moreover, she knew she looked good. She was the image of the photo she had posted with her Internet profile, and she was well dressed. She was a petite woman in peak physical condition. She had turned up in black leather pants, a leather jacket and a light blue silk blouse that brought out the color of her eyes. Again she tried to give her date the benefit of the doubt. Maybe he had to move his car. Maybe he felt ill. Perhaps he was a PETA member and was upset by her pants.

The waiter arrived at Bernice's table, looking sheepish. He knew she had been stood up. Bernice tried to smile confidently, and ordered a dry martini. Then she sat back and took stock of the situation. How could any man be so rude and boorish? How would any grown-up find himself unable to tolerate fifteen minutes of small talk, then make his excuses and say good-bye? We aren't all looking for the same package. We aren't all right for each other. But couldn't he spend fifteen minutes in conversation rather than running out like a coward?

As Bernice sipped her drink, things seemed to become clearer. She was accomplished, funny, independent . . . a catch! How dare he not like her looks! How dare he walk out on her! She picked up her phone and called his cell. It was turned off. What a surprise! But Bernice left a message anyway. "Who do you think you are? And who was your charm school instructor—Idi Amin? The least you could have done was stay for a drink, and then politely say good-bye. Thank goodness I know this is your problem and not mine."

She felt a little better after venting, but the experience left a nagging feeling that business remained unfinished. The next day, Bernice e-mailed the customer service department at the singles' site that had brought her and Ray together. She told the customer service representative her story and asked that an obvious scoundrel like Ray be kicked off the site. He wasn't, of course. Vengeance was not Bernice's, sayeth the webmaster.

When Bernice thinks back on the experience now, nearly a year later, it still stings. She remembers Ray's friendly hand-shake, his easy manner . . . and, oddly, the run-down state of his loafers. Yet somehow, that memory makes her smile. After all, time wounds all heels. And that's an unpleasant fact of life even Ray cannot outrun.

As I told Bernice, no singles website could ever rid itself totally of inconsiderate, socially inept men—or women. If that were to happen, there would be about three people left to match up, and one of them would be a monk who has spent the last twenty-two years on a mountain top praying constantly for the peace of the world.

Now, anyone who has ever seen me speak or read my previous books knows that I am normally a very optimistic person. Optimism is a requirement for any flirt. So what makes me think there are so few "stand-up" flirts to be found? Because I hear stories like Bernice's all the time, told from one side of the going-nowhere relationship or the other. And that has convinced me that, although the flirts involved don't intend to be cruel, many, many singles would rather take the coward's way out than confront a partner who is not right for them.

Consider this story. It was told to my collaborator, Barbara, the very week this chapter was written.

Steve was a mature, experienced single man who, for some reason, attracted more than his share of much younger ladies. Steve was in his early fifties and looked it; and he never set out specifically to charm the is-that-your-daughter set. Nevertheless, he did have that certain something—so it didn't surprise Barbara when he began to tell her about his dates with Erika, an assistant television producer fresh out of journalism school.

The relationship followed the usual progression. Lunch. A dinner. A night at the theater followed by dessert and a nightcap. Steve was as impressed with Erika's intellect as he was with her beauty. And Erika was dazzled by Steve's out-there humor and casual sophistication. They agreed that their fourth date would take place in a more personal setting. They would meet at Erika's apartment. She would make her grandmother's gnocchi and he would bring the wine.

A few nights later, Erika was pinching off pieces of dough in the tiny kitchen while Steve busied himself looking over the mementos scattered about the homey living room. Suddenly he came upon a series of framed photographs. The photos were of professional quality, like ads. And they featured a young woman dressed in very scanty clothing. It was Erika! Suddenly Steve wasn't sure what to do. He and Erika had not been intimate. Now he felt as though he had walked in on Erika while she was dressing! He finally decided to confront his date about the photos over dinner.

"Oh, *that*," she answered brightly. "I supported myself all through graduate school by working as a dancer! It's silly, I know, because I have a 'real' job now, but the money is so good I still perform on weekends. Otherwise I wouldn't be able to afford my own place."

Erika chattered on blithely but Steve found it difficult to chat. He finished dinner, excused himself politely and called Barbara.

"She's a stripper on weekends!" he hissed into his cell. "It's not a big deal, I know. I've been to strip clubs. I enjoy strip clubs. But I don't think I can go out with an exotic dancer. I know it's hypocritical. I know it's definitely not PC. But there it is."

Barbara understood. If attraction was an unpredictable mix of factors, so was disinterest. Steve's feelings had clearly changed now that he had the bare facts. "If it's a no-go, then it's a no-go," Barbara counseled. "You'll have to tell her."

"That's what I'll do. I'll tell her," Steve said. "I'll call right now and tell her that I'm not looking for a relationship."

What? If he wasn't looking for a relationship, why had he been seeing Erika? "You can't say that!" she argued. "It's made up!"

"Fine. Then I'll say I just don't want to be dating anyone right now."

"Steve, you just told me that Erika is intelligent. You've been calling her for dates! Telling her you don't want to be dating right now won't set off her BS detector? Are you kidding?"

Now Steve was clearly frustrated. "OK then, what should I tell her?"

"How about the truth?" Barbara suggested. "She has to know that certain things are deal breakers for people. While you aren't passing judgment on her, her sideline is a deal breaker for you! That's all there is to it!"

At last, Steve agreed. Everyone's boundaries *were* different. Erika had told him herself that she had refused to date a man because he had gotten a job in the same company where she worked. She simply didn't date coworkers. Period. Wouldn't someone who was so in touch with her own deal breakers understand his feelings?

That night, Steve did call. He lied through his teeth. And now Erika will never have a chance to understand anything about why such a warm relationship abruptly cooled. Was that fair? Was it kind?

* * *

No matter how open minded and accepting we think we are, our feelings can change when someone else's lifestyle choices clash with our own. Habits like smoking or drinking, geographical location, prior marriages, sexual tastes (mine are "normal"; his are weird!), physical condition, the absence or presence of kids and a host of other factors from the ridiculous (his 3,000-piece Matchbox car collection) to the sublime (her devotion to the spiritual teachings of a New Age guru) aren't "quirks" we assume we must endure—they are the hot buttons that can jettison a pairing. Since finding Mr. or Ms. Right is a lot like buying a pair of shoes—even Ray had to try on many pairs to find some with just the right fit!—it's important that flirts learn how to unload a relationship that isn't working without taking on a load of guilt.

Whether you're dating or relating, if your bond is disintegrating, I believe that honesty is the best policy. It can even make breaking up easier to do.

Rejecting others isn't easy. Doing it with grace requires courage and skill. Since flirting is a risk you have taken, you know you have the courage. As for the skill, the strategies I outline below will help.

♡ *Use "I" messages.* Beginning every sentence of your *adieu* speech with the word "you" (as in, "You just aren't right for me" or "You are the most exasperating backseat driver I've ever known and the next time you ride in my car, I guarantee you will be in the trunk!") places the blame for the relationship misfire squarely on your partner's shoulders—and that makes for hurt feelings.

Since it is you who have diagnosed the incompatibility, it is important that you admit your feelings and take responsibility for your actions. Make a conscious effort to use "I" messages, such as, "I feel we have little in common," or "I am looking for a different kind of relationship right now." There is no guarantee that your former date will leave with a smile on his or her face, but this technique will make the situation less painful and leave your partner's ego intact.

♡ *Do the easy thing—even if it's difficult.* Avoiding his phone calls, steering clear of her old haunts, blocking him from your buddy list, going miles out of your way just to keep from driving past her house . . . these aren't acts of kindness. They are acts of cowardice!

What requires more energy: running, hiding, evading and skulking around the Internet like the Invisible Man or simply saying, as kindly as possible, "I like you very much, but I feel no chemistry between us." Or "I have really enjoyed getting to know you but for whatever reason, there is no real love connection for me here. Do you feel the same?"

Stating your case, briefly and sensitively, cuts down on the wear and tear on both of you. It also earns you the respect of someone who may not want to waste time on you any more than you want to spend another minute with them!

♡ *Be brief.* If you've ever been on the receiving end of a breakup speech that turned into an analysis of your sins, failures and inadequacies, you will understand the merciful intent behind this suggestion.

Having trouble keeping your good-bye simple and to the point? These concise, compassionate "I messages" will ensure that you dish rejection out the same way you'd prefer to take it:

"I like you very much but this is just not a love connection for me."

"I know this is a cliché, but I really would like to be friends!"

"It's been wonderful getting to know you, but I don't feel we're right for each other."

"I'm not looking for commitment right now. Spending time together is keeping us both from finding the relationship we want."

"I feel_____." Just fill in the blank and move on.

Before you make your breakup public . . . A lot of singles prefer to take their parting shots in public in order to minimize the possibility of emotional overreaction. Speaking on behalf of those who may be seated at a nearby table, your goal is commendable—but is it attainable?

Here is some guidance that could preserve the peace *and* the glassware: If the relationship has played out in public— that is, if the two of you have done lunch, shared a couple of cozy dinners, spent a few evenings at the theater or passed time in any other public venue—then your pairing was more about "outings" than cocooning. A public setting for your final conversation is a safe bet. If, however, you have dried each other's dishes or washed each other's backs, if you have been seeing each other regularly and have met each other's friends, I recommend that you say good-bye in a manner befitting the intimacy of your relationship. If you don't want to end the liaison at home, at least seek out a quiet place that has meaning for both of you.

Week 14

My Seven-Day Countdown to Complete Rejection Recovery

Busy people live by their schedules. I am a great example of that. In order for me to get everything done that needs doing in the course of a day, I adhere to a self-imposed agenda that allows me time for all of my necessary chores: working out (upon waking, usually around 9 a.m.), appointments with clients (noon until dinner) and, of course, time for flirting (all the time!).

Of course, schedules don't just put you on track to meet your own obligations; they also put you on the social pathway. When you hit the local haunts at the same time each day, you tend to run into those people who also run their lives—and their errands—by the clock. That's how I first met Boyd. A young, busy dentist in private practice, Boyd took a break to walk his springer spaniel pup, MacDuff, every day at mid-morning, just about the time I get out and about in the neighborhood. Since familiarity breeds conversation, it wasn't long before Boyd and I would stop and exchange a few words.

After a few months, I noticed that Boyd had acquired a lithe, athletic-looking two-legged companion, as well. His girlfriend's name, he informed me, was Debbie. She worked at a ski shop in town, ran cross-country clinics on weekends, and, judging from Boyd's blissful glow, was wonderful in every way. I ran into them several times a week . . . hauling kibble back from the pet store . . . jogging along the sidewalk . . . sharing a sandwich at the deli around the corner.

Then, for a while, I didn't see Boyd anymore. Of course, Manhattan is a big, busy place. Although I thought of Boyd now and again, I assumed that he, Debbie and the impeccably groomed MacDuff had jogged off to a better situation in another town. But just when as I gave up on seeing my neighbor again, there he was, sitting alone on a bench in the park one Saturday afternoon. MacDuff lazed in the sun nearby. Debbie was nowhere to be seen.

True to his profession, Boyd extracted the painful details of his story. Things with Debbie had taken a turn and the relationship had begun to grind him down. He was thinking of ways to let her down easy when, totally unexpectedly, Debbie turned the tables and dumped *him*. She simply announced that she wasn't happy, packed her running tights and ski poles into a rented van and moved to Vermont. By making a preemptive strike, she had made it easy for Boyd. So why had he gone to pieces? Although he was planning for a breakup, the denouement he envisioned was on *his* terms. Debbie had caught him totally off guard. Now the usually upbeat dentist was down in the mouth and there wasn't a thing anybody—his friends, his family or me—seemed to be able to do about it.

"If I had been able to plan for this, I could have managed it," Boyd told me. "I would have scheduled Debbie's departure, made allowances for the things I would miss. Deb was a lousy girlfriend but she was a good roommate, one who filled the house with people and fun. Suddenly being without her made me feel like a camper without a counselor. My life was in chaos. My agenda was out the window and I had no idea how to get it back."

Boyd was right. When we lose a significant other, we don't just lose the affection and company of a specific person, we lose the lifestyle that we shared. And that can make you feel lost . . . adrift . . . with nothing to focus on but the gaping hole in your daily life where the routine you once shared used to be. That's why I believe it is so important to jolt yourself out of your post-rejection doldrums.

After a breakup, a day or two of self-pity is to be expected . . . but a week or two of negative behavior can become a habit! These tips, which I prescribed for Boyd, are meant to be administered like an anti-rejection vitamin: one each day to prevent post-parting depression.

♡ *Remind yourself that rejection is not necessarily personal.* Debbie may have had her issues with Boyd, but was her ski-bum lifestyle more compatible with the bustling streets of Manhattan or with the rolling hills of Vermont? Her abrupt departure left a hole in Boyd's life (and in his wall—when she left, she took her grandfather's mounted deer head with her) but, in the end, did she reject Boyd or his lifestyle? The question didn't keep Boyd from sulking but the answer might have saved him from months of self-flagellation.

Listen to what happened to my friend Marnie. To keep in shape, and to stay within her budget as a copywriter for a small, independent publishing company, Marnie bought an inexpensive membership to the local YMCA. She would swim there in the evenings after work, three or four times a week.

As Marnie and I discussed, a swim club is not necessarily a great place to get your feet wet as a flirt. Dedicated athletes rarely wish to be distracted from their regimens—and a woman rarely feels that she is at her best when her hair is dripping and winter pallor has turned her skin a uniform shade of mortuary yellow. Nevertheless, Marnie managed to get over her self-consciousness and chat amiably with Matt, a muscular young man, who swam evenings, too. The two of them had a great deal in common— they both worked in publishing, they were alumni of the same New England university, they both had tiny apartments with bathtubs in the kitchen—and, as far as Marnie was concerned, they were both treading water in terms of romance. One night, she gathered her courage and asked Matt if he'd like to stop for a cup of hot chocolate after their swim. To Marnie, this was no big thing. It was a friendly invitation and nothing more. She was surprised, then, that it seemed to throw her new friend for a loop. Giving her a peculiar look, he stammered out something inaudible. Then he disappeared from the pool forever.

Marnie was disappointed, to be sure. In fact, she stopped asking men out altogether, but she kept up her workout regimen. Almost a year later, she was looking very buff and seriously outpaddling the guy in the next lane. But when she stopped to catch her breath, she was shocked to discover the man she had left in her wake was Matt! This time he was as charming as he had been when he first met her. And although she had no inclination to ask him out, he *did* ask her. Over tea and pastries, he revealed the real reason behind his curious behavior and mysterious disappearance. Matt had been told just hours before his last swim with Marnie that the company he worked for was transferring him. He was reeling from the news. When she invited him out, he was totally nonplussed. Matt liked Marnie a lot—but to him, there was no point in getting to know each other better. Any possibility of a relationship was dead in the water.

Now that Matt is back in the city to stay, he and Marnie have become an item—but for Marnie, the episode has been a lesson she'll never forget. Her message to Boyd and every other flirt who has been "rejected"? Rejection is not necessarily about *you*—it could very well be about him, his current situation, his plans or his baggage.

People come together for any number of reasons, including loneliness, physical attraction, boredom, a common hobby, convenience and countless others—valid and otherwise. (I know a woman who moved in with a man because he had a dog that looked remarkably like her childhood pet!) Is it really so impossible to believe that your ex may have decided to hit the road for a reason that has nothing at all to do with you? No, it is not! How could she leave you? Spend a part of the day after counting the ways! You may end the day viewing the entire episode in a different light.

♡ *Write a thank-you note.* Every single man or woman has experienced at least one "nowhere affair." What's that? A luscious whirlwind with a paramour who wastes a few months of your life, then announces out of the blue that the relationship is "going nowhere." In a case like that, there's no question that rejection is a favor. That's why, on day two following a breakup, it is important to show your gratitude by writing a thank-you note to the man or woman who set you free. Load that poison pen and chronicle the many annoying habits you no longer have to endure. Pour out your appreciation for the future indignities you have been spared. Offer lots of evidence that the problem could not have been you! Be effusive. Be sincere. Be as scathing as you want to be! Just don't be quick to post your thoughts. This missive is for your eyes only. Do not, under any circumstances, send it.

♡ *Get out of the house.* To get out of your funk, get out of your house! Sure, it's recuperative to chill out, regroup—but unless you break your self-imposed exile, you may be hibernating alone for a very long time. Light a fire under that La-Z-Boy and get out of the house *tonight*! Then choose three more nights of the coming week and mark them as unbreakable dates with yourself on your calendar. Even strolling around the neighborhood is healthier than retracing your relationship's path to destruction.

♡ *Learn something new.* There is almost nothing as therapeutic as learning something new. Whether you decide to try your hand at landscape painting or ice skating or throwing pottery, whether you are learning a skill from scratch or picking up on a hobby you dropped somewhere along the way (undoubtedly so you could spend more time with Mr./Ms. Wrong!), mastering a new talent will focus your thoughts and absorb your attention. You will simply have less time to pine and yearn and wallow. But if you want to really send those roller-coaster emotions around the curve . . .

♡ *Throw a pity party!* No, I don't mean the quietly desperate kind only you and Ben & Jerry attend. I mean a real roll-up-the-rug-and-save-the-peasants, knock-down, drag-out party! I've spent some of my most upbeat evenings in the company of the dumped—and how could it be otherwise? The jilted are an endlessly creative—and delightfully vindictive—crew. One recently thrown-over gal treated her friends to a unique and festive party activity: "Pin the Blame on James." She simply amended a child's donkey game so that the face of her former flame was affixed to the *burro*'s body. She then handed out slips of paper on which she had listed her ex's most grievous flaws, passed out the pins and a rollicking time was had by all!

♡ *Pull out the spare.* When a pairing fizzles and goes flat, don't just sit there . . . pull out the spare! Who doesn't know at least one promising prospect that made you think, "If I weren't attached, I'd . . ." And how about that cutie your boss has been dying to set you up with? You've got nowhere to go! Why not make that call? Now that the extra baggage is gone, you're alone and in the driver's seat!

♡ *Inventory your assets.* On a sheet of paper, list nine "no"s and one "yes." Then, each time you get turned down, thrown over or just overlooked, cross out one of the "no"s and remind yourself that you're one step closer to "yes." You may have to kiss a lot of frogs before you find your prince or princess, but now there is one fewer than before!

Part Three

Approach

Put a Great Coach on Your Team!

One day last year, I found a very unusual message in my e-mail.

Sent from a foreign address, it read: "I just finished your books *How to Attract Anyone, Anytime, Anyplace*, and *101 Ways to Flirt*. I was wondering, do you do personal coaching on the telephone? I think I could use some professional advice on how to approach women who appeal to me." The e-mail was signed simply, "Gerhard."

Naturally, I was intrigued. I have coached dozens of people who wanted to learn to mingle but generally these clients came to me by recommendation or through the "personal touch consultations" link on my website, www.schoolofflirting.com. This man was contacting me directly, however, and he was clearly willing to cross international boundaries—at least by phone—to expand his social horizons. I fired off an e-mail asking a few pertinent questions—I needed to know exactly what he expected before I took him on as a client—and included my phone number.

By the time he called a few days later, I had spent hours speculating about my new friend. What could he possibly look like? He certainly didn't seem shy. I didn't have to wonder long.

"I am a man in my forties," Gerhard began. "Women say I'm attractive. I'm five-foot-eleven and athletic. I've been married and divorced. I have an adorable three-year-old daughter. I'm also what I call 'temporarily retired.' I sold my business last year and am looking now for a new investment. In my social life, I am the 'extra man.' Other people fix me up with dates all the time, but I want to choose my dates myself. That's the only way I'll find someone who really makes me happy."

By now, I was getting used to the idea that Gerhard was nothing like what I had expected, but his next comment took me by surprise.

"Most of all, I want to be able to pick up a woman in an elevator," he announced.

I laughed. "In an elevator? No one even makes eye contact in an elevator! Why would you want to flirt in such a difficult place?"

"Well, actually I want to be comfortable picking up women 'anyplace, anytime,' which is why I chose your book in the bookstore," Gerhard explained. "But the buildings where I do business are full of beautiful young women. I see them in elevators all the time. Unfortunately, I'm afraid to start a conversation. If a woman is my type, I fall mute."

I began to weigh Gerhard's issues against the funny, charming, successful persona he presented to me. Why was such a capable man so uncomfortable starting a simple conversation? Was he afraid of rejection? A poor conversationalist? And why were his friends so eager to step in and take over as matchmakers? Did they sense something awkward or "unapproachable" about Gerhard? The project had taken on a definite allure.

For the next two months, I coached Gerhard once a week by telephone. As a cognitive therapist, I uncovered his core issues quickly. Like many people, he needed to overcome the negative messages he had absorbed in childhood and adolescence. So we worked to reprogram these negative messages, turning them into positive new behaviors instead. But Gerhard was still reluctant to leap into the conversational fray.

One day, after role-playing a scenario that required Gerhard to strike up a conversation with a woman while ordering a latte at a coffee shop, he made an interesting proposal—to me.

"Talking to a stranger comes so easily to you. I would like to watch and learn. Would it be possible for me to come to New York so you could coach me in person? I'll fly down and pay you for the hours we spend together. What do you say?"

I said, "Why not?" And my new career was born.

The most adroit flirts always know where to go to "see and be seen." I immediately decided that Gerhard and I would develop our cultural awareness and our social contacts at the same time by meeting at the Metropolitan Museum of Art. A museum is an easy place for a single to visit alone. It encompasses a variety of prime locations for flirting: exhibits that invite comment, inspiring spots to people watch, great bookshops and usually a very nice cafeteria. In other words, a museum is not only a repository for some for the world's greatest art, it is a gallery where people can display themselves. Unfortunately, my student was a little intimidated by art. "I don't know a thing about it," Gerhard groused. "So what do I do? Say something inane, like 'I love the color red in that painting?'"

"No." I laughed. I reminded him of about the importance of asking open-ended questions (see week 23). Then I whispered, "Watch me."

I walked over to some Da Vinci line drawings and placed myself within hearing distance of the first man I saw. If there was a "code" to unlocking the secrets of flirting, maybe Leonardo would help me break it.

"The Da Vinci exhibit is so crowded," I commented to a man nearby. "I can hardly see the fine lines of these exquisite drawings." I leaned closer to the drawing, but not so close that I'd make him uncomfortable.

"I'm coming back in the morning," my new friend responded. "It's too crowded for me, too."

"Unfortunately, I can't. I work tomorrow." I gave him a rueful smile. The next thing we knew, we were discussing what I did for a living, what I loved about the Met and what had drawn me to this exhibit. (A classical physique! And I don't mean Da Vinci's anatomical studies, either.)

Now it was my client's turn. Since Gerhard felt more comfortable chatting over ratatouille than Rembrandt, I directed him to a table in the cafeteria near an attractive woman who was sitting alone. I seated myself nearby.

The woman was a striking brunette with deep-set brown eyes, posed somewhat like Rodin's *The Thinker.*

"Talk to her," I prodded from behind my menu.

"What should I say?"

"Anything you want as long as it's not sexual or threatening," I hissed. "And don't lean in too close. Give her enough personal space."

Gerhard nodded in the woman's direction. Finally, he caught her eye and said, "You're deep in thought."

The woman stared blankly at him. Was she irritated by the interruption? I was sure she would blow him off.

Gerhard persisted. "You must have a lot on your mind," he commented.

The woman seemed more perplexed than annoyed. She regarded my student quizzically, sizing him up. Would she speak? When she did, I was surprised at her candor.

"I'm an artist. I adore Da Vinci and I'm thinking about what a genius he has for drawing the human form. What a talent! And do you know he died thinking he was an absolute failure?"

I looked at Gerhard. He was trying not to look at me. I knew he knew nothing about art. Would he remember what I told him to do when in doubt about what to say?

He leaned toward the woman and smiled. "A failure?" he prompted.

I nearly applauded. Weeks ago I had shown my client how to repeat the last few words of a friend's statement and rephrase it in the form of a question—a foolproof way to add fuel to the conversational fire and draw out a new acquaintance. Gerhard was not only using what he had learned, he was working it!

Fifteen minutes later, they were chatting like old friends. Gerhard and the artist had nothing in common, but he was trying to follow my rules. He had found her conversational "hot button" and keyed into her interests. When she'd revealed a particular interest in Da Vinci's drawings, he personalized the conversation.

"Do you draw?" he asked.

The woman's eyes came to life, and she described her work as a botanical illustrator. At this point, Gerhard got a little tongue-tied over the technicalities—but he asked intelligent questions and made relevant comments. He even led the conversation to a related topic.

"I had an aunt who was an artist. She did sculptures in driftwood," Gerhard offered, and told her a bit about his eccentric aunt. Maybe a little too much, in fact, but he was obviously trying.

He extracted himself from the encounter by explaining that he had a tour to catch and had to be off. But he offered his friend a lovely parting handshake and a hearty, "Nice chatting with you," thereby ending the conversation with a compliment, just as I had suggested! What a student! What a flirt!

Now that Gerhard was warmed up, we moved on to test his skills in several other locations—a café (where he was extremely charming but failed to "close" [see week 51]), a large midtown bookstore, Saks Fifth Avenue, the Four Seasons and finally, a venerable Manhattan restaurant decorated in the style of colonial England. He made his moves; I took notes.

At last, we arrived at the bar at the Four Seasons, exhausted by our day of "charm-athletics" and ready for an honest review.

"So what do you think?" he asked eagerly.

This would be the hard part, I knew—criticizing gently and constructively. I used the "sandwich technique," cushioning the "meat" of my criticism between two cushy compliments.

"Once you broke the ice, your conversation was light and fun,"

I said encouragingly. "You are witty and interesting and, most of all, interested in others." Then I said, "I think you will be even more able to successfully 'close' when your body language is in closer alignment with your dynamic, confident personality."

"Even in elevators?" Gerhard teased.

"Especially in elevators—or anywhere else you must make a connection in what is known as a 'New York minute.'" We smiled at each other.

"Your posture and carriage don't exude self assurance," I said quietly. "When you approach, your head is often down, your eyes are looking down and your shoulders need to be more squared off. That will send a more centered message."

"I only do that because you are short," he joked.

"Vertically challenged, please. But don't look down. Keep your chin up and walk with certainty, Gerhard. You are a tall, nice-looking man; show it off."

I suggested that he have a friend videotape him so he could watch himself interact. He had a tendency to shuffle and stoop, a common trait among shy, tall men.

"When you get home, practice awhile—then send me a video so I can reevaluate your body language," I suggested. "In fact, you might consider taking a Pilates or yoga class—or a course in the Alexander Technique. Any skills that incorporate strength and stretching will enhance your carriage. Plus, there are lots of women in those classes," I urged.

The next morning, I reviewed my notes and sent him a follow-up e-mail suggesting specific strategies to boost his flirting efforts—especially in an elevator. I also thanked him for what turned out to be a mutually educational day. During our whirl-wind twelve hours together, Gerhard learned that he had what it took to flirt successfully in what might be the most competitive singles market of all. And I came away with a renewed belief in my life-long philosophy: Connecting with that special someone is really a matter of connecting with the amusing, uninhibited, natural flirt in each of us.

I came away with another very important realization: Whether we have been consciously flirting for six months or sixty years, whether we have been blessed with the animal magnetism of George Clooney or the blundering appeal of Mr. Bean, every one of us needs a flirting coach from time to time. Think about it. We are all subject to developing habits that, while small, may be off-putting to others. A truly objective observer will notice the unconscious tendencies, defensive habits, self-diminishing stances and social tics we tend to wrap ourselves in like old, comfy sweaters. And if your observer is a skilled "people person" himself, he can even point out some strategies you can use to reach out to the attractive singles that cross your path every day.

I know what you're thinking. "Great idea, Susan! Why don't I cash in my frequent-commuter miles and trek into New York? You can watch me try to put the make on people while I stand in line to buy a hot dog from a street vendor! We can really paint the town . . . with mustard." I understand that most people don't have the wherewithal to opt for transatlantic travel when they want to get their flirting lives off the ground. But the good news is that a great flirting coach is one luxury we can all afford! And the very best ones are not just close by; they are, in fact, usually those who are closest to us.

What makes a great flirting coach? If you asked Gerhard, he would tell you that the ideal trainer is someone who has an understanding of what makes individuals "tick" and what makes couples "click." Nobody knows what makes you "tick" better than your nearest, dearest friend.

You may not realize that you take on a "glazed" look when the conversation takes a political turn and you may not be aware that you tend to drum your fingers when you feel anxious, but your friends certainly do. Take advantage of that! A great flirting coach is someone who knows what you're like when you've got it going on—and what you're like when you don't. He or she is also someone who is always on your side. Invite a keenly observant, upbeat pal to check out your technique from a nearby table or to belly up to the bar while you chat up that charmingly clumsy line-dancer, and you're sure to get a new perspective on which of your lines work—and which fall flat.

Do you have a friend who simply can't understand why a catch like you hasn't been snapped up yet? Make it both of your business to find out! Stake out a couple of spots in a favorite hangout and let the coaching begin! The guidelines below will let you and your coach know exactly what to look for.

♡ *Ask for a sound check.* We could be reciting "The Charge of the Light Brigade" or reading from the periodic table of the elements; the truth is that whatever the content of our speech, our voices telegraph our emotions. Of course, in any flirting situation what we say is important; but no matter what the text of our message, it is the timbre, tone, pacing and pitch of our speech that broadcasts our enthusiasm, transmits our anxiety, shouts out our shyness or suggests our dishonesty. It is important then, that you have a good idea whether your voice is great or grating.

Since it's not just what you say, it's how you say it that counts when you're out to charm a new friend, it is important that your "flirting coach" take note of any changes in the way you sound when you're with someone you want to impress. If your coach suggests that your pitch becomes higher, that your voice takes on a "choked" quality, or if the sound of your voice seems somehow stressed, check out the sound check we suggest for week 30. It will ensure that you are seen and heard. A friend can alert you to the unconscious behaviors that might be keeping you from making a meaningful connection. And that's a lot of information for the price of a cup of cappuccino or two.

♡ *Could you please point that thing somewhere else?* There were no two ways about it: Miguel established himself as a hot stuff from the instant he entered my School of Flirting workshop. For one thing, he looked like Antonio Banderas. If that weren't enough, he humbly admitted that he had made the climb from an entry-level marketing job to a corner office in record time. He even danced salsa in his spare time. So why was he having such a tough time turning an initial conversation into a first date? I pulled two chairs up on stage and asked for a female volunteer. It was time for a role play.

The woman I selected to interact with Miguel was definitely not a natural extrovert. Just revealing her name to the audience—she was called Kerry—made her blush! Still, she and Miguel hadn't exchanged ten cordial sentences before Miguel found himself face to face with Kerry's assertive side.

"Wait a minute," Kerry demanded, stopping Miguel in mid-sentence. "Do you have to do that?"

Miguel was clearly bewildered. "Do I have to do what?" he asked.

"That pointing thing," Kerry complained. "You're jabbing your finger at me as though I'm being accused of a crime!"

Miguel looked at me for verification.

"She's right," I affirmed. "It's like something out of *Twelve Angry Men*! Have you heard about this from other women?"

"Just one!" Miguel said. "And she was a consultant my company hired to help me communicate!"

Now the audience was laughing; Miguel was not. Miguel was in sales. For him and a handful of people on his level, a memorable public speaking style was a must. A few months prior to our meeting, Miguel and several other managers were sent to a corporate trainer to brush up on their presentation styles. Among the techniques Miguel learned during that session was how to literally "point out" the parts of his speech he particularly wanted his audience to remember. Unfortunately, this was one strategy that didn't translate to the world beyond the boardroom. Women found it about as charming as being asked to punch a time clock before dinner and a movie.

As I explained to my friend the marketing genius, the medium is the message. The message—that you are your fascinating, charming and miraculously eligible self—isn't likely to come through if you're gesturing like a fascist dicta-tor. Nor are you going to win the day (or the date!) if you are sending any other nonverbal messages that are in conflict with what you happen to be saying. For instance, if you are shaking your head "no" while making a positive statement (gushing, "Oh yes, I adore opera!" while negating that opin-ion physically), unconsciously shrugging your shoulders (What . . . you don't know if you like the person you're talk-ing to?), drumming your fingers as though in boredom or tapping your feet as though you can hardly wait to make tracks for the door, your inability to sit still is making you ap-pear less friendly, less accepting and less attractive a com-panion than you really are. Ask the buddy who will act as your flirting coach to take note of the way you move and ges-ture while you're spending time with a new friend. It may be de rigueur for public figures to engage in finger pointing, hand waving, eyebrow raising or head cocking when issuing a statement, but use those gestures in a social context and you may soon find yourself waving good-bye.

Your friends would do anything to help you to create a happier, more fulfilling social life. Let them! This week, invite a trusted pal to take a peek at your technique. They'll pick up on what you can-not. And you will pick up on interesting "others" you never thought possible. There really is such a thing as constructive criti-cism. A few pointers from those who care the most about you and you may find yourself building a new outlook on life.

To Meet Interesting People, Be an Interesting Person

The Metropolitan Museum of Art is one of my favorite haunts. I have to admit, however, that, like Gerhard, my most successful attempts at the fine art of flirtation have taken place in the Met's newly refurbished cafeteria. The excellent food gives you a menu of delicious subjects to comment on, but best of all, the cafeteria checkout brings even hurried diners to a complete halt. I use that time to chat people up as they fumble for their change—or offer to put in my two cents if they're a tad short. Add to that the closely spaced tables, which make them perfect for tête-à-tête, and the Metropolitan becomes a masterpiece of opportunity.

One recent afternoon, I had just finished weighing my salad and was now doing the same with my seating options. I surveyed the tables. There he was: gray-haired, blue-eyed, well-dressed and age-appropriate. He even had a very nice frame! What were the chances of that? I put the paperback novel I had been carrying into my bag. It would keep until bedtime. This good-looking man might not. I walked to a nearby table and slipped into a chair facing his.

Opening a conversation with Mr. Blue-Eyes was easy. He happened to be wearing a very distinctive Southwestern-style bracelet and ring. I had traveled to New Mexico myself and recognized the Suni Indian pattern. In fact, I had a smaller version of the ring at home. He was wearing a prop, though I am sure he didn't think of it that way.

"Are you from the Southwest?" I asked pleasantly. It was a simple question; one that gave him the opportunity to answer in a single syllable or expound. I would follow his lead.

"No, actually I'm from Colorado," he answered with a smile. "I'm here for Christo's installation in Central Park."

Score! He not only chose to expand upon the question, he had moved into what was familiar territory for me. The contemporary artist Christo was adorning twenty-three miles of pathway through Central Park with 7,500 saffron-colored banners. But I would return to that subject later. Instead, I detoured into more personal territory.

"Oh! My ex-brother-in-law attended the University of Colorado, Boulder," I exclaimed. With that remark I had covered three bases: I continued the conversation, established commonality with him and revealed that I was divorced.

"No kidding? I teach art history at the University of Colorado, Fort Collins," he responded.

Things were going well. My gentleman friend revealed more with each exchange. He wasn't just being polite; he clearly wanted to talk to me. I offered something empathetic to help him along.

"I've never been there, but I know Fort Collins is close to Boulder. You're far from home."

He nodded. "I am. But I love the Met and Christo's exhibit gave me an excuse to spend some time in New York. I am working here, so my expenses are paid."

"What are you doing for the exhibit?"

"It doesn't sound like much but I'm giving out samples of the orange fabric the artist used to anyone who asks." My new friend grinned. And I was happy with the weave of the conversation, too.

The bits and pieces of information people gather throughout their lives may seem disparate and unrelated at first glance, but the truth is that these very different pieces fit together like a beautiful collage. Since people love to share the information they have chosen to explore and make their own, all a smart flirt really needs to do is find a thread that binds these interests together. Follow that thread and it will lead you to the very heart of what your partner believes gives life meaning. It will also provide you with virtually limitless opportunity for conversation.

"I actually met Christo and his wife when he gave a guest lecture at the university," he volunteered.

"What is he like?"

"He's had a fascinating life! He was born in Bulgaria and stowed away on a ship to Paris at a time when defection was simply not allowed. He painted portraits for a wealthy French family, making his living as their resident artist."

I considered what I knew about this very avant-garde artist. First, there was the installation and simultaneous opening of 3,100 blue and yellow umbrellas in Ibaraki, Japan, and the California desert. Then there was the project he called *Surrounded Islands,* in which eleven islands were surrounded by wide collars of pink fabric. He didn't seem to be the kind of artist who would be into painting bowls of fruit—or even a portrait of cranky Uncle Henri.

"I didn't think he did representational art," I commented.

"Oh, yes! He still sells his representational paintings today," the gentleman explained. "In fact, it was while painting portraits that he met his wife, Jean-Claude. She was one of the family members he painted! Of course, Jean-Claude's mother didn't approve. But it didn't matter. Now she is his partner in art and in life."

At last, a relationship story! Now we were really off and running. From that point on the conversation meandered through a vast and varied terrain. We talked about Christo's bad-boy allure and his modest lifestyle in a fourth-floor walkup. From there, we explored the issue of artistic integrity and the author Ayn Rand, whose life and books were variations on that theme. For me, *The Fountainhead* had been required college reading. Decades later, the assignment had finally paid off. We ended the conversation with a discussion of values, and why basketball players earn $81 million and teachers only $40,000, an issue close to his heart.

That afternoon I learned a great deal. Unfortunately, I also learned that my new friend was married. Still, I wouldn't have missed the encounter for anything. He was good company, and we made a date to meet again during the summer, at the Delacorte theater in Central Park. He'd bring his wife. Maybe I'll ask her if she knows any more like him in Colorado—or, better yet, on the East Coast. Even if she says no, the connection will have brought me tremendous pleasure—and possibly, a future connection.

When I was in college, surrounded by students who were investing every waking moment in developing expertise in their subject of choice, I was embarrassed that I seemed to be a jack of all trades and master of none. True expertise, I knew, was what earned professional respect—not to mention the big bucks in an increasingly specialized world. It wasn't until later that I realized how lucky I was. My interests, which ranged from books to beaches to odd professions (I am the only person I know who has met two professional "noses" in the perfume business—and I won't even go into the professional wrestler ...) seemed scattered, to be sure—but people who collect bits and pieces of information find it easy to pick up on a conversation! Whether or not I ever made the big bucks, I would always be able to make my own luck in the romance department—and, except when there's a great sale at Bloomie's, that's good enough for me.

So what did I learn from my conversation with Mr. Blue-Eyes? A certain amount about art and literature and my new friend, of course. But it also reminded me that there are two kinds of knowledge: The first is one mile wide and ten miles deep. This is the type of knowledge demonstrated by my erudite acquaintance, the art professor. The second kind of knowledge is one mile deep but ten miles wide. This is the kind of information a smart flirt scatters about like confetti whenever a chat needs some color. The good news is that no matter which type of knowledge you happen to possess, you can use it to become a fascinating flirt.

This week I am asking you to become the most interesting, interested flirt you can be. How do you begin? By following the trends and subjects that pique your curiosity and by sharing what you learn with others—and by putting these simple, effective tips to work for you:

♡ *Be a five-minute expert.* You don't have to be able to expound indefinitely on a subject to be an interesting person. All you need to do is be ready and able to chat for a few minutes on a wide range of subjects.

  Conversations aren't lectures or monologues; they are two-part processes. Develop a wide range of interests and you'll always be able to hold up your end.

♡ *Give your curiosity free reign.* To be interesting, it is not enough to go with the conversational flow, you must add to it! Allow yourself to collect bits of information. Subscribe to magazines, read books, go to movies, try new hobbies, and follow your curiosity wherever it leads. The latest Hollywood gossip or a piece of television trivia might seem too "fluffy" to share, but these are the tidbits that can keep a conversation afloat!

♡ *Don't nod if you don't know.* Nodding is a great nonverbal technique to let a conversational partner know that you understand what he or she is saying. But are you still nodding when you don't? Rather than admit to ignorance on a subject, people nod. The problem is that when you gesture "yes" in these instances, what you are actually saying is "no": No, I will not ask you to explain something to me. No, I will not do what it takes to become fully engaged in this talk with you. And most of all, no, I'm not going to let you in if that means confronting my own ego. Ask! People love people who are interested in them! Asking demonstrates interest.

 Remember: There are no failed flirtations, just flirts who fail to network! So what if he's married? Big deal if she's gay! You've gotten to know each other. It's only a matter of time before you get to know his friends . . . or her friend's straight friend!

Week 17

Pick That Special One from the Crowd

As you no doubt suspect, I'm not one to pass up an opportunity to socialize. So, when a few of the fledgling flirts from my workshop asked me to join them for a drink after class, I couldn't say no. I put on my coat and my purple hat (flirting prop . . . never leave home without it!) and followed Heather, Gina and the quiet, good-looking Peter into the night.

While the others perused the menu wondering what to order, I perused their body language and wondered, too: Had they learned anything at all at my flirting workshop? Gina, a woman who clearly didn't need a crowd to have fun, chattered incessantly to no one in particular, without ever seeming to draw a breath. Peter turned a cold shoulder to both Gina and me and focused his eye contact entirely on Heather. What was I, chopped liver? If I had been, that would have been just fine with Heather. She was so busy calculating the carbohydrate content of each appetizer on the menu that she seemed to entirely lose her appetite for chat.

Often when relative strangers gather socially for the first time, it takes a while before the acquaintances really "click" as a group. None of us were teenagers anymore, and I was just beginning to wonder whether another birthday might pass before Heather, Peter and Gina found common ground when the women headed off for the traditional group excursion to the ladies' room. (Clearly, they had missed my earlier admonishment never to travel in "herds," as well.) I was left to scrape up a conversation with Peter over the dirty plates.

A few hours earlier, Peter had distinguished himself at the workshop by demonstrating some very seductive interdigitation—the man had developed a "flirting handshake" so potent it would melt a wax model from Madame Tussaud's—so I knew that, underneath it all, Peter had a sensitive soul. I decided I'd use the moment to hone his abilities as a flirt.

"I know you're interested in Heather, but it's not good flirting to focus entirely on her . . . at least not when you're in a group," I offered, as gently as I could. "Remember, flirting is a numbers game. Since anyone at the table could turn out to be 'the one' for you, it's a good idea to spread the charm. That way all of your options remain open."

Peter's fork hovered in midair. He looked at me quizzically. "What?"

"I know that the workshop is over," I began again, "but I wanted to remind you that flirting, at its best, is a playful pursuit—one that is totally without serious intent. I just wanted to let you know that when you're in a group, it's more polite to keep your body language open to the entire table, even if you are interested in someone specific."

Peter looked utterly confused. "I am not interested in Heather!" he finally sputtered.

Now it was my turn to be surprised. "You're not?"

Everything about Peter—his position, his expression—had convinced me that our food-conscious tablemate was his *plat du jour*. If an ongoing friendship with Heather was not on Peter's intended menu, what was? What feelings were his nonverbal messages masking?

"Well, you could have fooled me," I laughed. I demonstrated

how, simply by turning his body slightly, he had inadvertently closed himself off from me and Gina.

Now Peter was smiling. "The funny thing about it is, I am interested in someone at the table. But the person I'm really interested in is you."

I certainly would never have guessed! Still, his mistakes turned out to be serendipitous. I found him to be every bit as attractive as he had found me. We were able to exchange cards quickly before our classmates returned to the table.

His body language was much more inclusive—at least toward me—after that. In fact, we had a romantic relationship that carried on happily for nearly two years and has since morphed into a warm friendship. Yet, when I think of him, I am always reminded of how difficult it is to make meaningful contact with an individual when you're a part of a group—and how easy it can be to let that special someone slip away into the crowd.

When did dating become a group effort? Group dating, alternatively known as "hanging out," has always been regarded as a great way for young people to learn to socialize. If one prospect doesn't speak to you and you're out with twelve people, you are provided with a fallback position. Most people prefer targeting their attentions, mixing and mingling among a prescreened crowd, to leaving their romantic options to happenstance. And who can blame them? Aren't we all looking for a certain someone who shares at least some of our interests?

Of course, there is no age-related cut-off date for group encounters. Singles of all ages gather all the time . . . to suck down a few pre–Super Bowl brews . . . to commiserate after a particularly grueling professional meeting . . . or simply to blow off steam after a long, hard week. Whatever your age, these get-togethers can create amorous heat, if you know how to "work the crowd."

The gaggles of friends, coworkers and colleagues who count

us as "one of the gang" give context to our lives. They reassure us that we belong. But, as we have seen from Peter's story, finding and attracting that special someone while you're in the company of . . . well, a company, can be tricky. This week, try these techniques when you're out with your "peeps." They'll help you make your admiration known while maintaining the friendly ties that bind.

♡ *Keep your eyes on the prize!* Group outings are understood to be social rather than romantic events. Consequently, it is important that you make and maintain affable "glancing" eye contact with everyone within your conversational group even while you're focused on one particular individual. To stay "in with the in-crowd," I suggest you follow my guidelines for using the "flirting triangle" that you will find in week 21. This will keep you in playful, energetic eye contact with everyone at the table. If a certain someone at the table really interests you, hold his or her gaze just a second or two longer. If you can't do so subtly, move to a position where you can make more direct eye contact. When she adds to the conversation, ask a couple of open-ended questions based on her comment. This will not only draw her out but will let her know she has your attention. Smile at her, certainly, but remember to remain an active part of the interaction around you. These may be old friends of yours but they are also friends of hers. You might be surprised to know how many singles would not date someone they felt had ignored or mistreated or otherwise dissed a friend.

♡ *Maintain inclusive body language.* Whether you're at a party or in a club or simply in some conversational setting, it is not pleasant to find yourself on the "wrong side" of a couple that has formed its own "huddle!" Think about it. Two minutes ago, you were chatting amiably with these people. Now they have melded into the corner and turned at least one back toward you—not to mention the rest of the group. Why wouldn't those who have been excluded feel like intruders? That's precisely what they've been turned into!

When propriety tells you that it wouldn't be wise to seek out "someplace more private," it can be tempting to form your own little quiet corner. Don't. It's uncomfortable for everyone involved. Find a way to make your new friend feel special without turning your back on the world.

♡ *Spread the wealth.* How do you tell which is the most sought-after appetizer at the party? It's on the plate that keeps getting passed around and around! Well, the same is true of people. If you want to whet the appetite of that certain someone, make sure everyone gets a taste of your convivial persona! Ask all the girls to dance even if only one catches your fancy. Chat up every man in the room with ears. You'll get good word of mouth—and remember, you can always return to the one you're attracted to.

♡ *Make your feelings known.* Younger flirts will sometimes purposefully ignore someone they like, or play hard to get, but these games aren't a good idea. Ignore someone long enough and they may very well disappear—with someone more emotionally forthcoming! Besides, playing with someone else's feelings is manipulative—and manipulation is never good flirting. If you feel you've sent mixed messages or that your signals might have been too subtle to sink in (Hint: Is he pausing to say good night to the waiter but not to you? If so, your approach might have been a bit too restrained!), you must make your interest known before the end of the party. Make it a point to say good-bye and get his number. Send her off with a sizzling, flirtatious handshake. You might even mention that you were really taken by him but didn't want to slight the other guests. Whatever you do, make sure you hit on that unique individual before he or she hits the streets.

Do Talk to Strangers

"Is that seat taken?"

"I hate weather like this. It wrecks my hair!"

"Do you have a light?"

"Before I left, I had to tell you—your smile just lights up a room."

"You're a Yankees fan? How can you possibly be a Yankees fan? I like you!"

What are the quotes above? The latest messages sent by Koko, the "talking" gorilla? Outtakes from the best-selling guide *When Bad Lines Happen to Good People*? Believe it or not, this is a sampling of the simple, mundane, even inane comments real people have used to break the ice, and, in some cases, charm a future spouse.

Every flirt has stood in the bank line, at the party, at the sugar-free Slurpee machine, groping for a clever, unforgettable thing to say to that friendly-looking man or woman nearby. Every flirt has continued groping for that memorable zinger long after Mr. or Ms. Wonderful has completed his or her transaction and moved on. Considering the silly, routine lines that have gotten people over that dreaded "hello hurdle," why do so many singles find it so difficult to start a conversation?

Michelle, an advertising executive, explained her case of terminal tongue-tie this way: "It's not enough to make a statement. I feel like I have to make an impression! I've seen copywriters struggle for weeks to find one perfect line. How can I come up with a punchy one-liner in a split second?" A man I know recently described his tendency to be the too-quiet type this way:

"The instant I open my mouth, I feel vulnerable. I might be rejected. I also might be making a fool of myself! I'm not just putting the make on someone—if I'm in public, I'm putting my interest out there for everyone else to see."

No doubt about it, breaking the ice can be daunting—particularly for those of us who feel that the ice is the only thing that is keeping us from sinking over our heads in chilling conversational waters! But contrary to what flirts like Michelle may think, it isn't really what we say that creates a good impression—it's the way we say it. The cleverest line will fall flat if it isn't backed up with a sincere smile and open body language. And while we might feel like we are putting our feelings "out there" when we speak to a friend we haven't yet met, I'd like to say this: Nothing ventured, nothing gained! Keeping your distance will immunize not only against rejection but against a thriving social life as well.

Human beings are social creatures. We interact with each other—and often, with total strangers—many times a day. So many times, in fact, that these risk-free, impromptu encounters hardly even register.

"Oh, maybe other people just strike up conversations on the street, but I don't," argued my friend Trina. "I just can't bring myself to interrupt some guy's solitude."

Oh, no? When I began to press Trina on the details of her day, a much different scenario emerged. As it happened, Trina was late for work that morning, the victim of a city bus that simply did not come. Did she keep her frustration to herself—or did she indulge in a bit of mass transit motor-mouth? Trina admitted that she did comment to her fellow commuters about how buses tended either to arrive at the stop in groups of two or three or not at all. A man standing nearby put aside his *Wall Street Journal* to tell Trina—and everyone else at the stop—that in physics, the tendency for moving objects to leave a starting point at different times yet arrive at certain locations in groups was known as "random clumping." The buses weren't just tardy—they were proof of a theory! Trina found this interesting and even wondered if the man might be a scientist himself but, rather than ask, she hailed a cab.

Was this the only opportunity Trina took to shoot the breeze with a perfect-enough stranger? Absolutely not! In the grocery store after work, she asked a man stacking mangos what an unfamiliar vegetable was. He explained that it was a "chayote"—a type of squash grown in Mexico. Later, in the same store, Trina chatted with a warm gent she met in the frozen-foods aisle. He was reading and rereading the nutritional information on a frozen dinner trying to figure out the meaning of the term "net carbs." (Frozen dinner? Net carbs? Earth to Trina! Could this be a single man holding a flirting prop? Sheesh!)

Even that was not the end of Trina's socializing. Before she got to my door, she chatted up two new neighbors in the lobby of her building, a guy selling Yves St. Laurent knock-offs on the corner and even the doorman in my building! Was this what Trina thought of as conversational deprivation?

"OK, fine—so I'm a closet chataholic," Trina laughed. "But if I'm such a social butterfly, why am I still single?" Easy. As I explained to Trina, she and flirts like her tend to think of chance encounters as unimportant. Unless flirting is characterized by stress, unless the approach is a planned one—often complete with sweaty palms and moments of panic—it simply isn't flirting! How wrong-minded that is. Most of all, what a waste of the countless opportunities to flirt—in the theater lobby, at the dog run, on a field trip—anywhere!—that are handed to us every day!

As for those of you who stand silently by, paralyzed with fear that you will be ignored, passed over or possibly even dismissed, fear no longer: You will almost certainly be snubbed at one time or another! Rejection is not a blot; it is the mark of the true master flirt! Wherever I go, whatever I'm doing, I make it a practice to speak to anyone, regardless of age or gender, who will stand still long enough to hear me out. For my trouble, I have been overlooked, underappreciated and even discounted. So what? I don't know these people! Their opinions of me couldn't matter less. What *does* matter is that flirting is a numbers game. Every time I am slighted by Mr. Wrong, I know I'm slightly closer to finding Mr. Right!

And there's more good news: We are hard wired for interaction. We want to speak to each other and connect. That's why when you say a cheery hello to someone else, you are very unlikely to get stony silence in return. In fact, the encounter may turn into something much more than a casual fly-by.

Of all the flirting techniques I know, speaking to strangers has brought me the most joy—and virtually no risk. Think of it this way: Words scrawled in haste last as long as the paper they are written on endures. E-mail messages, written in seconds, can be ferreted out by the FBI long after you think you have deleted them. But the few friendly words we exchange with a passerby, a nodding acquaintance or someone we may have seen but don't know are literally neither here nor there. They may make an impression on the mind or the heart, they may touch the soul or tickle the funny bone, but they are intangible. They are gone as soon as they are spoken. So what are we really risking by tossing a comment or an opinion to the wind? If no one speaks back, we've lost nothing. But if a certain someone responds, we have a meeting of the minds—or maybe more—to gain!

For every woman hoping that some significant other will break the silence barrier, there is a man hoping the same. And for every single man wondering whether that lovely woman might respond to an impromptu greeting, there is a woman with a welcoming smile just waiting to use it. Give those attractive strangers the chance to respond to you!

This week, I am asking you to put your fears aside, forget your mother's warnings and speak to several hand-picked "strangers" every day! I am also asking you to extend yourself to as many new types of people as possible. To ensure that you do, approach this week's assignment the way a student might approach the college application process. Mentally divide the men and women you encounter each day into two groups:

♡ *The "Easy-ins"*—people you have already developed a silent familiarity with: for example, that robust clerk with the great pecs who sees you at the organic grocery or the woman with the energetic walk you pass on the corner each morning while walking your dog;

♡ *The "Reaches"*—the drop-dead gorgeous steward who offered you a "sweet" on your red-eye flight to London or that buff beauty at the reception desk you've heard earns extra bucks as an underwear model in her spare time. (Hey—these people are always kvetching that nobody ever talks to them because they're too good-looking! Isn't it time you gave them a break?)

Make up your mind to exchange a few words with three from each category every day for the next week. The world can be a lonely place. Let's hear a little chatter out there!

Week 19 Turn Those Greetings into Meetings

"I'm a salesman. I can talk to anybody," announced Tony, an easygoing middle-aged guy in a perfectly tailored charcoal suit. "Give me thirty seconds and I can walk into your office, shake your hand and become your best friend. And when I walk out again, I'll have you scheduled in my Palm for a golf date on Saturday and delivery of five thousand units of my company's latest widget."

Suddenly the smile seemed to evaporate from Tony's face. He leaned toward me conspiratorially and lowered his voice. "So why are things so much different when I'm trying to sell myself to a nice woman I've just met? Oh, I can get past the first few seconds alright. I say, 'Hello—it's a pleasure to meet you.' But after that, my mind goes blank!" Tony shrugged his shoulders. "No wonder I have so much time to wine and dine clients! I don't have too many dates cluttering up my Palm!"

No matter what we do for a living, whatever our situation in life, we all have "scripts" we rely on to get us through life's stickier, less comfortable situations. Whether we are selling "widgets" like Tony does, convincing a stubborn two-year-old to put on a shoe or offering condolences to someone who has recently suffered a loss, there is a kind of "patter" we rely on to finagle ourselves an "in," deliver a message and leave a good impression. In certain situations, usually those straightforward, formal events that have a distinct beginning, middle and end, polite—even impersonal—address is enough to get you through. But flirting follows a more meandering path. In order to get where he or she wants to go, a successful flirt must be agile enough to pick up on any clues strewn by a partner, and quick enough to keep up with the conversational flow no matter how many times it changes direction. He or she must possess the adventurousness to eagerly explore a virtual stranger's inner landscape and the tenacity to search out that all-important common bond, even when none appears to exist.

"And what else does the successful flirt do, Susan? Go rappelling down the side of a romantic cliff without a safety rope?" commented Diana, a women I met at a singles event in California. "Call me chicken, but that's what it seems like to me."

Diana laughed when she said it, but I could see that the idea of "boldly going" wherever a flirtation took her made her anxious—as it does many flirts. Unless you are blessed with a silver tongue and a quick wit, you may find yourself dangling mid-conversation with nothing to say. But the good news is there are strategies that work together to form a safety net for unsteady flirts—and they are all predicated on a simple, comforting idea: staying relaxed.

Many pitfalls can undermine a fledgling relationship—but none is quite as pervasive or socially toxic as that heart-pounding anxiety. Think about it. The laid-back flirt can settle comfortably into his own body language. He leans on his self-confidence like he would a lamppost and watches and listens for positive signals. Meanwhile, the anxious flirt is caught up in his own panic. He is so busy wracking his brain for just the just right thing to say, he may never really hear his new friend's ideas and opinions at all! And because tension etches itself on our faces and bodies, we don't just experience it ourselves . . . we telegraph it to others! Who wants to go out for a latte with someone who has just served them a double shot of ill at ease?

As cute and charming as you may be, you are unlikely to get your feet wet as a flirt unless you are willing to go with the conversational flow. How can you transform yourself from "that guy/girl who sort of mumbles hello when she/he passes on the street" to that very hot prospect he/she can't wait to see on Saturday night? Here are some simple techniques that always work to get us to hello and beyond:

♡ *Introduce yourself!* Sure it seems obvious, but if everybody thought to do it, would each of us be carrying around that little catalog of men and women whose faces we see all the time—in the neighborhood, at the supermarket, in the elevator, in the hallway—but whose names we do not know? What a waste! Familiarity doesn't breed contempt—it breeds trust! So why not break the ice with someone you've already established what I call a "nodding acquaintance" with? It doesn't take much thought or effort. A simple smile and a brief intro ("I see you on this block all the time and I just wanted to introduce myself. My name is _____ and I live around the corner.") will do.

♡ *To be memorable, be human.* If you're feeling clever, you might even throw in a little self-deprecating humor like my friend Stan does. Stan had been crossing paths with the same slender brunette at the organic grocery for years. When he decided to break the silence between them, he didn't just establish his presence—he introduced his wit. Standing near her at the checkout, Stan patted the pocket where he usually kept his wallet. Finding it empty, he leaned across the counter and commented to his new friend, "My name is Stan and I have just realized that you must be a neighbor because I've seen you here every week for the last six months. I've also just realized that I cannot pay for my bok choy because I left my wallet at home." Then Stan smiled at his new friend and said, "Since I live just a few doors down, I predict that you'll be seeing me again in about ten minutes."

He passed his new friend, Lisa, a few minutes later on the street. This time he had enough cash to pay for his veggies and a sheepish grin. Lisa had a perfect excuse to continue the conversation. Although it was not a love connection, Stan and Lisa are more than "nodding acquaintances" now. Lisa pet-sits Stan's English bulldog when he's away on business—and Stan has introduced his new friend to the new natural foods co-op in the area. They may not have fallen into each other's arms (yet!) but they've turned a greeting into a series of meetings. Who can predict what they'll be checking out next?

♡ *Take a risk.* Patti is an effervescent redhead who studies landscape architecture by day and waits tables at a raucous Creole restaurant on weekend nights. Her personality is as spicy and warm as the crawfish étouffée she serves and I have never seen her when she was not dead center among a group of gregarious friends. It surprised me, then, when Patti confessed that when it came to turning her greetings into meetings—and a waitress in a popular spot can collect a veritable menu of new acquaintances every single day—she was a dud. And she isn't the only one. How many men are unwilling to take the risk of moving beyond that first hello? Judging from the number of attractive single women I see as clients and friends, a lot!

If you find that you are making contact with plenty of new people but not making a reasonably equal number of dates, ask yourself this question: If that cutie you just met was "just a friend" or a newly met pal of the same gender, wouldn't you invite her to sweat out a lap on the running trail with you? Ask him to join you at that free lecture at the local bookstore? Suggest you stop for a drink or a cup of coffee? Why shouldn't you treat the eye-catching singles who attract you like friends? At this point, that's what they are! Now that you've said hello, you've opened a door that was previously closed to you. Invite that certain someone to walk through! Greetings, warm smiles and casual nods provide us with our minimum daily requirement of human contact; turning those first few stammering words into a meaningful, mutually satisfying dialogue can max it out! Go for the gusto!

Week 20

Smile When You Say That! (And Especially When You Don't!)

It was a Saturday night and I was headlining one of my trademark School of Flirting events at a nightclub in Manhattan. The subject of the moment was creating "approachability"—that ineffable quality that seems to draw an endless procession of men, women, children and beasts to certain, particularly compelling individuals. I noticed a willowy young woman waving her hand at me from a front table. She had a question. I wasn't surprised.

"Susan, I am out with my friends all the time. If we aren't out to dinner, we're at the theater or dancing at a club. On weekends, we're off skiing or at a museum or wandering through a neighborhood we've all wanted to explore." The woman looked around, as if to ensure that no one was around who could possibly use the information she was about to share against her. "What I can't understand is my friends are getting hit on all the time. Old men, young men, men who are there with a woman . . . my friends draw them all. But no interesting stranger ever seems to come over and talk to me!" She smiled wistfully. "I know I'm not bad looking. And I'm a friendly person. So why am I always the one holding the seats while my friends are holding court?"

She was certainly beautiful; there was no doubt about that. Lanky and slender, with flawless skin and an incredible mane of chestnut hair, she had every qualification that would make most men want to approach: except for one. Her lips drooped noticeably at the corners. Whether due to some fluke of genetic engineering or simply because it had become her habit, this otherwise lovely woman was continually "down in the mouth." No matter how she was feeling, no matter how upbeat, friendly and open she was underneath it all, her perpetually peeved expression was so off-putting that I knew it must be the reason men were passing her by. I asked her to meet me after the session so I could speak to her privately. I explained as gently as possible what she could do to consciously change her expression and she promised that she'd be in touch if she felt she wasn't able to correct the problem. Since I haven't seen her since, I assume she's looking and feeling much happier.

Human beings are only weeks old when they become aware of the tremendous power in a simple smile. A gummy grin is one of the few communication tools available to a baby, yet it is the key to fulfilling all of that baby's basic needs. Think of it: Using only a toothless smile and without ever uttering a single word, a baby is able to attract the adults around it, compel people to feed it, entertain it and nurture it in every conceivable way. Now, although most of us have outgrown our baby fat, the fine art of flirting still works in precisely the same way. Broad or demure, toothy and unabashed or flickering and transitory, our smiles mark us as people who not only draw contentment from the people around us but who wish to share it—to bounce it playfully back at the men and women we encounter.

The way you smile and the amount of beaming you do can be a direct result of your cultural background. That's why people of more reserved nationalities (you know who you are!) feel uncomfortable with Americans' tendency to smile. Studies show that we all tend to be most comfortable among people whose expressions neither exceed nor fall short of the frequency and intensity of our own. Smiles allow us to transcend cultural differences, soothe away shyness, overcome language barriers and even bridge generation gaps. This week, I ask you to go to your happy place and put this cozy, comfy nonverbal tool to use in your life. But first, a few guidelines:

 I like to say that smiles are like greeting cards—there is one for every occasion. We smile when we feel shy, diluting an otherwise inviting expression with teasing eye movements or a covert glimpse through lowered eyelashes. We smile sheepishly when the checkout clerk tells us that our credit card will not go through. We smile when we squeeze past someone in a tight space, as if to say, "I'm sorry, but you know how packed this room is!" The embarrassed smile we adopt when we're caught looking at a stranger in an elevator apologizes for us—and the brief, nonthreatening smile that passes between people on the street says simply, "I see you there. Hello!"

It follows that there are smiles that are more likely to make us "run thither" than "come hither." These include the leer (a wolfish look that speaks of things no good flirt would speak of until the time was right); the gritted-teeth grimace (you know the one—it seems to say, "This is painful but I will withstand it!") or the closed-lipped grin so reminiscent of those smiley faces that smirked from virtually every surface in the 60s.

Before you embark on this week's smile-athon, take a moment to consider what message your expression conveys. If you aren't sure, take an honest look at some candid photographs of yourself. Is your grin affectionate or affected? Pretty or somehow pained? The expressions we assume can be a function of habit. The time to make an adjustment is now.

♡ *Check out your pearly whites.* Could they be more attractive? I realize that I am writing this at a time when the glare off of most starlets' preturnaturally whitened teeth can pose an ocular hazard to the unsuspecting passerby; nevertheless, the relative health and appearance of your smile merits a check. The fact that a flirt should maintain a kissable mouth may seem obvious or even superficial, but there remain those who do not—to their detriment. One very successful attorney I knew dated very little after his divorce simply because the cigars he was so fond of had discolored his teeth! What would you rather sit through: a couple of tooth-cleanings or a yawning future of frozen dinners in front of *Law & Order* reruns? I rest my case.

♡ *Is expressionlessness paralyzing your social life?* I have been a student of nonverbal communication almost as long as I have been alive. Imagine my reaction, then, to this comment made recently by a revered movie executive. To paraphrase: "Thanks to Botox, we now have an entire generation of actresses who are simply unable to look convincingly angry or happy!"

One thing that human beings have over their counterparts in the animal kingdom (other than opposable thumbs and credit cards to hold in them) is the ability to use facial expressions to telegraph every nuance of our constantly evolving thoughts and emotions. A little cosmetic "tweak" may actually help in that effort. Certain techniques can erase lines that make us appear drawn, angry or otherwise unapproachable. Still, we have come to expect the human face to be constantly informative and we look to a person's mouth, in particular.

A blank, expressionless face may be dermatologically perfect, but others can interpret it as portraying a total lack of interest! Whether that placid, level-eyed gaze is the result of practice or a skilled surgeon, an absence of normal expression is off-putting to others—and that is never good flirting. Let your feelings show! If your smile is saying, "Hello," "I'm interested," "I've seen you before," "I like what I see" or simply, "You seem like a person who is like me," engage your entire face in the effort. You may create a few laugh lines but who needs a porcelain complexion if the cost is an expression as blank as the pages of your date book?

♡ *Look for leakage!* A "social smile" is definitely better than no smile at all, but "put-on" expressions can make it difficult to accurately read and interpret the sincerity of other people's smiles. Is that a manufactured happy face or is he glad to see you? You'll find the clues in his "emotional leakage," the subtle crinkles that reveal every wrinkle of his deepest feelings. If he's "smiling with his eyes" and pairing his grin with an excited eyebrow raise or comfy eye contact, his smile is the genuine article.

Smiles: The Real Deal

A smile's message is simple and warm. It says: "I may not know you well, but I like you. I'm making this first gesture in the hope that you will let me know you better." The following anecdote demonstrates the way the most basic flirting techniques work to establish commonality between people who were, just a few seconds earlier, complete strangers. It is predicated on a smile. You have one of those, don't you?

It is a dark, rainy day. A woman dashes through the lobby of an office building and squeezes into an elevator just before the door closes. She notices that she is sharing the car with a man. She smiles.

"Your smile brightens this horribly rainy day," he says.

What a lovely thing to say! The woman considers her options. She likes the man's unassuming good looks. She is also impressed by his willingness to compliment. She knows that if they simply arrive at their destinations and get off the elevator, there is virtually no chance of ever seeing him again.

She scans the elevator buttons. The man has pressed 4. She presses 9. But that doesn't mean she intends to get off there.

When the elevator arrives at the fourth floor, the man gets off; so does she.

"What a coincidence!" he says. "Can I help you find the office you're looking for?"

"I'm looking for Sachs and Weintraub," she says.

"Oh! They are not on this floor," he tells her.

She pulls a business card from her pocket and looks at it. "Isn't this the ninth floor?" she asks. The man shakes his head. "I guess your lovely remark in the elevator must have distracted me," she explains, laughing.

If she has gotten distracted, he's glad she did—and he tells her so. They make a date for coffee where they smile and talk some more. They are now married—and have been smiling ever since.

The Flirting Triangle (Tri This!)

Seeing eye to eye can be risky business for a fledgling flirt. Need proof? Look no further than the tale my business colleague Lidia told me not long ago.

Lidia had put in a lot of late nights in her job as a marketing executive and now she was in the market for a condo. Her Realtor urged Lidia to see a particular space that day before the condo appeared on the multiple listing system.

"I had already lost two places I had bid on, so I knew that time was of the essence. Although I had never been in the neighborhood where the condo was listed, I wasted no time," Lidia told me. "When the clock struck five, I left my desk and went straight to the subway station. Wherever that condo was, I would find it.

"It was a big station and, at rush hour, it was very busy. I didn't know which subway stop would take me closest to my destination. I wasn't even sure which train to take. I sort of went with the flow of the people in the station while I mulled all of these issues over. The next thing I knew, I was walking down a flight of stairs toward the subway platform. That's when I noticed the cute guy waiting for the train. He happened to look up from his newspaper as I was coming down the stairs so I knew he noticed me, too. He smiled; I smiled. I needed directions from someone who knew the subway route. So I decided I'd flirt.

"By now there was a huge crowd on the platform and people were moving in every direction. I knew it wouldn't be easy to get someone's attention in a mob scene like this so I did what I thought I was supposed to do—I held the man's gaze. As I made my way through the crowd, I made sure I didn't look away. I thought it would be sexy, like something you'd see in a movie. You know, two people drawn together in the middle of this mob . . . but that isn't the way it worked out. He stared down at his newspaper like it was the Rosetta Stone. He moved a little closer to the steel stanchion he was resting against. He seemed like he wanted to hide.

"Just then, a train pulled into the station so I put on my friendliest smile and popped the question. 'Is this the shuttle to Times Square?' The man folded his paper. He didn't smile back. The train brakes screeched.

"Shuttle? Yes, this is your train!" he announced, a little too loudly. The doors slid open. He directed me toward the opening. The current of the moving crowd carried me inside. Before I had a chance to ask any further questions, the doors closed between us. The man had thrown me into the train car like I was a hot potato! He chose not to take the train himself though it was obvious he had been waiting for it. In short, the whole experience was a flirting derailment."

Lidia shook her head. "I've read a lot of stuff on flirting and that's not the way this is supposed to work, Susan! I made eye contact and this guy couldn't wait to get rid of me. Oh, and by the way, I didn't get the condo, either. I got to the address twenty minutes after somebody offered full price.

"So what do you think?" Lidia's smile was wistful. "Am I going to get where I want to go as a flirt or do I need further directions?"

Lidia had the right idea. Nevertheless, further directions were certainly in order. Eye contact is essential when you're trying to catch someone's attention. The trick is to not catch flak while you're at it!

Used with sensitivity, a glance can make someone feel noticed and nurtured; applied carelessly, a look can feel like a slap. How can such a brief exchange between strangers resonate so deeply? Each time our eyes meet someone else's, even for a split second, we send a message. Think about it: As two people simultaneously observe each other's eyes, an intimacy is created. Even if you are in a roomful of people, if only for just that moment, you literally only have eyes for each other. And in just a few seconds, you exchange a tremendous amount of information. Are you "looking"? You must be! Do you like what you see? That, too, is apparent. Are you seeing something in an acquaintance that might hint at long-term happiness? Or are you disinterested? Surrounded by the most pliant, sensitive skin on the human body, framed by equally expressive brows, our eyes have a remarkable ability to transmit each nuance of emotion we experience long before we are aware we have even felt it. They are the limitlessly expressive barometers that telegraph our feelings and thoughts. And although this type of encounter is known to raise stress levels in participants, it also raises the questions that are so elemental to us as human beings: Do you see me? Do you like what you see? Would you like to know me better?

We have all heard the saying "the eyes are the windows to the soul." According to researchers, friendly eye-to-eye contact continues less than three seconds before one gazer or the other politely retreats and looks away. You can imagine, then, how unnerved people feel when someone stares into those "windows"! Since eye contact is the first contact we make with the available men and women around us, it is important that the messages we send are always positive and affirming rather than confrontational or threatening. While I can't be certain how Lidia's advances felt to the man on the platform, one thing *is* certain: Something about her look made him want to reach for a can of Mace rather than his date book. That is evidence enough that some eye-contact modification is definitely in order.

If you are concerned that your eye contact is a bit too hard focus, I suggest that you use the Flirting Triangle technique. Instead of making only eye-to-eye contact, think of your partner's face as a triangle with the widest points at the corners of his forehead, tapering down to the tip of his chin. Now imagine that you are an artist and that the flirting triangle—from hairline to jawline—is your canvas. Instead of staring directly into your partner's eyes, allow your glance to wander from his brow to his temples, from his earlobe to his chin. Now and then, allow your gazes to meet—you might acknowledge this with a slight nod or smile—then continue with your exploration, moving your eyes over his face lightly, playfully and always respectfully.

At first this technique may seem a little strange to you. If you are the direct, eye-to-eye type it might not seem like real contact to you. If so, I suggest that you defer judgment until you have tried this technique at least three times. This wonderful stare diffuser makes it impossible to unintentionally skewer a partner with your gaze. It also leads you through the first steps of the complex dance that leads to intimacy. Isn't that the perfect reason to learn a few new moves?

And while you're looking for just the right partner to charm, consider these tips to further finesse your technique:

♡ *Be sensual but not sexual.* When sexuality begins, playfulness ends. That means no winking, no sultry sidelong glances (those are creepy, anyway) and most of all, no eye contact with any of your partner's body parts between the neck and knees. Eye contact is not a full-body sport and it should never have a "morning after."

♡ *Keep it steady.* Beware of quick or darting eye movements. These can make you seem "shifty" or suspicious.

♡ *Know when to end it.* A well-timed glance communicates a simple message: "Hello. I see you." To keep the exchange friendly, maintain eye contact only as long as it would take to make that statement aloud. Then "retreat" by glancing away briefly before engaging your partner again. This gives him or her time to regroup—and to consider trying a few flirting tricks out on you.

If that certain someone seems reluctant to make eye contact with you . . . don't assume you're being rejected! Though a lack of eye contact can signal disinterest, it can also communicate physical discomfort (like too-tight shoes or impending illness) or extreme shyness. You should also bear in mind that not all cultures see eye to eye on this icebreaker. The Japanese, for example, are encouraged to focus on a person's neck in order to avoid eye contact. People of other cultures find such looks to be "forward" or aggressive. To correctly interpret your partner's intentions, I suggest that you check his or her body language. If your new friend is smiling, leaning or turning toward you or displaying preening behavior, you need not worry about eye contact. He or she has already given you a second look. Go for it!

Week 22 | Mirror, Mirror

Chris is a thirty-seven-year-old computer programmer who has had plenty of good fortune in his life. He has a job that makes him happy. He owns a spanking-new condo near the beach. He has a large extended family and a pair of season tickets to Boston's Fenway Park. To top it off, he and a recently divorced friend have just gone halvsies on a small cabin cruiser, giving Chris what he calls "a hole in the water where I can pour my money." Even Chris would admit that he's a guy who has everything—except for luck in the romance department.

Chris spent almost a decade with a woman he met in college. The relationship was comfortable enough—his entire family adored his ex—but it had no spark. Unfortunately, the spark-free theme seems to have carried over into Chris's third decade.

"I can't figure it out. I think that I've found someone I have a lot in common with but then, a week or two up the road, we're sitting across a table over our second or third dinner, and something just isn't settling right." Chris looked perplexed. "It's not that we don't get along. It's not even that we have discovered that we really don't have anything in common. It's just a feeling that even though we have the right wiring, we don't quite connect."

What is this thing called chemistry? How is it possible to look into a stranger's eyes and know, in an instant, whether this pairing will sizzle or fizzle? Of course we are disappointed when we arrange to meet a promising prospect for tapas and know before the sangria arrives that attraction is not on the menu. But it can be a life-changing event when it is.

Consider the story of Bill and Hillary Clinton's first encounter. They were students at Yale University law school when, suddenly, their eyes met across the law library. The stare-down continued until Hillary marched over to Bill and said, "Look, if you're going to keep staring at me, and I'm going to keep staring back, we might as well be introduced. I'm Hillary Rodham. What's your name?" Bill Clinton has said in interviews that he was so thoroughly shaken by the encounter he couldn't remember his name.

That is chemistry. Some describe it as magical, others as an irresistible magnetic attraction drawing together two people who know each other's deepest yearnings but, curiously, not each other's names. If you're lucky, it's what happens on some enchanted evening when you meet a stranger across a crowded room. And if you are not the type to rely on luck? You should know that chemistry can be coaxed.

Smart flirts know that people are drawn to people who like them, and especially to people who are like them. Being in synch—or getting in synch—with others, which is the basis of chemistry, is something most of us work at every day. Establishing commonality—discovering and reinforcing the links between us and the men and women we like—is what we are doing when we run through the verbal getting-to-know-you drill. ("Where did you go to school?" "Do you like golf?" "I have a subscription to the ballet, do you like classical dance?" "Oh, do you know Tom? I do, too—great guy.") But that's not the only way to show someone you're on his or her wavelength. In the singles' world, where time and patience are limited, nonverbal communication can build rapport more quickly than words, and, as I explained to Chris, it is best accomplished by using an incredibly effective yet very simple technique called "mirroring."

What is mirroring? It is a nonverbal strategy that creates a feeling of simpatico through the conscious matching or mimicking of a partner's gestures, stance, facial expression or behavior. Skillfully done, mirroring transmits two positive messages to a partner: The first is, "I like you." The second, and most important, is, "I am like you." In my opinion, there is nothing you can say or show to a potential friend or lover that will give you greater, more immediate bonding power than this technique.

Is mirroring the latest pop-psych fad? Hardly! Matching another's movements is a mating ritual that dates back beyond the flirtation of Adam and Eve! Anthropologists have observed matching rituals in chimpanzees and other socially evolved primates. And if you would like to see an example of mirroring in action, all you need to do is tune in to the body language of happily married couples you know. Emotionally bonded couples routinely stand at the same time, lean toward each other when speaking, or display unconscious facial expressions or physical gestures that are so similar, they can drive us independent singles to distraction.

Mirroring has withstood the test of time. But could it help Chris turn his next date into a meeting of the minds and hearts? He wasn't convinced. Mirroring, I explained, isn't always unconscious. Because it is so effective, it has become not only a mainstay in building rapport for counselors and therapists but also a way to create a feeling of commonality between clients and suppliers in business negotiations. While there was no guarantee that Chris's date, a surgical nurse named Diana, was indeed "the one," mirroring would certainly help Chris give the pairing one great shot! Chris had dated Diana the week before. Their time together was cordial but uninspired. Since Chris was planning to see Diana in the next few days, I outlined a strategy for him and sent him on his way.

He phoned me way too early on Sunday morning with the good news. Imitation was not only the most sincere form of flattery, Chris told me, it was the key to unlocking the barriers between him and Diana. While I made myself a cup of coffee and tried to wake up, he happily described what had happened. Diana began the evening sitting back in her seat, her hands resting on her lap. This, Chris knew from his discussion with me, was a distancing position common to people who don't know each other well. He also knew that, unless he was able to draw Diana into a mutually shared space, this date was going nowhere. Summoning the waiter, Chris quickly ordered an appetizer to share. Soon Diana was pulling her chair closer to the table, reaching into Chris's personal space.

As she became more comfortable with Chris, Diana began to lean forward across the top of the table as she chatted with her date. At one point, she rested her chin in her hand. Chris leaned into the conversation, too, indicating his willingness to create a shared space with her. When Diana lowered her voice to relate a personal story about her father, Chris responded in kind, turning down the volume, softening his tone. When Diana tilted her head sideways, lifted her wineglass and swirled her drink playfully, David did, too, joking that he was a wine connoisseur—and asking her whether it was true that the best wines came in cardboard boxes.

All in all, the evening went swimmingly. When, at the end of the night, Diana patted Chris's arm, he took hers. And before going their separate ways, they made a date to see each other again—this time for a romantic picnic on Chris's boat. The relationship that just a week ago had seemed beached was still afloat. And although Chris didn't know if his pairing with Diana would last forever, he had learned a technique that would buy him the time to find out.

I have used mirroring in business, in friendship and as a therapist, a teacher and a flirt, and I can say without hesitation that my faith in this technique is unshakable. I believe it can expand your social circle, enhance your career and make you a more successful communicator. Just remember as you flirt, that first or second date doesn't yet know you. Your future depends on whether or not he/she feels you "connect." This simple, nonverbal technique reaffirms the message that you share his interests, empathize with her feelings, care about his or her needs and, most of all, that you can be trusted. You become a person to get to know.

One last point: Casual dates will rarely reveal their less-than-positive feelings about you. No one will ever tell you that you made them ill-at-ease for a reason they can't put their finger on, or that you didn't seem to "fit" with them. They will simply stop calling. Mirroring will prevent such "unexplained disappearances," thus ensuring that you always have a pool of likely prospects to choose from. Just bear these tips in mind and you'll be certain that every move you make reflects well on your character, your motives and your skill as a fun, respectful flirt:

♡ *Be subtle.* There is a big difference between mirroring and aping. Your movements should never seem contrived or obvious. If you fear you might go overboard and come off as parodying your partner's movements, here's a buffer that will help you to polish your mirroring technique: Stay aware of your partner's body language and, as it changes, adopt a position that is similar but not identical to his or hers. For instance, if she smoothes or flips her hair ("preening behavior" is always a very good sign!), you reflect the movement by straightening your tie. If he reaches over and touches the stem of your glass, wait a minute or two then offer an appetizer from your plate. You're sending the same message as he did—literally, "I'm meeting you more than halfway across the table"—but you're not matching his every movement.

♡ *Know what not to mirror.* We all have little flaws that we don't necessarily want to see in the mirror. If he is slouching in his chair or if she is making a strange whistling sound with her teeth, one thing is certain: These are behaviors your partner would rather not see parodied! Be sensitive about what you mirror.

♡ *Put your partner at ease!* A stiff, stony appearance or a guarded posture may not indicate that your partner doesn't like you. What he or she may be showing you is a nervous habit! Before you write this date off as a lost cause, look for other signs that he or she is not relaxed. And while you're at it, check your own body language. Is he or she unconsciously picking up on some stiffness or nervous habit of yours? If so, take a deep breath. Ensure that your arms are not folded into a "barricade" position. Put him at ease by modeling relaxed, interested behavior. Then, when your partner loosens up, you can reinforce the good vibrations between you by mirroring his happy, flirtatious gestures.

Use the Three Rs

I noticed the man in the black trench coat as soon as he entered the restaurant. He paused just long enough to stomp the snow off of his shoes, then walked past the hostess and into the middle of the room with three huge strides. His brow was knitted into a deep furrow, and he began to scan the crowd, glaring at each of us as if we were suspects in a police line up. Although I didn't know this man, I was sure of two things: First, the person he was looking for was me. Second, this fix-up might be beyond repair.

I nodded in his direction and he made his way to the banquette. I put out my hand for a shake and got a brush-off instead. He tossed his coat into the booth, waved for the waiter and placed an order for a double Dewars and water. Then he sat back and looked me over.

"Hardly seems worth coming out in this weather, does it?" he said finally.

I stared back blankly. Was that what passed as a greeting on the planet Obnoxious? He wasn't the only one to have braved the winter elements. I searched my repertoire for a reasonably pleasant response. I needn't have bothered.

"I tried to call and cancel but apparently you had your cell turned off," my unhappy companion groused. "I've always wondered why people carry phones at all if they're not going to turn them on. I mean, if a cell phone isn't on, is it a phone? Or a paperweight?"

By now the waiter had arrived with my escort's drink. Generally, I stayed away from hard liquor but right now, the scotch was looking good to me—as something to pour down my stroppy companion's pants. I took a deep breath and considered the situation. The weather outside *was* frightful. My date was not delightful. But since there was no place to go—and mostly because a former client had been trying to arrange this meeting for months—I would try to give my companion the benefit of the doubt.

Mustering my friendliest smile, I leaned toward my tablemate. "I'm so sorry if I caused you any inconvenience. I spent the afternoon at an estate auction in a brownstone on the Upper West Side. I didn't want to be the one with a ringing pocket. But it was thoughtless of me not to turn it back on." So far, so good. I was keeping my cool. I extended my hand once again. "But it's nice to finally meet you, Jim." I winked conspiratorially. "You *are* Jim, right?"

My date leaned back against the banquette and rested his hands on his knees. "Oh, yes, I'm Jim. I'm also a total idiot for venturing out on a night like this," he answered tartly. He looked distractedly around the room for the waiter. "I don't suppose you're ready to order, are you?"

I had been perplexed and I had been angry but now I was curious. I had served up the sweetest possible conversation opener and he *still* wasn't having any! What had happened to make this man as blustery as the February weather? Although it was tempting to grab my jacket and flee, I decided that I would try to find out. I repeated and slightly rephrased his challenging statement and fed it back to him.

"You don't like going out in this weather?" I prompted.

For the first time, Jim met my gaze. The deep furrow in his brow seemed to soften. He shook his head. "To tell you the truth, I hate the winter! The snow and the sleet just seem to go on forever. And by February, I am just so tired of being cold!"

At that, I nearly laughed aloud. He was tired of being cold? He embodied cold! Install him at the top of Killington and there would finally be some decent skiing in the northeast! Nevertheless, I was intrigued. What could possibly have happened to create such a maelstrom of emotions? Keeping the focus clearly on Jim, I reflected his statement at him one more time.

"The snow and the sleet get to you?"

"They sure do," he answered, this time in a softer tone of voice. "Of course, I didn't always feel this way. I used to like the change of seasons, no matter what they brought. But in December I had a car accident, and frankly, I've been spooked by the winter weather ever since." At last, Jim looked up at me and smiled. "It sounds ridiculous, doesn't it? There was only a thousand dollars worth of damage to the car. But my social life was almost totalled!"

By now, the conversation was out of its skid and Jim was able to chat more easily about his experience. The accident had been his first in a lifetime of driving. The feeling of being out of control in a fishtailing car had been traumatic. Nevertheless, things were moving along a great deal more smoothly between us. Jim was focused on the here and now rather than on an incident that had occurred months ago. And since we had gotten to the root of his problem, we could now move on to subjects we had in common: an aversion to slush, the pros and cons of moving to a warmer climate . . . and how delightful blind dates can turn out to be.

So what are the three Rs and how did I use them to draw Jim out, without judging, giving an opinion or even adding to the conversation in any substantial way? The three Rs are the elements of a powerful conversational skill based on verbal mirroring. Rather than responding to a question or comment with your thoughts and ideas, you *Repeat* your partner's words back to him or her, *Rephrase* each statement as it comes and *Reflect* the attention back upon your conversational partner.

The three Rs technique is a well-known method for opening people up and inviting deeper discourse. It works for everyone who tries it, but it is especially useful for the fledgling flirt because it is an all-purpose, foolproof method. By simply repeating and rephrasing a speaker's words, you give validity to his or her feelings. This makes him/her want to elucidate further. And by constantly steering the focus of the discourse away from you, you encourage an acquaintance to reveal more and more of him or herself, allowing you to see the needs and emotions that underlie his or her opinions.

For a look at how the three Rs can rescript a conversation gone amok, you need only refer to the story of my date with Jim. The date turned out to be the first of many. (He did, eventually, relocate to southwest Florida where, he told me, he inadvertently overturned a golf cart but suffered no grass-related trauma.) Best of all, this strategy can help you turn superficial first-date conversation into the kind of in-depth chat that builds lasting friendship. All you have to do is keep the focus on your partner and bear these bits of advice in mind:

♡ *Don't mimic . . . mirror!* People love to talk about themselves. Your date will be so delighted and flattered by the chance to speak without interruption that he or she will be very unlikely to notice that you're simply reflecting the conversation back upon him. Just make sure you don't start mimicking your companion's tone, inflection, accent or speech pattern, as well. If he expresses himself with a labored John Wayne–esque swagger, if she tends to turn a statement into a question?—a tendency that is increasingly prevalent today?—he or she may very well notice the same tendency in you. To be successful, try not to pick up on a new friend's idiosyncrasies . . . just his or her ideas.

♡ *Don't be a sell-out.* You don't have to agree with everything a date or conversational partner says in order to validate him or her. (Yes-men and -women are too wishy-washy to be really good flirts.) Remember, validation simply means accepting another person's point of view as real—and that should require no compromise on your behalf. Simply repeat, rephrase and reflect and you will offer your new friend all the encouragement he or she needs to open up.

♡ *When in doubt, butt out.* Funny thing about silence—people simply can't keep themselves from filling it! And this can work in your favor when you're drawing a new friend out. Silence acts as a gentle prod nudging a person toward deeper disclosure. Think about it: What happens when a companion makes a statement and you react, not with a comment, but with amiable silence? He refocuses on his statement and reconsiders what he has said. If he is like most people, he will dig deeper into his thoughts and feelings. Then he will share those thoughts and feelings with you.

You can learn more in a minute of silence than you can in an hour of mindless chatter. Bear in mind, however, that effective silence is active; unproductive silence is just plain monotonous. If your eyes start to take on a zombielike stare, or if you notice your companion drumming her fingers on the table, it's time to liven things up a bit.

Practice Asking Open-Ended Questions

Recently I found the following message from my friend Roberta on my answering machine: "Susan! I just rode home with Richard Gere! What a *dud* he turned out to be!"

Before the undoubtedly delightful Mr. Gere slaps me with a libel suit, let me explain. For weeks I had been hearing from Roberta about one of her fellow train commuters who reminded her of Richard Gere. Apparently, she had finally broken through her mute adoration of his charms to converse with the look-alike.

I settled in with a glass of wine and called her back to get the details. A dud? What unfortunate traits or ugly comments could have exposed the trashy novel hiding under that fairy-tale cover? This was going to be good.

"So, what's his story? What did you find out about R.G.?"

"Nothing!" Roberta replied. "Nothing at all. He was just a big zero. No matter what I said, he kept giving me one-word answers. After a while I started feeling like a pest and just gave up. It's weird, though, he didn't seem to mind my talking to him and he flashed me an amazing smile, but he just wouldn't open up. I thought, 'He may be great to look at, but this is just too much work.' What kind of bugs me is that I watched him have quite the animated conversation with one of the conductors before he got off at his stop. Maybe he has a thing for men in uniform."

After some gentle probing, it became clear to me that Roberta had sabotaged what might have been an opportunity to costar with a real winner. I'd suspected as much as soon as she'd mentioned his "one-word answers."

One-word answers come invariably—and appropriately—in response to yes-or-no close-ended questions: "Isn't it awful the train's so late?" "Hasn't it been cold lately?" "Do you know you look just like Richard Gere?" No wonder he didn't have much to say! Roberta's conversational approach had the tone of an interrogation rather than an invitation.

To be fair, a close-ended question isn't the worst way to start a conversation (at least you've said something instead of nothing) but if the other person doesn't pick up the baton, it's one of the best ways to end one prematurely. The better alternative is the open-ended question, either as a follow-up to a yes-or-no question or as the icebreaker itself.

Open-ended questions ask more than yes or no. They ask *how* or *why* or *when* or *where* or *who* or *what*. Open-ended questions encourage details, explanations, opinions, suggestions, elaborations, stories, memories, advice. Best of all, open-ended questions encourage ever further conversation; they expand outward instead of collapsing in on themselves like a simple yes-or-no.

How do you formulate an open-ended question? Don't. Don't formulate or belabor it. Open-ended questions tend to spring naturally from being present in the moment. You probably ask a dozen or more open-ended questions every day of your life. (If you cook, for example, I'll bet you've asked the person next to you in the supermarket checkout line how to prepare the unfamiliar vegetable they've got in their cart.) So rule number one is simply this: Pay attention to your surroundings, your impressions, your curiosity and especially to your present company.

Take your first cue from common experience. If you're in the same place with someone you'd like to speak to, you already have something in common. Find out what brings him/her there.

Look around and inquire about something interesting, perplexing or unusual that you see. If you're taking a French class, ask the *mademoiselle* sitting next to you why she chose to learn French rather than German, or see if she's planning a trip to France. If you're at the bowling alley, inquire of the fellow who's caught your eye if he knows about the local leagues or if he has any tips for keeping your ball out of the gutter. If you're waiting in the ticket line at the multiplex, find out what movie that obviously solo film buff is going to see and why. And always remember that most people in most situations like to be noticed and like to be spoken to.

Speaking of movies, here's a perfect example of how to gracefully wield an open-ended question. You might remember this bit of dialogue from *The American President*. Annette Bening's character notices that the guests of honor at a White House state dinner—the president of France and his wife—are sitting at the table silent, left out and on the edge of boredom. Bening says—in French—something to the effect of, "Here we are in this beautiful room, with an orchestra playing such beautiful music, but there's no one on the dance floor. Why do you think that is?" Delighted to be addressed and brought back into the scene with such an evocative description, the visiting dignitary then very happily shares an intriguing historical anecdote about the consequences of daring to dance under Marie Antoinette's rule. Ask an open-ended question and you never know where the answer will take you.

If it seems unlikely that you'll be invited to dinner at the White House, let's go back to Roberta and see what you might make of her situation. Imagine yourself in her shoes, on the train with "Richard Gere" (or his female equivalent). Now think of twenty-five open-ended questions that might have gotten a conversation on the right track. Here are a few to get you started: "I've noticed you ride the train every day, too. How do you make this commute look so easy?" or "What do you do that makes it worth enduring this commute every day?" or "I see you have a BlackBerry. How has it changed your life?"

This week, see what doors to people's psyches, personalities and expertise you can open simply by asking open-ended questions. Pose them wherever you go of whomever you meet. Make it a habit and you'll find yourself making all sorts of surprising and gratifying connections.

Here are a few more suggestions for opening your world with open-ended questions:

♡ *Learn from the pros.* If Oprah, Dave, Jay, Katie or Matt asked yes-or-no questions they might fit twenty more guests into every program, but we'd never know anything about any one of them. Start watching your favorite morning news or late-night talk show with the eyes and ears of a flirt in training. The masters of the talk-show universe are always asking questions, and very often getting wild and unexpected answers to them. But they never give the impression that they're interrogating or even interviewing their guests. It seems more like they're having a cozy, freewheeling conversation. It also seems utterly unplanned. But if you really listen, you'll hear they all have a formula that you can learn, imitate and adapt to your own personality.

♡ *Don't make your questions* too *open-ended.* Questions like "How was your day?" or "Tell me about yourself" don't just leave the door open, they take the whole side off the house. They ask for too broad an answer, leaving the other person fishing around in an ocean of information to come up with something to tell you. Be specific enough to make the other person's response comfortable and spontaneous.

♡ *Keep up your end of the game.* As we've discussed, open-ended questions just keep opening up new avenues of conversation. So be sure you really listen to your companion's responses and be ready to send the ball right back. She/he will certainly be lobbing some questions your way as well. Let the conversation volley and bounce wherever it may. Stay in the moment and you'll stay in the game.

Keep a few lucky charms in your pocket. Although it's usually best to use the trappings and impressions of the moment in unplanned flirting opportunities with strangers, there are situations in which you might want to have some surefire reinforcements on hand. If you've already dispensed with the weather or other matters at hand, and you still have the time and attention of your new connection for a while, pull out the fantasy query—the sort of open-ended question that can be a source of shared delight and a real window into someone's worldview. Here are a few examples: "If you could plan the ideal dinner party and invite ten people, living or dead, real or fictional, who would they be?" "If you could live anywhere in the world, where would that be?" "What would you do with your life if money was no object?" "What would be your perfect day?"

Week 25

Soften Up the Hard Sell

I was recently asked to appear as a speaker (on the subject of flirting, of course!) on a singles' cruise to Bermuda. Since the man I was seeing was tied up with business and couldn't go along, I took my totally available friend Meredith instead. Just because I was exclusively involved, there was no sense in missing an opportunity to make some waves as a flirt.

On the second night, as the ship steamed toward Bermuda, the passengers were also busily "cruising." Some lingered over dinner, where each table included an array of attractive strangers to sample alongside the asparagus *vichyssoise* and coconut shrimp. Some joined the "Nasty Public Breakups Trivia" game being led by a personable Australian crew-member in the Egyptian-styled bar. (Breakups can be a lot of fun when there is a prize involved!) My friend and I opted to follow the sounds of a reggae band to the lido deck where there was a party going on. It didn't take Meredith long to spot the catch of the night, an extraordinarily tanned and dapper man sipping a drink from a plastic cup.

"What a handsome guy," Meredith crooned. "They don't make them like that in Manhattan, do they?"

In fact, a man of this quality would be a rare find in Manhattan, particularly in the month of November. At a time when most men in the city had already lost their Hamptons tans and beach physiques, this guy was bronzed and fit.

"Catch his eye," I urged my friend. "And when he looks over, don't forget to smile."

It may be "every man for himself" in the event of shipwreck but, on a cruise for singles, there isn't a man on board who isn't looking for companionship. All Meredith had to do was flash those baby blues and her hunk was making his way nonchalantly through the crowd, strolling along the rail, sipping his Bahama Mama, pausing now and then to watch the flying fish skim the surface of the waves. When he crossed the room, I knew it was my turn to fly. I left Meredith and her new friend to get acquainted and joined a group of fledgling flirts from a talk I'd given the night before.

It was an interesting group. Like-minded souls who had been brought together by the flirting workshop the night before, the three men and two women were now debating whether to spend the next day swimming with the dolphins or snorkeling near the remains of a shipwreck. But before I had a chance to voice my own opinion, Meredith was standing beside me—alone. "What happened?" I asked her. "Wasn't he interested?"

Meredith grinned. "He was too interested."

What did that mean? I waved for the waiter to bring us a round of drinks with umbrellas and settled in for Meredith's report.

That dashing man who looked as though he had the world on a string and the phone number of every woman on board wasn't quite the casual charmer he appeared to be. He was a close talker, which is to say, he was in Meredith's face long before she had invited him to be there. His compliments were too effusive. (As Meredith recapped: "He said my eyes were the 'same turquoise as the ocean.' Excuse me! My eyes are hazel!") And that was just the beginning. In the relatively short time they'd spent together, Meredith's new friend had also stared deeply into her eyes ("as if he were charming a cobra"), walked her into a location that made her feel physically cornered, then massaged her bare shoulder ("the way you'd grope a chicken leg you were about to disjoint"). In other words, he may have had a glorious tan, but socially he was toast.

"I understand what you mean by 'too interested,'" I commented.

"Right," said Meredith. "What I meant was, he's too desperate!"

It's flattering when people try to win our hearts. It can even turn our heads when their only real interest is our bodies. We went to schools where they gave points for extra effort, so what's the problem with flirts who try too hard?

A hard sell is stressful—and that is true no matter which side of the dialogue you're on. If you're a flirt who feels pressured to impress, you are spending too much time thinking about yourself—your compliments, your manner and your overall style—to really be successful. And if you happen to be on the receiving end of a coercive approach, you feel pressured, too—to stop the games, to try to make some real contact or, finally, to escape.

This can seem like a very hard, cold world—especially when you're looking for love. As the days tick past, it can be easy to forget that finding love "only takes one." When that happens, when we replace an upbeat, optimistic mantra with a plea ("Are you the one?") or worse, an unspoken demand ("I've waited so long. You must be the one!"), we begin to act from fear. And fear is a powerful emotion that everyone around us can sense.

Naturally, we are more attracted to those people who seem to offer some "warm fuzzies" than we would be to those who delegate stress. To put you in the frame of mind to radiate relaxation, I suggest that you keep one word in mind: S.O.F.T.E.N.

♡ *S—Smile!* There is nothing like a pleasant smile to put whomever you are speaking with at ease. There are two reasons for that. First, a sincere smile makes you seem familiar, like an old friend. Because your conversational partner associates you with outgoing, cheerful people he or she has known in the past, you establish instant rapport. You know that open, easy feeling you get when it seems like you've known someone all your life, even if you met her ten minutes ago? This is the root of that sentiment. Make the most of it!

The other reason a smile has a feel-good effect on those around you is that it relaxes you—and that makes you more attractive to everyone around you. When we are stressed, our emotions are face-front. Our jaws clench; our lips purse; our facial muscles are tight and drawn. And Botox wouldn't be nearly so popular if our brows didn't furrow. But the act of smiling is nature's antidote for that strung-too-tightly look. Put on a happy face and your muscles appear soft rather than stiff. Your jaw relaxes, your cheeks lift and your impression on those around you heightens. Doubt that? Then think back to the last time you stood near someone who was seething with anger or resentment. It's likely that you picked up on those intense feelings immediately. And so it is with an agreeable grin. Smile and the world really will smile with you. (To remind yourself of how and why a smile works, see week 20.)

♡ *O—Open posture.* Most people are naturally attracted to men and women whose facial expressions, verbal communication and body language are welcoming. The O in the acronym S.O.F.T.E.N. reminds you that an open posture opens the door to meaningful conversation. Make sure your shoulders are square and facing your partner but at ease. Stand with your feet apart and your hands loosely behind you, down at your sides or in your pockets. Most of all, don't sway. Swaying can make you seem edgy or telegraph a sense of instability. (See week 27, on body language.)

♡ *F—Forward lean.* Inclining your body slightly toward a new friend is one of the most effective ways to demonstrate your interest. What does the forward lean say? It subtly says, "There may be a lot of stimulating people in my world, but I'm leaning toward you!" Since people tend to like those who like them, that's good flirting in any language!

♡ *T—Touch.* Touch can be a very touchy subject—and for a lot more people than just my friend Meredith. As you will see in week 26, some people don't like to be touched by casual acquaintances at all—and often, for good reason. For the rest of us, however, touch remains an electrifying sensory experience that conducts a feeling of intimacy, security, approval and affection.

To stay on the safe side, limit yourself to a "touch of touch," especially at the getting-to-know-you stage. Restrict yourself to touching a new friend only from his or her fingertips to elbow. Does that seem like too small a region to let your fingers do the walking? Perfect a sultry, memorable flirting handshake and you'll see that it's not. A great shake ensures that you'll go just far enough to make a lasting impression but not so far that you hit a nerve. A poor handshake can shut down communication before it begins. A limp, dead-fish, bone-crusher, wiggle-waggle or aggressive-pump handshake is a definite turn-off. Men, remember women wear jewelry, so watch that squeeze. If you squeeze her fingers together, she may not shout, but disengage and be on her way.

♡ *E—Eye contact.* As you will see in my recommendations for week 27 (and this is such an effective technique!), eye contact is a powerful, ages-old method for attraction. But the object of your affections may never see you for the hottie you are if you're short-sighted about this strategy.

Psychologist Monica Moore, PhD, of Webster University in St. Louis, Missouri, has spent more than two thousand hours observing women's flirting maneuvers in restaurants, singles bars and at parties. She has identified three distinct types of eye contact flirts rely on when they want to see and be seen. First, there is the room-encompassing glance. Anyone who has ever been to a large party has seen a man or woman use this technique. The new arrival enters the room, perches at the perimeter of the gathering then visually sweeps the area as if searching for a friend. Why have we all seen this strategy? Because in actuality, it is an attention-getting tactic the confident flirt uses to make eye contact with an entire roomful of people! The net result is that he or she gets more attention focusing on no one than if he or she picked one or two targets from the crowd.

The second type of eye contact is the short, darting glance. On its own, this kind of hit-and-run technique can send a mixed message. The two people involved meet eye to eye so briefly that the recipient of this look can't really be sure whether the sender is merely curious or truly interested. In week 27 I show you how to team it with a cluster of friendlier nonverbal techniques to send precisely the message you intend.

The final strategy, the fixated gaze, is more problematic.

No one is comfortable being the subject of a stranger's stare. Threatened and uneasy, like Meredith, your target will feel she has no choice but to run.

When it comes to expressing our emotions, the eyes have it! To make sure you are sending positive, friendly signals, reread my guidelines for week 20. If the movements I suggest seem too subtle to you, you may be telegraphing an emotion you did not intend. An adjustment in technique will enable you to make your presence—and your interest—known without coming across as obsessive or fascinated in an unhealthy way.

♡ *N—Nod when the other person is speaking.* This simple gesture not only indicates that you hear what an acquaintance is saying, but it also implies that you agree. Since most of us are looking for a like-minded partner, appearing to have a viewpoint in common can only help your case. One caveat, however: Don't nod constantly or you may appear to have a tic! Seem far-fetched? I've seen flirts who waggle like bobble-heads! So be aware of the tendency to appear too agreeable.

In the animal kingdom, quiet confidence is the mark of a leader—and stress is an incredibly potent emotion that compels entire herds to bolt!

A flirt who is trying too hard is trying for everyone. Your assignment for this week is to eradicate any conscious or unconscious urgency by S.O.F.T.E.N.ing your stance, your glance and your overall approach. Then simply let nature take an exciting, positive course.

Personal Space Is Personal!

Does she or doesn't she . . . want you to come closer, that is? And if she does want you to cozy up, how much closer can you get before you're too close for comfort?

Personal space—the invisible but very real buffer that forms a "comfort zone" between yourself and others—is the "understood" distance a person maintains to ward off unwanted or premature intimacy with casual acquaintances. It's also a barrier that differs from culture to culture—and one that exists in our minds rather than in the real world. Therein lies the difficulty for the respectful flirt. Since there is no chalk outline on the sidewalk to refer to, we have no idea what constitutes the limits of someone's personal space. Indeed, what is acceptable contact for one date can seem like an intimidating "space invasion" for another. If, as Robert Frost wrote, good fences make good neighbors, then indeterminate, loosey-goosey barriers can make for some very bad reactions. Not knowing the exact location of a date's "do not enter" sign places even the most sensitive, thoughtful flirt literally one step away from an inadvertent faux pas.

This story sent to my website by a woman I'll call Dolores illustrates just how powerful and visceral the reaction to a breach of personal space can be.

Dolores met Bob at a surprise birthday party for a mutual friend. Bob and Dolores had begun their relationship as most of us do—in a vertical position. In fact, they spent over an hour chatting happily about their mutual friend, their travels and even about the mystery meat in the caterer's mini-tacos, when Bob suggested that they grab a pair of recently vacated seats. Since the seats Bob indicated were positioned face to face, the couple was able to move their conversation to a cozier location without missing a beat. The connection between them was so strong it had attracted more than a few curious looks and sly winks from Dolores's friends. Things were rolling along smoothly until Bob made what turned out to be an attraction-ending error. In an effort to bowl Dolores over with a single romantic move, he grabbed hold of the legs of Dolores's chair and pulled her, seat and all, as close to him as he possibly could. Suddenly, they were knee to knee and eye to eye. Dolores felt her heart drop. In less time than it took to say "how do you do," Bob had brought the conversation—and the relationship—to a screeching halt.

What did Dolores do? Did she scream out loud, "Who do you think you are? I hardly know you!" Did she slap Bob? Of course she didn't. Dolores simply moved her chair back, stood up and walked away without ever looking back. As for Bob, I'll bet he has looked back on that pivotal moment more than once. It never occurred to him that his maneuver might upset Dolores. He was clearly stunned.

In many cultures, particularly those where people are used to being crowded into public conveyances or herded along bustling streets, it is considered perfectly acceptable to stand very close—six to eight inches apart—when conversing. Here in America, however, the general rule is to allow twelve to eighteen inches of air space between you and a casual acquaintance. Interestingly enough, this is approximately "handshake distance" for most people.

If you're looking to meet a mate, it's crucial that you get a clear idea of what it feels like when an uninvited guest crashes your personal space. It's also important that, as a fledgling flirt, you are able to slip up once in a while without getting slapped! In my School of Flirting workshops I demonstrate the differences in people's boundaries with the following exercise.

I choose a female volunteer and position her on the stage. Then I select a male volunteer and place him facing the woman, about fifteen feet away. As I'm walking him to his mark, I instruct him that, unbeknownst to his partner, he is to move as close to the woman as he possibly can. Then I turn to them both and ask them to walk slowly toward each other.

As they set off, both participants are relaxed and smiling. When they are about two feet away and still moving, the grins begin to look more like grimaces. How close should I get? How close will he get? The female volunteer gets noticeably more unnerved with every step. Finally, the man is practically in her face. Lo and behold, the woman steps back—sometimes in a state close to panic. On one occasion, the female volunteer became so desperate to escape the encroaching man she lost her balance and practically fell off of her feet.

As for the male volunteer, he's usually laughing—until I remind him that if this had been a real-life meeting, he would be toast before he ever had a chance to say hello. And that's a crummy way to end what could have been a beautiful friendship.

"All of that makes perfect sense," said Matt, one of the many men who have volunteered to play the space buster in the previous exercise over the years. "But if none of us ever entered each other's personal space, wouldn't the human race become extinct?"

Matt's comment earned him a huge laugh—but it also introduced a very serious topic. How does the deferential flirt know when he or she is being invited into a date's personal space? Should you RSVP to that invitation with a word or can you accept with a touch?

There are many steps that make up the intricate dance that leads to intimacy. If you misread your partner's cues, it becomes extremely easy to get off on the wrong foot! Each subtle change, every minute gesture, either draws you closer or signals your partner's need to retreat. Here are a few guidelines to keep you on the right side of a new friend's barriers:

♡   *If he leans toward you or inclines his head toward yours, he wants you to move closer.* A tone of voice that draws you closer sends the same signal. If she is whispering or if he is confiding in you quietly, you are free to move about your partner's personal space.

♡   *If he crosses his arms or if she puts her bag between you and her body, it's a sure sign you're coming too close.* Back off for now.

♡   *Test the waters.* Rather than reaching directly for your partner, penetrate his space by gesturing at something nearby (a painting, or some other object of interest). If he seems to flinch or takes a step back, you've been too forward.

♡   *If you're at a restaurant or seated at a table and you want to find a friend's comfort zone, slide some of your personal belongings— perhaps a book or your reading glasses—to your date's side of the table.* If he or she allows the "invasion," the light is green. (Note: Never, under any circumstances, should you reach your fork across the table and spear a piece of food off of a date's plate! This behavior not only breaks every rule of etiquette, it is spectacularly boorish and rude. If you've always wanted to taste a certain dish, order it and pay for it. It may not be the best plate of food you've ever eaten but it will certainly be easier to digest than cold shoulder.)

When in doubt, always allow a female to set the pace for increased intimacy. Women are very sensitive to power plays. Most women find it extremely intimidating—and even physically threatening—to have a man barge into her personal space. To stay on the safe side, maintain a hands-off policy until she touches you first. Once she takes your arm, straightens your lapel, brushes against you or makes physical contact, you are free to respond in kind.

Send Your Message Without Saying a Word

Nancy stumbled into the coffeeshop in a burst of wind and rain, her outermost package crashing to the floor. As she pushed her hood back and not so delicately pulled a strand of hair from her mouth, she managed to mumble a "thank you" to the man who handed the bag to her, with a smile. A very good-looking smile, she realized as she imagined her mascara streaming toward her chin. She blushed, then blushed at her blushing. She sat nearby, ordered a tea and bolted to the rest room for emergency repairs. She returned, composed and focused, smiling at her hero, and managed to hold that eye contact for the all-important moment extra.

She sat, crossed her legs gracefully, leaned her head on her hand so that her hair fell forward at just the right angle, and casually paged through the magazine. The fact that she wasn't reading any of the words meant nothing. He was looking and she could feel it with every fiber in her body. He cleared his throat, and they both gratefully looked up as another drenched soul tumbled in, seeking shelter in the warm and close-quartered coffeeshop. "Nice weather," he said. She laughed and gave the all-important eye contact again. "Oh, I know. The beaches must be packed." When in doubt, shared moments of useless sarcasm can be great bonding tools. He then praised her, in a friendly, mocking way, for being brave enough to have accumulated so many shopping bags on such a bad day. She barely heard him, though, because she was watching how he shifted in his seat and leaned forward on his elbows. The intensified eye contact triggered her blush again, and again, and she mumbled out something about being a dedicated player, not daunted by wind and torrential rain. A shopping postal worker, of sorts.

An hour later, they were exchanging business cards. His name was Sean, and he was new to the city. He had played football in college, but now he enjoyed building furniture. Bad knees, he laughed. She laughed, leaned forward and shared an embarrassing but entertaining ski accident story from her twenties. They commiserated about soreness on days like this. They laughed, they leaned in, then comfortably back. She played with her hair, tucking it behind her ear, and noticed how his eyes searched her face. They never talked about anything important, yet much was said and understood from the way they moved, looked at one another and filled the air between them. There would most certainly be another date. It would definitely require more shopping for Nancy.

Silent movies had a great advantage. An attractive man or woman didn't have to be brilliantly witty or embarrassingly forward, or stutter something barely understandable to get their message across. In that world all the attention was on body language. With the batting of glued-on eyelashes, the dramatic clench of a fist or an unfortunately funny fall through an ill-placed hole, worlds were conquered, fights were had and hearts were forever carried away.

So what did the glamorous, heavily madeup stars of old have that we do not? Nothing. We all have the ability to read distinct messages from others that are sent with body language alone. The depth of communication between a couple is intensely connected to facial expressions, postures and body placement. Is it interest? Is it love? Is it the more steamy chemical reaction of lust? Do you smell funny? The nuances of this unspoken language are there for all of us, and they are necessary tools in the science of flirting.

As in any form of communication, of course, the possibility for confusion looms large but our movements provide context for what we say.

Eye contact is primary. It is the pièce de résistance in the matters of communication. As I have said, it should be used respectfully and with a specific plan. Look up. Connect. Hold for a bit. Look away. Quickly glance up again. Look away. Evaluate the target. The ball should be bouncing right back to your side of the net any minute now. If not, look up and repeat, reevaluating the target and its viability. Is there, perhaps, a wedding ring? A partner sidling into the space between you? Is he leaving soon? The point is, eye contact acts like the Navy SEALS of flirting. It establishes territory and lays the groundwork for the next phase.

What you do with the rest of your body is also incredibly important. When Nancy crossed her legs and leaned oh-so-nonchalantly to read her magazine, Sean perceived a woman who was relaxed, approachable, but not obviously dying to talk to him. The challenge was set, yet the danger was relieved by her relaxed posture. When he initiated conversation, her body turned to his, and the talking proceeded from there. The unspoken message was that they both wanted to talk to one another; Nancy's magazine never had a chance. Leaning forward, relaxing back against the seat, laughing, eye contact and a general sense of comfort with the situation are the scaffoldings upon which the conversation rests. Basically speaking, anyone can do it, because we have been unconsciously practicing it and watching others since we were babies. We learn the nuances of body language before we learn the vocabulary to express our emotions, thoughts or great jokes . . . but that doesn't mean we don't need a reminder! To reiterate:

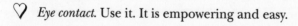 *Eye contact.* Use it. It is empowering and easy.

Be conscious of your body language. But present it to the world as if you have never thought about it for even a second. Recognize your situation. If sitting, sit casually, but in a way that suggests confidence: shoulders erect, body open to the room.

♡ *Tear down the walls.* Crossed arms, a newspaper or magazine held stiffly upright, a leg crossed ankle to knee: These aren't just casual positions, they are physical barriers. Tear down the walls! Flirting is all about inviting someone into your life, not building a barrier between you.

♡ *Don't take up space.* Whether you are sitting or standing, don't sprawl! Draping yourself over a piece of furniture or taking up a conspicuously large section of floor suggests self-importance and superiority. And the more you spread out, the less room you leave for someone else to squeeze in. Show that you have room in your life for a significant other.

♡ *Watch your stance.* According to body language expert Patti Wood, a very approachable woman should stand with her feet no farther than six inches apart with toes pointing slightly inward. If you are a man, however, it is a more dominant look that attracts the opposite sex. You should stand with your feet six to ten inches apart, toes pointing outward.

♡ *Show your interest.* When engaged in conversation with a person you're interested in, maintain eye contact and position yourself in a welcoming way: Turn to face her, shift in your seat or lean forward, and you will send the message that you're interested in what she wants to say. It will also give her a moment to think of a brilliant reply.

♡ *As with anything else, don't overdo body language.* Physical communication is powerful. People instinctively move away from things that approach like freight trains.

When Body Language Goes Wrong

My friend Stephanie is frequently a few minutes early to meet me, while I am usually about fifteen minutes off cue. On one occasion, she arrived fifteen minutes early and secured herself a nice seat in the corner of the bar. She ordered her drink and began people watching to pass time until I arrived. She was tired from several long work weeks; caring for her mother, who had recently suffered a mild stroke; a crowded subway and a headache; so she relished the opportunity to be quiet and wait. Suddenly a man appeared out of nowhere.

"Is anyone sitting here?" he asked, gesturing to the empty stool next to her.

She looked up for a fraction of a second. "Yes," she said with a half smile.

"Are you sure?" he persisted.

"Very sure," she countered, with a slightly more chilly, little-less-than-half smile. She placed her coat on the back of the chair, and returned to studying the bar menu with enough intensity to make it levitate.

"I've never seen you here before. My name is Tom."

She sighed. Although she was not outwardly impolite, the image of Munch's *Scream* came to her mind. "I have never been here before. I'm waiting for my friend to come—we haven't seen each other in a long time." With that, she smiled (sort of), shifted in her seat (again) and returned to her visual attack on the bar menu.

Tom made three more half-hearted attempts before I burst

> through the door. I sensed danger immediately. I was able to scurry Tom away with little ceremony, and talk Stephanie off the proverbial ledge.

Poor Tom. In his eagerness to make a connection, he couldn't see the signals Stephanie broadcast so clearly. Remember, a person's body language tells us more than hours of conversation. Quite simply, someone who does not turn to face you does not want you to perceive a welcome opening. A person who will not maintain eye contact with you is nervous or uncomfortable. A person whose face is emotionless or flat does not feel anything they would consider sharing. The best thing to do is say "Next!" and move on to more fertile flirting grounds.

Consider whether you might be misinterpreting your conversational partners' signals. Here are some potential pitfalls:

♡ *Lack of eye contact.* It's likely your acquaintance is trying to shut down your interaction.

♡ *Folding arms tightly and leaning back.* Someone who pulls into themselves is generally not suffering from a sudden chill. They sense or feel discomfort of some kind. Use it as an opportunity to excuse yourself.

♡ *The "cold shoulder."* Someone who does not turn to face you while you talk is going for the body language touchdown in the disinterest column. They don't want to engage, so don't continue trying. Besides, eye contact with a shoulder blade has historically been found extremely unsatisfying.

♡ *A stiffening of the upper body.* If she stiffens or if he pulls himself up to full height, you have literally gotten his or her "back up." It is probably time for you to back down.

♡ *A lone verbal cue.* Don't set too much store by a single encouraging verbal cue. It's like RSVPing to a party before you've really been invited. Press your intentions only after you've received a cluster of positive messages.

♡ *Mixed messages.* A smile should not be taken as an invitation if it is teamed with crossed arms or any other "blocking" behavior. And stay on the lookout for the person who is verbally saying "yes" but simultaneously nodding "no." He or she is either revealing an honest case of ambivalence or telling a lie.

Week
29

Overcome Your (Conversational) Gender Issues

I met Jenny, a nurse somewhere between thirty-eight and forty-two years old, after a talk I had given at a West Coast bookstore. She seemed to have had some kind of a revelation in the course of the workshop. In her hand she held several sheets of hastily scrawled notes. The pages were decorated with so many exclamation points they could have been written in some kind of sideways Morse code.

"Let me cut to the chase," Jenny blurted after introducing herself. "I have no problem getting first dates. That's the good news. Unfortunately, nearly all of my dates are first dates. In fact, if not for first dates, I'd have had no dates at all this year!"

Jenny was vivacious, enthusiastic and honest to a fault. I had the feeling that even I wouldn't mind having her as a dinner companion! I asked the obvious question. "Do you have any idea why?"

"I do now!" Jenny said brightly. She rummaged through her notes and thrust a page under my nose. "Listen to this . . ."

She cleared her throat and began to read what sounded like bits of quoted conversation.

"I would have been here earlier but I had to pick up the twins and drop them at their father's."

"I used to work out every day until I developed this terrible bursitis."

"I have a 1992 Ford Taurus. What kind of car do you drive?"

She looked at me and grinned. "And now for the pièce de résistance . . . 'With your coloring, I think you look fabulous in blue! Did you ever think about getting a similar sweater in say, cobalt?' "

She looked at me expectantly. Even proudly. "No wonder I never get a second date! Judging from the information you just gave me, everything I say is wrong!"

I laughed and complimented Jenny on her candor. I offered to stay awhile and discuss the subject further but Jenny had other plans.

"I'd love to but I'm going out for coffee with a group from class," she said. She nodded in the direction of a small group of men and women gathered by the door. As she did, a tall, handsome man caught her eye and smiled.

"I see," I said with a wink. "So what are you planning to do differently, then?"

Jenny smiled and slipped into her jacket. "That's easy. Everything!"

My School of Flirting events are always high-spirited affairs. No matter where they're held, no matter what the demographics of the crowd, virtually everybody who participates seems to learn something new about dating and relating. How do I know? Because so many of my guests come in unescorted but, two hours later, leave in pairs!

How do these fledgling flirts learn so much in such a short time? For one thing, they're motivated learners. (Do you think any unattached person really wants to use the passenger seat of his snazzy two-seater as a place to store his unfolded map collection forever? I assure you, they do not!) In addition, learning to flirt is not just fun, it's practical! It's not like algebra or any of those other subjects people swear you'll use eventually. Every tidbit of information you pick up at a flirting workshop can be put to use immediately . . . with your fellow students . . . with the coat-check clerk . . . with the waiter tallying your bill . . . even with your flirting instructor! (Need proof? See week 17!)

As Jenny learned, flirting is all about communication—and communication is a two-part process: First your mouth is open, then your ears. If Jenny had been "listening" for her dates' verbal and nonverbal messages about their interest in the conversation, she would have maximized her chances at second and third liaisons. But there was another problem with Jenny's chatter: She spoke to her male escorts the way she would a trusted girlfriend. She wasn't aware that conversation is, in many ways, gender specific.

Why can't a woman be more like a man—or vice versa—when it comes to simple banter? The communication gap between men and women has been the subject of countless books and the source of many flirting failures. Still, experts disagree on what prevents males and females from connecting in conversation. Some believe it's because women are brought up to be more social and familial, and therefore more focused on the "softer" emotional issues. Others believe that men are biologically programmed to transmit facts rather than feelings and, therefore, are more direct in their speech and behavior. No matter what the reason, men and women do not always find the same kinds of topics meaningful nor do they know what subjects might raise a red flag for a member of the opposite sex. Both situations are hostile to flirtation.

I believe that the conversational gender gap is a combination of nature and nurture. But identifying the reasons why a man tunes out "touchy-feely" talk or why a woman shrugs off male-speak is hardly the point. Unless you can separate the hot topics from subjects that are strictly hands-off, you will not be successful as a flirt.

So what do you say? This week, try these gender-specific guidelines:

Talking Points for Men

♡ *Do reveal your feelings.* I am not suggesting that you laugh, cry and emote like a character in a vaudeville melodrama. But would it kill you to give a woman some idea of how you feel? If there is something you like about her—her eclectic jewelry, her taste in art, her off-tune singing or her slightly off-color jokes—why not say so? Feelings don't have to talked to death; they can even be expressed nonverbally. It is when they are neither verbalized nor shown, that your intentions—and therefore the reason for the relationship—become murky.

♡ *Don't reduce her to a number.* Age may be casually traded information among your group of buddies but that may not be the case for her. Ageism is very real and there are few women who have not experienced it. Never ask a woman a question—"What year did you graduate from high school?" "How old are your children?"—simply to determine her age. No woman wants to be discriminated against because she's too old, too young or too in-between.

♡ *Ask her what she thinks.* Your forty-five-minute monologue about the rigors of your job, your diatribe on the mind-numbing effects of techno and even your harangue on the proper preparation of a whiskey sour might become tolerable if, at some point, you ask her what she thinks! Some men tend to overlook a woman's opinions. Show some respect for her thoughts and she'll think the best of you.

♡ *Let her know you're listening.* Nod, smile, maintain interested, active eye contact—do something to let her know you're listening! When women complain they can't "talk to a man," what they're often really saying is that they don't feel heard.

♡ *Don't fix it immediately.* Women often work through a problem by airing their feelings. Listen to her before you give her what you think is the obvious solution.

♡ *If you find yourself trying to convince, stop!* Grandstanding, table pounding, repetition and outright insistence may have scored you points when you were on the debate team, but it won't get you the girl! Would you rather be right or happy?

♡ *Watch out for the bombshells!* When you hear a leading question like, "Do I look fat in this?" don't even look up! That only acknowledges the possibility that she may look fat in some article of clothing. Instead, look her straight in the eye and say, "Absolutely not. You always look wonderful!" And mean it.

♡ *Never kiss and tell!* She may not like or even know your ex, but things you say about your past dates may color your romantic future. Bragging about your sexual conquests (even if you don't think you're bragging) will make your current lady feel like one of the crowd. And spilling the beans about a former wife or girlfriend's secrets may make her think twice about sharing intimate moments with you.

♡ *Keep sex off your lips even if it is on your mind.* Women like sex but they don't like to be sex objects. You may admire certain aspects of her physique (just as she may admire bits of yours!)

but she will want to know that you think of her as more than the sum of her parts. There is a fine line between compliment and innuendo. To stay on the right side of it, keep the come-ons to yourself.

Guidelines for Gals

♡ *Don't blab about everyone you know.* Women tend to personalize conversations. Even when they start out talking about things, they can end up talking about people. Of course, the friends and foes you've collected are meaningful to you, but to him they can be more difficult to sort out than the cast of characters in a Russian novel! Does he want to know about your best friend, your aunt Betty or you? Stick to the subject at hand.

♡ *Don't ask too much about what he does for a living until you know him well.* If women resent being addressed as "sex objects," men bristle at being treated as "success objects." What type of car he drives, where he bought that beautiful suit, where he spends the summer, even which schools his kids attend may seem like innocent questions to you, but they may translate to "How much money do you make?" to him. Don't dig for info, or gold.

♡ *Keep your maladies to yourself.* You may be living quite comfortably with your herniated disc, water on the knee, migraines, chilblains and allergy to red wine, but this depressing litany of illnesses, conditions and complaints may make him wonder if you are going to make it through dinner! Not even a defibrillator could revive this dead-end conversation. Spare him the story about the orthotics in your shoes or he might walk.

♡ *Leave your kids with the sitter.* They're smarter than average; cuter than the rest. You gave them life; but could you give this guy a break? He asked you here to spend some quality time. When does it begin? I know you adore your kids. But he may have offspring of his own he believes are—can you imagine?—just as exceptional. Besides, the goal of flirting is to date, relate and possibly meet your mate. Just for tonight, focus on yourself.

 Do talk about your job . . . especially if you love it. Men find independent, accomplished, attractive women fascinating. So be yourself!

 Week 30

Do a Sound Check

Reina was soaking up some rays when she saw him: the man not of her dreams but of her fantasies. He was nice looking and about her age (twenty-two), and best of all, he was looking her way. Trying not to appear obvious, Reina adjusted her Ray-Bans and did a covert full-body scan. The man was, indeed, the physical specimen she had hoped for—and the book in his hand told her that he might be intelligent, as well! But what was he reading? She peered at the cover of his book. Could it be? They were reading the same novel! Fortune was certainly smiling on her today.

Reina knew just what to do. She pushed her sunglasses down on the bridge of her nose so she could make eye-to-eye contact. Then, when she knew she had caught his gaze, she smiled coyly—and lifted her copy of the popular bestseller. He lifted his in response, as if in a literary toast to their future. Reina cleared a spot on her blanket. She knew he'd be visiting soon.

Sure enough, he put the book aside and sauntered across the hot sand. The closer he got, the more Reina was certain that someone had taken her wish list and compressed it into a single toned and bronzed package. But when he plopped down next to her and began to speak, it was clear to Reina that it was time to wake up and smell the cocoa butter. He may have had the body of a marble sculpture, but he had a voice like gravel. Worse yet, the grating sound was interrupted only by strange little squeaks that crept in and out of his sentences like scavenging mice.

She loved what she was seeing. Could she possibly overlook what she was hearing? She was mulling that possibility when she became aware that her vocally challenged swain had asked her a question—and was awaiting an answer. Would she be in the beachfront clubs that evening? Could they hook up in a specific place at an appointed time?

Reina smiled and promised she would be around but she knew she wouldn't. Her beach boy had the look of love—but a soundtrack sound that set her teeth on edge.

Some of us are so busy putting together the right appearance that we forget to consider the way we sound. Just how much influence does our vocal personality have on the people we meet? You need only consider your own reaction to these types to know: The fast-talking salesman. The raspy smoker. The chronic whiner. THE LOUD TALKER. The inaudible whisperer. Who would willingly sacrifice their eardrums and patience in an effort to know these people better? I know I wouldn't.

But what if the conversational types that bug us *are* us? How can we recognize these irritating tendencies in ourselves? And can the way we talk be the reason our romantic lives aren't much to talk about?

Consider Greg's story. Tall, dark, handsome and accomplished, Greg was an extremely successful pharmaceutical chemist who parlayed a gift for gab into a lucrative sales career. A Tufts graduate, born and raised on the coast of Maine, Greg was a big hit in the east, socially and professionally. But when he took a job in

Kansas City, suddenly success didn't come so easily. His sex appeal seemed to lose its potency. In addition, he was no longer considered the wunderkind at work. When important presentations needed to be made, he was asked to sit on the sidelines. The entire situation was a bitter pill . . . until his boss suggested that he attend classes to diminish his distinctive New England accent! Turns out that the flat As and dropped Rs that were perfectly acceptable on the east coast were totally unintelligible to midwesterners. Greg took the classes and has enjoyed more harmonious personal and professional relationships since.

When we explore the way we sound to others, we don't usually tune in to our regional idiosyncrasies—but we should. Once, when I lectured in the South, a man in the audience politely interrupted. "You're talking too fast. I don't understand you. Would you mind slowing down?" I admit I was a bit miffed at the time, but now I realize that I, too, need a sound check now and then. I've lived in the city my entire life and tend to get things said in a "New York minute." I was in the South to help people build rapport. If I hadn't controlled the speed of my delivery, I would never have connected with my audience.

OK—so what is perfectly acceptable speech in one region is completely unintelligible to people from another. But we don't hear ourselves as others do. So how are we going to tell what we sound like when no one tells us?

I suggest you try an exercise I use in my School of Flirting workshops. Find a partner—a friend or colleague who can be honest with you—and ask him or her to honestly critique your tone of voice, pitch and verbal speed.

While it can be fun to chatter or go with the conversational flow, this can actually distract your coach. You don't want him or her to be so absorbed by the content of your monologue that he/she ceases to hear the sound and rhythm of your speech. Instead, I suggest that you repeat one simple phrase—I usually use the sentence "What is that?"—and that you imbue the phrase with a range of different emotions . . . anger, curiosity, boredom and surprise. After several minutes of practice, repeat the sentence to your partner and ask him or her to guess which emotion you are portraying.

Participants at my workshops find this exercise to be fun and valuable. Often, it gives them their first experience of how their intonations, volume, pitch, nasality and resonance reflect their feelings and influence others. It has also elicited unexpected comments like these:

"I don't know how to tell you this Lynn, but you whine. Maybe you have a deviated septum and can't help it, but my sense is that it is just a habit."

"Your voice is too soft and seems tentative. I am almost sitting in your lap trying to hear you! You need to speak up, especially in a group."

"Where were you born? You have a very unique accent but it bothers me that I can't really place it."

Since research has shown that people converse most easily with those who share their verbal patterning tendencies, it is important to know what yours are. If you're uncomfortable asking a friend to critique your personality, there is another way to give your speech a fair hearing. Most people hate to listen to their recorded voice. Indeed, the anticipation of being recorded can create so much anxiety, it can actually change a speaker's pacing and sound. That's why I suggest that you give a close friend a pocket tape recorder and ask him or her to tape your voice—without warning—during one of your conversations. Then you can tune into the tape for clues on how your voice or speech pattern might be affecting your flirting.

As you listen, ask yourself the following questions:

♡ *Is your voice a turn-off; either too high, too low or extremely nasal?* Although these tendencies aren't intimidating, as excessive volume or speed might be, they can be grating.

♡ *Do you speak in a varying pitch or are you a boring monotone?* A monotone voice can make you seem like an emotional "flatliner" or even be downright soporific! Need proof? Think about the lullabies we sing to soothe babies to sleep. Most are melodies composed of very few notes. You'll never rouse your love life if you're putting your listeners to sleep.

♡ *Does your voice project well?* A man whose voice is too soft can seem "mush-mouthed." A woman whose voice has a breathy tone can be simply too hard to hear. A conversation with her can seem too "high maintenance."

♡ *Do you put a "smile" in your voice?* If you sound happy to be in a conversation the person you're talking to will be happy, too.

♡ *Do you speak too fast, too slow or at a comfortable speed?* If your speech is rapid-fire or staccato, you can sound like a television pitchman. Don't be surprised if dates think you're trying to sell them a bill of goods!

We all want a lovelife that is worthy of discussion . . . or even gossip! Since most communication breakdowns are habitual rather than physical, they are easily eradicated. How? Practice! Simple exercises like these can help:

♡ *Stretch your vocal cords by inhaling and exhaling.* Open your mouth and throat wide and relax your jaw. Next, exhale through your vocal cords. Try first with a high-pitched sound and then drop it down to a low pitch and then a large yawn.

♡ *Practice breathing from the diaphragm.* Breathing correctly is the key to a pleasantly pitched, comfortably paced speaking style. Place your hands on your midriff, just below the rib cage, and inhale deeply through your nose until your lungs fill with air. Then exhale slowly though your mouth, forcing the air out from the rib cage. This exercise is designed to help you breathe deeply, evenly and correctly. Repeat this technique three times, several times a day, and your voice will become clear, resonant and well-modulated.

♡ *We cannot hope to put our conversational partners at ease unless we are relaxed ourselves.* This exercise works wonders to loosen up speech that sounds "choked" or "tight." Relax your head. Tilt it to one side as if to touch your ear to shoulder, and then to the other side. Repeat five times, and then turn your head right and left. Rotate it slowly. Practice each step five times a day.

Part Four

Action

Assemble Your Flirting Kit!

My friend Steven is a power-systems engineer at the top of his field. Always meticulous, he carefully plans everything—whether it's his latest project or a social outing—to the nth degree. When he and a group of friends, including me, decided to take advantage of the low off-season plane fares and spend a long weekend in northern Italy, Steven called ahead to ensure that there would be beds ready for all of us jet-lagged travelers when we arrived. And when we dawdled over grappa so long in Padua that we missed the last train back to our hostel, it was Steven who pulled enough granola bars out of his bag to provide us with an impromptu breakfast.

You can imagine how surprised I was, then, to discover that Steven may have crossed romance off of his agenda by not planning for flirtation.

It happened on the island of Murano, a short water-taxi ride from Venice. We had just spent a few minutes watching a man spin a delicate horse from a lump of molten glass when we wandered into the gift shop. We weren't there more than a minute when an animated brunette at the jewelry counter began to check out the glass beads for which Murano is famous—and also Steven.

She picked up one colorful necklace then another. She sighed. Then she turned to my friend.

"You're an American, aren't you?" she asked, nodding toward Steven's MIT alum polo shirt. "I don't mean to disturb you, but I'm trying to choose a souvenir for my sister. She's very picky and she never likes anything I buy her. My sister has nearly the same coloring as I do. The question is, which of these neck-laces do you think would be more complimentary to her? The blue? Or the green and blue?" She held each of the strands to her throat. Steven suggested that the green would play up her hazel eyes. Then the conversation turned to the woman's plans for further travel in Italy.

The woman, Eti, would be in the northeast of the country for the next four days. Could Steven suggest some places to visit? Steven had been researching the off-the-beaten-track vistas and quaint villages in the area for the last few weeks. Could he suggest an itinerary? You bet he could! Soon he was regaling his new friend with the all the sights and sounds of Verona—home to a spectacular Roman amphitheater dating back to the third century and the setting for Shakespeare's greatest love story, *Romeo and Juliet*. Did Eti have time to visit Padua? If she did, she could take in some of Giotto's greatest artworks then top off the day with a plate of some delicious regional specialty, like *polenta con baccala*, at an outdoor café near the scenic *Prato della Valle*.

Eti and Steven chatted like old friends until one of our group checked the time. We had a tour scheduled in St. Mark's Square—and if we didn't hurry, we were going to be up the Gulf of Venice without a water taxi to get us there in time. We let Steven know that it was time to go.

"I'd love to meet up with you and your friends this weekend," Eti suggested. "Where will you be heading next?"

Steven shrugged. Group travel is a wonderful treat but adven-turing on the fly with a group of friends means that everything is subject to discussion. The next day's destination was still unde-cided.

Eti was definitely interested—and she would not be deterred.

"Do you have a card, then?" she asked. "I travel on business all the time. Maybe we could meet for lunch the next time I'm in New York."

Steven went blank. A card? As a matter of fact, he did *not* have a card! Since this was a pleasure trip and not business travel, he had left his cards back at home along with his cell phone and pocket protector.

By now, there was no time to search for a pen or a piece of paper or anything else to assuage the situation. We had to dash for a water taxi chugging up the canal toward our stop. We made our tour, but Steven failed to make the most of a great encounter.

When we got home, Steven went straight to a local printer and had a simple card made for just these kinds of impromptu social encounters. But it was curtains for this star-crossed pair. A connection with potential had become just another vacation memory.

The moral of this story? A straightforward card presenting basic contact information is a passport to your second encounter with an interesting, attractive person. Never leave home without it! Of course, a business card is acceptable. Many flirts prefer to keep their private information private until they get to know a new friend better. But if you'd rather not encourage social contacts to phone you at work, or if you wish to direct calls from new acquaintances to a specific or easily screened telephone number, I suggest that you have some inexpensive calling cards made.

Here are a few guidelines to consider before committing your come-on to type:

♡ *Don't sweat the text or graphics.* A card doesn't have to be clever or funny to be successful. In fact, what is a laugh to you can be off-putting or even offensive to someone who doesn't know you well enough to accurately interpret your sense of humor. Keep your card friendly and informative. You'll have plenty of time to display your wit when you're face to face.

♡ *Daunt? Don't!* An impressive list of lofty credentials might prompt a headhunter to reach for the phone, but for social success this kind of information may be a wrong number. Think about it. Will that happy-go-lucky surfer type check out your list of professional affiliations and wonder whether you might be all work and no play? Will the looker manning the next booth at a professional conference think you're trying to make a social connection or drum up business? Why risk that kind of confusion? Your name, perhaps some indication of a hobby or job, a telephone number where you accept messages, and an e-mail address that you use for social purposes is more than enough information for a new acquaintance to go on.

♡ *If he/she seems to need a written invitation to call . . . provide one!* There is nothing that softens a card's hard edges like a personally scrawled message—and that is especially true when the note acts as a reminder of a moment you and the recipient have shared. Did you meet at a baseball game? Jot a little something like "Thanks for passing the peanuts!" and it will serve as a reminder of a pleasant afternoon spent in adjoining seats in the upper deck. If you crossed paths at the park? A few handwritten words on the back of your card ("Next walk, the water's on me!") and he'll remember why a companion might be what he needs to light a fire under his exercise regimen. Go ahead and jot down a description of him on his card so that when he calls, you'll remember him.

It is human nature to like people who like us. Adding a few choice words to a preprinted card takes only seconds—but it's a great way to snag first place on that certain someone's "to-call" list.

♡ *And when you can't think of a thing to say . . .* a nicely designed card can speak for you. If you are feeling tongue-tied or shy, send your card along with a drink or a rose to an intriguing person at an adjoining table in a local restaurant and you've opened the door without ever getting out of your seat! What could be easier?

♡ *An iffy alternative:* A Realtor I know was mailing refrigerator magnets advertising his services to potential clients when he had a brainstorm: Why not produce his social card in a form with more "stick-to-it-iveness"? It seemed like a great idea until a woman he had recently "carded" saw his picture and number on a close friend's refrigerator! It just goes to show you: A paper card may get tossed aside but a greeting in a medium that is meant for public display may bring a chilly result. A card may seem old-fashioned but it slips easily into a pocket or wallet. That keeps the encounter cordial, non-threatening and blissfully private.

Week 32 — Give Flirting Props Their Propers

At first glance, Vince looked like the type of man you'd cross the street to avoid on a dark night—or even in broad daylight. He was six-foot-five, well-muscled and generally menacing. He was also irresistible.

Why? Because when I met Vince, this hulk of a man's man was frolicking in the park with a pair of perfectly coiffed and beribboned toy French poodles. Now, French poodles are known to be very smart dogs. And as I soon discovered, in the case of these two, their handler was even smarter. It turned out that Napoleon and Josephine were not Vince's dogs at all, but belonged to his mother. He borrowed them on a regular basis for the express purpose of meeting people.

"Let's face it," Vince told me, "as far as first impressions go, I come off more like King Kong than Prince Charming. I'm a competitive body-builder but I also have a master's in British Romantic Poetry . . ." He smiled charmingly, almost blushing, then continued, "You know, I even have a real sweet tooth for chick flicks! The dogs—who I do love dearly—make me more approachable. They help me meet women who otherwise wouldn't give me the time of day."

Vince had discovered the power of the flirting prop. In fact, he deserved another degree for having devised and mastered the use of a "value-added" prop. By being big enough, so to speak, to acknowledge he had forbidding physical presence, he had found a brilliant way not only to soften that first impression but to transmit a sense of humor about himself and a good dose of easy self-assurance along with it; the sight of this gentle giant paired with these prissy poodles would bring a smile even to the face of a passing sourpuss.

Flirting props are the easiest and most successful items in the flirt's arsenal. Dogs, of course, are high in the pantheon of flirting props. Not only are they natural flirts themselves, inviting familiarity and even immediate displays of affection from strangers, but their instinctual responses to people can often separate the good guys/gals from the bad. And just ask an intriguing stranger to hold on to to your beagle's leash for a moment while you locate your keys and you'll know right away if she/he is a dog lover or a Fido-phobe. I've lost track of the number of romances, marriages and long-term friendships I know of that began with the wag of a tail. But of course, don't get a dog just to use as a flirting prop. If you don't have the time, space, love and attention to properly care for a canine collaborator, follow Vince's lead and borrow one.

Once you learn to connect the idea of flirting with props, you'll probably find that you already carry a few with you on a daily basis. What can serve as a flirting prop? Virtually anything that can spark conversation, incite interaction or communicate common interest or experience. In the next chapter I'll present a long list of them, but for the moment, let's look at how even the most mundane items can be turned into flirting gold.

I love this story told by my nearsighted buddy Lucinda. An intrepid flirt, Luce had gone ahead by herself to a large party—where she knew not a soul—when the friend who was supposed to accompany her bailed out at the last minute. She made a feast that night of delicious encounters with new acquaintances, several of whom she's seen since. But she found herself bested in the flirting department while she was standing in the buffet line and heard someone say, "Excuse me, four-eyes, but would you mind passing me a fork?" Lucinda's first impulse was to fire back a surprised and slightly offended, "Hey! What's the big idea?" (And she *was* armed with a fork, after all.) When she turned to confront the scoundrel, she found only the grinning face of a very attractive man wearing a screamingly obvious pair of thick, black-framed glasses. He had totally and ingeniously disarmed her, turning something as ordinary as eyewear into the perfect flirting prop, and turning a shared vision problem into the bond of a private joke. Once they had stopped laughing, Lucinda and David danced much of the night away.

So this week, take stock of the things you normally have with you to see if you're already packing some great flirting props. Are you a reader? Make sure the title of that riveting best seller or history of ancient Greece is clearly on display to the like-minded-looking fellow on the next beach blanket. But don't be so absorbed that you don't notice him trying to catch your eye; and go ahead and laugh, or sigh, or let out a thoughtful "hmmm" as you look up, to let him know you'd love to share what you just read.

Flirting props can be an especially fine means for the novice flirt to attract attention, interest and conversation. If you're a shy artist, take your easel and supplies outside and paint a landscape; there's no telling who might arrive on the scene. Whatever your hobby or passion, carry around its accoutrements—be it a tennis racket or a trombone—and you're likely to spark the interest of someone who shares or is curious about a talent or activity you love.

But don't use props only as a passive device. If you take your knitting everywhere, don't expect to be asked what stitch you're using. Do go ahead and ask that hunk sitting next to you on the bus to hold your yarn, or see if he'll let you measure the sleeve of the sweater you're making against his arm—adding, of course, that it's for your father.

Another wonderfully interactive prop is a video camera. My single friend Alan had a brainstorm for his sister's birthday present one year that turned out to be a perennially favorite flirting technique. He hit the streets with his digital video camera asking virtually everyone he saw if he could film them wishing a happy birthday, by name, to his sister. Sure, a lot of people looked at him like he was crazy and hurried on their way. But the sort of fun, outgoing women Alan most enjoys jumped right into the spirit of it. One pair of his "actresses" was so intrigued by the project they tagged along for the rest of the day's shooting! Since then, all of Alan's old friends and family members receive wonderfully daffy and personalized birthday greetings, while Alan's circle of new friends and dates is approaching a cast of thousands.

But not all flirting props are created equal. Some things are simply inappropriate or self-defeating. Others, like the Force in *Star Wars*, can be used for good or ill, depending on the particular circumstances or personality of the flirting-prop master. Here, then, are a few guidelines on the potentially improper use of props:

♡ *Be aware of unintentional props.* Do you always have a cigarette dangling from your hand or mouth? Is chewing gum your primary food group and do you snap it or chew with your mouth open? Do you keep putting off that trip to the dry cleaner and keep putting on the same stained or tattered suit? Bad habits and carelessness in personal presentation can become second nature to anyone with a busy schedule. But you'll never get a second glance if you don't take the time to assess the message you're sending with the sort of accessories you—and potential companions—can live without.

♡   *Go slow with slogans and logos.* Although you're sure to draw lots of attention by wearing a tight-fitting T-shirt proclaiming, "Want to know if these are real?" . . . get real. Today's marketplace is full of garments bearing titillating and supposedly humorous phrases and illustrations. But no matter what the words or pictures actually say, the message they often send is, "Not on your life." Even something as innocuous as a football team logo can backfire if your idea of hell is Super Bowl sunday. (Of course, if you do have a favorite team or a genuine interest in sport, the right prop might score you a flirting touchdown!)

♡   *A baby . . . maybe.* If there's an icebreaker on earth that's better than man's best friend, it's man or woman in infancy. Anyone who can resist the innocence of a baby or the charm of a toddler probably isn't worth knowing—unless, of course, you don't like children yourself. But there's something smarmier about "borrowing" a baby than borrowing a dog. If it's your niece or nephew or a friend's child you'd be out with anyway, go ahead and see what encounters your outing might bring, as long as the little one remains the main focus of your attention. The fact that you're babysitting will reflect well on your character. If, however, your main purpose is to use the babe as bait, let it go (the idea, I mean). Then again, if it's your own child and you're actually approached by a friendly stranger—especially one who's also on parental duty—you might owe some small someone an ice cream cone.

♡   *Make sure pets are pettable.* Please do not put kitty on a leash and pull her around town for your own amorous purposes. Likewise, don't parade around with an exotic or intimidating species of animal just to gather a crowd; you'll be remembered as the freak with the tarantula rather than as someone to take home to mother. If you have a dog that is temperamentally unpredictable or of a breed that has a reputation for viciousness, be sensible; don't expect anything other than a wide berth and don't fault those who step out of Bowser's way. And if you do meet a brave soul, be sure that she/he and your dog are properly introduced.

Flirting props can be almost anything, anywhere. Start paying attention to the honest advertisements for yourself you already carry and to those objects you run across in the course of a day that might bridge the gap between you and someone else. Remember, too, to notice and respond to the flirting props of your fellow flirts in waiting!

In fact, I wouldn't have written this book had it not been an encounter involving my pink jockey hat. At the Madison Avenue Café a man held the door open for me—still a polite and welcomed gesture. It was crowded and the waiter asked, "Are you one or two?" The man asked me if I'd like to be two. I smiled and nodded.

After a very pleasant lunch I asked, "Why did you suggest being two?" He replied, "You were wearing that crazy pink hat and had a great smile." Props at work! I knew I had to share my discovery!

Fifty-two Fabulous Flirting Props That Work!

"A flirting prop? What do you mean, Susan?" groaned my friend Darlene. "A T-shirt that reads, 'Make a Senior More Secure—Marry Her Daughter'? A sign that says, 'Will Date for Food'?" She shrugged her shoulders. "Listen, I know you say that flirting props work, but I have never been able to accessorize. Just tell me—what am I supposed to carry if I want to carry on a conversation?"

Darlene is right—an interesting, eye-popping flirting prop is a boon for the bashful! And since it is simply a conversation piece—something that invites (or sometimes even demands) comment—it can be nearly anything at all . . . a turquoise necklace that brings out your eyes . . . a travel brochure to an exotic locale . . . a jingling charm bracelet . . . a top hat . . . a bass drum. So if you've got a prop that works for you, flaunt it! But if you haven't, here are enough ideas to try—one for every week of the year:

At Work:

1. Photos of the "off-hours you" (golfing, kayaking, surfing . . . whatever shows off your fun side).
2. A fruit bowl (not a candy dish!) in your office.
3. The softball team/company picnic sign-up sheet.
4. Really good coffee. (French press: $25. Appeal at 3 p.m.: incalculable!)
5. A lunchbox. (A friend has two fabulous tin lunchboxes—a vintage Roy Rogers and a new one with a parochial school

motif. She's forty-nine years old and carries one every day. The commentary is delicious!)

At the Beach or Park:

6. A colorful kite.
7. A Frisbee.
8. An interesting tattoo.
9. A one-of-a-kind hat.
10. A friendly pet.
11. A sand sculpture or group project large enough to attract help.

On the Commuter Line:

12. An intriguing book. (Hint: The flirts in my workshops have told me that the covers of my books work like a charm!)
13. Jelly beans, hard candy or anything to share.
14. An extra schedule.
15. Anything awkward. (I once met a man just by putting some bulky holiday gifts in the overhead compartment of a train.)

At a Sporting Event:

16. Marshmallows and skewers. (Inexpensive, toastable on a hibachi and totally irresistible to nearby tailgaters.)
17. Any finger food you can personally pass around.
18. An extra blanket or a thermos of hot cocoa and extra cups. (Spread the warmth!)

At the Laundromat:

19. A pocketful of quarters.
20. Current issues of popular magazines.

At a Party:

21. Any piece of jewelry or article of clothing that lights up.
22. A prop cast on your arm or leg. (Bring a Sharpie marker!)
23. A guitar.
24. Something touchable. (A suede shirt attracts tactile flirts like crazy!)

On the Street:

25. Art of any kind.
26. Weird flea-market finds.
27. A shovel, a jack or anything else that might turn a friend in need into a date indeed.
28. A sketchbook. Yes, sketch something.
29. An umbrella that's big enough for two.
30. Memorabilia: a vintage Grateful Dead T-shirt, Civil War memorabilia . . . a lapel-full of buttons from past political campaigns.
31. Anything that's out of season. (Carry a pair of ice skates in July.)

At Play:

32. A tandem bike.
33. A dripping ice cream cone.
34. A camera. (Would he/she mind taking your picture? I've *never* seen this fail.)
35. A costume.
36. Media. (Nothing attracts a crowd on a hot news day like a battery-operated TV.)

At the Grocery Store:

37. His/her cart (Whoops!)
38. The cart with a funky wheel.

39. A live lobster.
40. A peculiar piece of produce (Ugli fruit . . . choyote . . . grapples . . . What are these? Ask!)
41. A helping hand.

For Men:

42. A happy child. Leave an unhappy child at home.
43. Interesting or unusual neckwear, vest or suspenders.
44. Cookware. (Works best when these gadgets are teamed with a confused look.)
45. Flowers.
46. Any peculiar ability, including magic tricks, juggling, ear wiggling, etc.

For Women:

47. A unique piece of jewelry.
48. A tie and the necessity to tie it.
49. Something to drop. Still works!
50. A unique or vintage car.
51. Jackets and shirts with team logos. (Shows you'll be a good sport during the season!)
52. Food. (It may not be the only way to a man's heart, but it's a darned direct route.)

Invite Opportunity into Your Social Life

Every flirt, no matter how natural or bubbly he or she may be, hits a lull now and then. As Danna explained it, her "dry spell" had dragged on so long dust had begun to collect on her telephone. I asked her what she intended to do about her social inertia.

"I don't know," she moaned, cupping her chin in her hand. "I wish somebody would do something fun . . . like have a party!"

I reminded Danna that if wishing made great parties happen, the word "soirée" would be auto-added to every line of our PDA calendars! Nevertheless, Danna was definitely on to something. Parties have all the ingredients for enjoyable flirtatious encounters—so there is no better way to shake off a wet blanket that has settled on your social life than to throw a party yourself!

Of course, it's waaaay more relaxing to wait around for somebody else to stock the bar, choose the guests, mix the music and hunt down those irritating invitees who refuse to RSVP until they're absolutely convinced that no better invitation is likely to turn up. When it's not your bash, all you're really required to do is show up and smile. But think about what you're missing. Hosting a party gives you open access to crowd of eligible people that can be as large and as lively as you like. And if a party is the kind of social vehicle that can put your life back on the road, then the host or hostess is the hub of that activity. And since this is your show, stage it your way. Eliminate the possibility that you'll spend forty-five minutes between the wall and a potted plant, cornered by someone who makes your eyes glaze over in boredom. Include the kind of people you like and don't include those you don't. Play the kind of music that energizes you and pulls you out of your shell. Schedule your get-together at a time you can be truly relaxed, when you don't have a visiting relative to worry about or a zit in the middle of your forehead or anything else going on that might detract from your ability to circulate, relate and meet a possible mate.

Your goal as the host of your own party is to sample the guests as if they were the buffet. It's important, then, that you provide yourself with some interesting selections you haven't tried before. It may surprise you to learn that meeting someone new will be a great deal easier if you ensure that at least a few members of that "old gang" of yours are also in the house.

Old, comfortable friends are like well broken-in shoes: They put us on steady footing but make every step in a new direction a pleasure. Lively banter between you and those who know you best will draw out the most exciting aspects of your personality, put your unique wit on display and provide new friends with interesting, intriguing pieces of information about you. (Your old pals have been waiting a long time for a forum where they can reveal the funniest stories they know about you. If you ever put a lampshade anywhere but on your lamp or if you have a talent for, say, hamster puppetry that reveals itself only after several margaritas, your friends will make sure your guests hear about it— and learning about these foibles will make you easier for new acquaintances to approach.) To ensure that plenty of eligible new friends attend, ask each of your old "regulars" to bring at least one person with them that no one in your group has ever met. If your peer group is like mine, that shouldn't be a difficult assignment.

Successful flirts are nonstop networkers—and whether you are currently "working" your web of acquaintances or not, your friends could be instrumental in making some important connections for you. Think about it. Most of us don't draw our friends from a single group of people but from a number of very different groups of contacts. One friend of mine gathers three times a year with a group of people she worked with in the publishing industry more than a decade ago. She also meets regularly with a group of "workout friends" she knows from the gym, has breakfast once a season with the stalwart men and women who make up what she calls "the crack-of-dawn dogwalkers," reconnects with friends from high school and college, spends an evening a month with her reading club . . . well, you get the picture. And she's still making new friends every day! Since every one of your invited guests has access to a virtually limitless web of unique individuals, chances are good that you'll be entertaining someone at your party who can be pretty entertaining in return. I've even known hosts who have asked each guest to bring a friendly old flame along as "new blood." And it works! Another person's ex is always someone else's bright, promising future. Provide yourself and your guests with an infusion of people previously undiscovered; who could hope for a more memorable or practical "party favor?"

And don't tell me that arranging such a get-together is simply impossible for you. My client Georgia lives in a thumbnail of an apartment on Manhattan's Upper West Side. Rather than jam her friends, new and old, into her tiny space, she cohosted a gathering with her next-door neighbor. Not only did this give her access to a whole new set of people to schmooze, it allowed her party to flow from apartment to apartment and into the hallway between. And if your neighbors are not amenable to going with the social flow? Not a problem. One single man I know whose ever-expanding guest list long ago eclipsed the size of his available space took his party on the road. He is now the organizer of some of the hottest and largest networking parties in New York. If your party plans aren't quite that ambitious, why not simply gather your friends—and their friends—at a local restaurant or bar? A neighborhood establishment where a gregarious group can interact and attract others is a prep-free, stress-free solution for you and a windfall to the business owner.

In case you need a few more hints to make your party a hit (while you get "hit on" in return), try these:

♡ *Introductions can be awkward for some people.* Take that responsibility off of your guests' shoulders by using a strategy I learned from the ultimate party-planner, Hugh Hysell. As each partygoer enters, provide him or her with a name tag that states his/her first name and profession or area of interest. Most people are proud of what they do for a living. And if they're not, they have a story about how they came to hold a job they dislike that they would love to tell! In any event, whether a person's work is meaningful to them or just another four-letter word, knowing someone's profession gives a savvy flirt an easy "in," a reason to ask personal questions and, most of all, a nonthreatening way to express your interest in a new friend.

♡ *Create your own reason to party.* You don't have to wait for Arbor Day or National Flirting Week (February 12–18) or even, if you are the swashbuckling type, National "Talk Like a Pirate" Day to throw a party. One group of friends I know makes it a point to get together at least three times a year for something they simply call "Games Day." This core group of people—including lawyers, publishers, writers, illustrators and other friends—come together to enjoy each other's company and to play the kinds of games that enable them to break with decorum, stand up in front of a crowd and behave in very silly ways, all in the hopes of winning a game whose outcome doesn't matter.

There are several reasons why these days have become such valuable flirting opportunities. First, no stuffiness is allowed. Indeed, no stuffiness is possible when you're acting out a phrase like "ball four." And since the games are played in teams, a "the more the merrier" approach prevails. There is rarely a Games Day that doesn't include several "friends of friends" or curiosity seekers. Getting to know these newcomers is a snap since team members must interact enthusiastically in order to play. In addition, because Games Days are scheduled every few months, everyone involved has begun to anticipate them. They know that wherever the party will be held or however many people will be attending, a good, no-holds-barred time will be had by all. Consequently, no one hesitates to invite an attractive friend to come along—or to chat up any newcomers that have been introduced to the mix. Games Day isn't a serious event; so what better setting could there be for acting and interacting without serious intent?

♡ *Don't leave all the work—I mean, fun—to the caterer.* Who could possibly be more popular at a party than the person who is passing around a platter of food? Repeat after me: Munchies are the ultimate flirting prop at any gathering! Not only does passing around the aioli or onion dip make you seem generous and caring, but serving up the grub along with a few friendly words can make you the special of the day!

♡ *Remember: Food gives you something to chew on.* Conversationally, I mean. Is she hot for the sate? Ask her if she's traveled in Asia, if she is interested in cooking or whether a preference for spicy food reveals something about a person's personality. Is he chowing down primarily on pâté? Is he a gourmand? A recent convert to a low-carb diet? Is he one of the ten people on earth who can possibly identify those ground-up, greenish chunks? Ask!

♡ *There is one more benefit to being the dude with the food: You simply must circulate—and that gives you plenty of opportunity to scout for the best possible candidates.* Make some observations as you make the rounds and you'll quickly see which guests to zero in on and which are simply, well, zeros. If that good-looking guy in the corner has managed, for three rounds of very potent caprinhas, to expound on the fall of Imperial China (or on anything, really) he's probably a drag. Pass the rumaki and, while you do, make a mental note of those "dishes" you do want to go back for later on.

This week, I am asking you to do a not-so-difficult thing: Set aside a little time to party! Your party need not be elaborate. The food doesn't have to be a gourmet spread, and the entertainment can be as simple as an awards show on TV or a boom box in the corner. Just supply yourself and your guests with plenty of interesting, new people to meet and everyone will be in a festive mood.

Flirting is a talent that comes naturally to all of us. Throwing your party your way enables you to flirt in the place and the manner in which you're most comfortable. Enjoy! With a little effort, you're next get-together will be a deux.

Week 35 — Go Where the Flirting Is Best

Patti likes to be where the action is: She constantly looks for new places to flirt. So she decided to shake off her winter doldrums—and a stubborn romantic "cold spell"—and sign up for a Saturday morning tennis league at a nearby indoor court.

Patti had been working out regularly for years so she knew she'd cut a trim figure behind the net. But how would she be in action? She hadn't played much tennis since the preceding summer—and even then, only when the humidity was low enough that her hair wouldn't frizz. Still, when it came time to fill out the application, she felt confident that she could hold her own. Patti considered her "level of ability." Since she had been playing tennis since she was a teenager, she wasn't a "beginner," was she? Patti checked the box marked "intermediate" and moved on to the next question. Was she interested in joining the competitive, round-robin league? Patti didn't hesitate to check "yes." She felt an organized league made up of skilled participants would put the bounce back into her social life. But it was not to be.

When Saturday rolled around, Patti arrived ready to serve up some sprightly conversation with a sinewy teammate. There were plenty of men in the group but, as it turned out, they were too focused on the game to entertain Patti with conversational zingers. Nor were Patti's new cohorts impressed with her abilities. In this league, an "intermediate" was a dedicated, accomplished heavy hitter who could tear the fuzz off the ball while flossing his teeth with cat gut. Patti found herself not only eliminated from the round robin but sidelined socially. When the next Saturday rolled around, she decided to drop by her local gourmet market instead and chat up the clerk about the lox. At least *he* made her feel she had something on the ball.

As I have said, a flirt with finesse can make anyplace work for her, but be forewarned: The Olympic symbol is not made from entwined wedding rings. Dog-eat-dog, to-the-death competition is not usually conducive to romance! Still, flirting *is* a numbers game. The more people you interact with, the more likely you are to meet that "significant other." But where should you begin? Right here, with this list of happy hunting grounds that have worked for so many of my friends, workshop graduates and me.

In my opinion, the very best places to flirt are informal, friendly and conducive to conversation. (Frankly, my dear, that eliminates the movies.) To help you choose the best locations for love, I've put my all-time favorite destinations into handy categories. This week, I urge you to pick and choose several among them. I'm sure you'll find an environment that is just right for you.

♡ *Great places for group flirtation.*

There is safety in numbers! That's why group encounters make for fun, nonthreatening experiences that appeal to the shy as well as the more gregarious flirt. Best of all, events that attract a crowd allow you to pick and choose. I suggest you try:

> Bicycling clubs
> Book discussion groups
> Bridge, backgammon or chess clubs
> Churches and synagogues
> Cross-country ski tours
> Gyms
> Hiking trails
> Marathons
> "Parents Without Partners"
> Singles organizations and events
> Tours
> White-water rafting
> Classes of any kind (acting, aerobics, computer, creative writing, cooking, foreign language, line dancing, oil painting, Rollerblading, sculpture . . . Heck, I even know a woman who met three very nice men when she took a course in defensive driving!)

♡ *Cozy spots where you can be coupled up.*

Group flirting is a lot of fun but it still takes two to tango! Whether you wish to pick a partner at a ballroom dance class or prefer to play in another type of duet, there are places where singles can go to be thrown together in pairs. One caveat: Limited partnerships mean limited opportunities. You can spend considerable time discovering that you and your partner don't really click. Nevertheless, if you prefer to meet your match one-on-one, here are some avenues to try:

Dating services
Dances
Internet matchmaking services
Personal ads
Ski-lift lines
Yoga class

♡ *Places where flirting props are provided.*
Here are some places to flirt where props are either provided or welcomed.

Conventions
Craft fairs
Paint-your-own-pottery shop
Dog-walking park
Parks and recreation areas
Playgrounds (A happy child is a great conversation
    starter! An unhappy one? Better luck tomorrow!)
Scenic overlooks (Ask that interesting stranger to take
    your picture.)

♡ *Spots that are conducive to conversation.*
What makes a place great for conversation? An environment stimulating enough to excite comment yet quiet enough to hear and enjoy it! These locales offer plenty of opportunity for chat, and make it easy to say a cordial good-bye if the conversation flags:

Antiques shows
Auctions
Bus stops
Bookstores
Coffee shops
Discussion groups
Flea markets

Garden tours
Jury duty
Museums
Reunions
Sporting events
Wine tastings

♡ *Places that invite questions and answers.*
Ask and you shall receive! These suggestions should make
it easy:

Antiques appraisals
Art gallery openings
Classical music lovers' clubs
Comedy club open-mike night
Financial seminars
Grocery stores
Hardware stores
Hotel lobbies (Ask where the locals eat!)
Hobby shops
The Laundromat (Oh, come on—does anybody really
    know how to use a centrifuge?)
New-age conferences and workshops
Real-estate seminars
Trade shows
Weddings

♡ *Opportunities to help.*
Who could possibly pass by a flirt who extends a hand to
those in need? Volunteering brings like-minded people together. Why not give it a try? You might do your community
and your social life some good!

Animal rights groups
Beach or highway clean-ups
Charity functions

Community organizations
Ecological groups
Fund-raisers
Outdoor activity
Habitat for Humanity house-raisings (Want ongoing
    contact? Try an ongoing project!)
Political organizations
Sierra Club meetings
Support groups
ASPCA dog walks

Hint: Some of the places singles go most often are the worst for flirting! Meditation retreats, noisy bars and clubs, harsh, competitive activities (like Patti's tennis league) and restaurants where people do not circulate freely are unlikely to expand your options. Rethink your haunts. Choose those that give you at least a ghost of a chance to meet someone new!

Week 36

Say What You Feel

Although he was average in every way—height, weight, even the cut of his "weekend casual" khakis—Shantae noticed him as soon as he joined her small book group at the local library. What was it about such a typical man—slender but with a slight paunch; unremarkable brown hair, thinning in the back—that made him so memorable? It is hard for Shantae to pinpoint it now. What happened in the course of that first two-hour meeting has since colored her memory.

The group was just digging into the first few chapters of *The Lovely Bones* when the man came in. He looked around at the group gathered on large pillows on the floor. He stopped to whisper something to the group leader, then, noticing an empty space, made his way over to Shantae's corner. He smiled a hello at the men and women around him then settled in to listen.

The Lovely Bones is the story of a young girl's murder and its aftermath, told from the point of view of girl's spirit. The discussion was following a rather predictable path—what went on in the minds of criminals . . . the emotional trajectory of family life . . . the unique depiction of the girl's experiences in heaven . . . until Shantae spoke up: What interested her, she said, was how lonely the main character was in heaven. Paradise, she noted, was perhaps too lofty to sustain the tangible needs of a human being. It might be heaven, she summed up, but the experience wasn't really heavenly . . . was it?

Suddenly, the group was alive with controversy. Shantae was sure the library's patrons could hear the buzz all the way to the reference desk. But did she care? Not for long. The man sitting next to her leaned toward her and smiled warmly. His name was Stan, he said. And while he had enjoyed the book, Shantae's take on it had added to his enjoyment. "Heaven is where you find it, isn't it?" he concluded. Then he threw himself into the discussion, which went on unabated for nearly forty-five minutes.

The group leader had just regained control of the conversation when Shantae saw Stan glance up at the clock on the wall. He jumped to his feet and got his coat. He apologized to the group for "bailing" so abruptly and began to pick his way through the bodies sitting on the floor.

But before he reached the door, he stopped. He turned, looked straight at Shantae and said, "You know, I have another appointment. I was supposed to leave early. But I have the feeling that if I do, I'll regret it for the rest of my life."

Stan returned to his seat and stayed until the end of the

meeting. When he left, he did so with the book in his pocket and Shantae on his arm.

One moment of sublime honesty had turned what would have certainly been an engrossing night into a life-changing one. Shantae and Stan are now engaged—but there is an alternate scenario. They could have walked in and out of each other's lives without much notice. But Stan didn't let that happen. He changed it all simply by saying what he felt.

We all say we want truthful relationships. We all say we want lovers who allow us to be ourselves, speak our minds, express what is in our hearts. But when we have the chance to go out on a limb, say our piece and reveal our feelings, do we? We do not!

It isn't hard to see why more singles don't come clean when they feel drawn, often for no explicable reason, to someone else. One woman in my workshop summed it up this way: "People who claim to love you hurt you all the time! Am I really going to hand my heart and soul to some guy who could be dating someone else? Or gay? Or married? Or just a jerk?" Revealing our feelings makes us vulnerable. Should those people decide to use our feelings as weapons against us, it cuts us to the core. But if they don't? If they welcome our emotional openness and reward us with theirs? It is an unmatched gift.

Mahatma Gandhi said, "Be the change you want to see in the world." What does that mean to a flirt? It means that people give back what they get. Approach them with honesty and vulnerability and they will feel safe enough to respond in kind. But if you encounter that perfect stranger and keep your thoughts to yourself, your new friend will remain exactly what she was when you met her: perfect . . . perhaps perfect for you . . . but a stranger.

Confession may be good for the soul but it isn't always easy on the ego. Is there any way a flirt can make his or her feelings known without getting emotionally trampled?

There is risk in everything that's worth doing. Isn't it time you spoke up for the relationship you want? Here are some strategies for you to try this week:

♡ *Realize that revelation doesn't have to be gushy.* A soul-stirring pronouncement like Stan's can sweep a prospect off her feet but a simple statement of interest—like, "Can we talk?" or "Would you care for some company?"—can be just as effective! A friendly, no-strings-attached approach teamed with a hopeful smile is all you need. And there's little or no ego investment required.

   If you're there because of him or her . . . shouldn't you say so? Stan's gambit might seem over-the-top at first glace but come on . . . who among us hasn't changed our plans just to be close to someone special? He may be handsome and she may be charming but neither are mind readers! A simple statement like, "I was hoping to speak with you before I went home," or "You're a great dancer! I didn't want to leave without letting you know," will remind your new friend how nice you are and give you a chance to "close" the deal (see week 51).

♡ *Smile when you say that!* A sincere smile (rather than a lecherous one) can make the difference between a compliment and a line. Check your grin to be sure it's friendly, not frightening. While you're at it, remember not to wink, raise and lower your eyebrows (á la Groucho Marx) or let your gaze shift and dart. Careless eye movements can make you appear duplicitous even if you're completely sincere.

♡ *Expect a response.* Now that you've made your "profession of like," prepare for a response! He may be married or attached. In that case, you simply say, "Lucky girl!" or "At least I tried!" and go on your way. She may be taken aback by your directness. If so, give her time—and your card. She'll wish she had your number when she realizes she's always wanted a gutsy, expressive man. He may react like an oaf and shoot you down. If that happens, just smile, wish him well and mean it! Mr. Wrong didn't reject you; he doesn't even know you! All he's done is set you free to find someone who will make you happy! The next hot prospect is around the corner. Take your shot.

How Not to End a Conversation

Setting: The dining room of my collaborator, Barbara Lagowski

Characters: A group composed mainly of forty-somethings, half of them single, half of them committed couples

Premise: The relatives had flown off to warmer climes. Now it was time for friends to get together and celebrate the holiday season. Among the group was:

NIKKI: A droll curator of a museum for the performing arts in a major city. Nikki had recently extricated herself from a tortured long-term relationship and come out on the other side looking every bit as sharp as her wit.

ANDY: A perennially single, wildly gregarious travel-industry writer who is more than able to charm the husks right off of the corn—but, in a pinch, will not hesitate to resort to a corny joke if that's what it takes to get a laugh.

PHIL: A divorced engineer, usually quiet and retiring.

By mid-evening, mountains of food had been washed down with several bottles of wine and the company was relaxed and happy. The conversation turned to the subject of work—then to the dazzling array of memorably bad bosses each person at the table had barely survived.

My collaborator had known Nikki for more than twenty years.

She also knew that Nikki had worked for one of the classic bosses from hell—and recently that she had the scorch marks to prove it.

"Tell them about Lana, Nikki," Barbara urged, knowing that no one at the table would be able to best Nikki's real-life saga about the "Little Draconian That Could"—as long as there was schnapps in her desk drawer and some unlucky underling around to abuse. But as soon as Nikki began to describe this tortured woman in the most colorful terms, Andy interrupted.

"When I was in college, I used to paint houses for extra cash. Did I ever tell you that?" he cheerfully butted in. "The guy who owned the business was terrified of heights. Can you imagine? A house painter with acrophobia?"

"I heard it was his fall-back position. He really wanted to be a tightrope walker," suggested Phil, reaching for another bite of tiramisu.

Barbara elbowed Nikki. Her story was too good to go to waste. Reassured that someone at the table was still listening, Nikki plunged into her saga with renewed vigor. She had just begun to reveal the details of the day her boss, a minor radio person-ality with a major ego—had actually undergone a full-body wax while she was on-air, when she was interrupted once again.

"Why do women do these things?" Andy feigned a shudder. "Don't females suffer enough without subjecting themselves to physical violence just for the sake of beauty?"

"That's right," Phil nodded. "Beauty is only skin deep! And besides, what man would complain about a woman who comes with her own fur coat?"

Barbara looked at Nikki. Violence? Violence wasn't something that came from the spa. Violence was what was about to erupt right here—over cappuccino!

Nikki stood up, leaned across the table, glared directly into Andy's eyes and announced, "I don't care what I have to do—I am going to finish my story." Then she smiled as sweetly as she could and retook her seat.

"You are?" Phil joked. "When? You've started it twice already!" Then he pretended to check his watch. "I have to leave in the next couple of hours. You might want to step it up a little."

With that, Phil and Andy laughed heartily. To them, the entire scenario had been a good-natured joke. To Barbara, it had been a shocking eye-opener. How could two usually, urbane men have behaved so boorishly? Barbara had hand-picked these people hoping that one of them might "click" with Nikki, but there was no way Nikki would date one of them now. She couldn't get a word in edgewise. Although the men might be more solicitous and sensitive in a one-to-one situation, why would she give either of them that chance?

Barbara chalked the episode up to testosterone overload and vowed to readjust the hormonal balance at the table the following year. What could have been a great flirting opportunity was lost forever.

We work so hard to start conversations. We overcome shyness, chip away at lifelong barriers, loosen cases of "tongue-tie." We conquer our fears of the unknown, try on opening lines like pairs of low-rise jeans and manage to smile, smile, smile while we're doing it. So why don't we realize that we'll never be "lucky in love" until we learn not to end the conversations we've taken such pains to begin?

Successful flirting is about making the people around us comfortable. We reach out; they reach back. They let their guard down, and so do we—and that's good. But when we abandon the idea of putting our conversational partners first (instead of our impulses!) that's not so good.

Because we can't watch ourselves in action, it isn't always easy to see why our conversations detour, but the symptoms of conversation bail-out are hard to miss. If you are just getting to hello, then suddenly find that your new friend is saying good-bye . . . if you are turning on the conversational flow only to find yourself drowning in awkward silence after a few stumbling, stammering minutes . . . if every time you launch the "love boat" your first mate abruptly abandons ship, it is time to consider whether your communication style might be mucking up your chances for romance.

Good flirting is about showing interest in others and giving them good reason to develop an interest in you. I suggest that you examine your recent conversations for symptoms of the conditions below. Are they cramping your social style? This week, ask yourself:

♡ *Are you the sunshine of your life?* Do most of your sentences begin with the words "I" or "My"? Do other people's stories tend to remind you of experiences you've had? Things you've done? Thoughts that have flickered through your consciousness?

Nature provided you with two ears and one mouth. Use them in proportion and you can make an impression without monopolizing the conversation. Flirts score big when they focus on the interesting people around them. Performing solely for your own entertainment is absolutely out of bounds.

♡ *Misery loves company, but company does not love misery!* Maybe you don't think it's fair that you've been passed up for promotion at the lingerie design firm (the thong market has hit bottom). And maybe you have been wrongly evicted from your sub-human hovel of an apartment, overlooked by your insensitive, self-centered relations and troubled by chronic post-nasal drip, but don't we all have troubles of our own? Who needs to go out to hear yours?

There is nothing interesting, redeeming or, most of all, attractive about somebody's complaints. Make it a point when you close your door to lock your troubles inside.

♡ *Are you critical or judgmental?* Here's another one for the books—at least for the flirting books. Hillary worked as an account executive at a public relations firm. One day, in the art department of that company, she met a very shy illustrator named Joe.

Joe was a sweet guy—quiet, introspective and not given to casual chatter. This posed an unusual challenge to Hillary. Gregarious and uninhibited, Hillary knew she would have to tone her boisterous nature down to fit in with Joe, whose talent, good looks and solitary nature had piqued her curiosity. For weeks, Hillary felt she was getting nowhere with Joe. Their conversations were stilted and short; he seemed to have little interest in her. She was dumbstruck, then, when he unexpectedly invited her to a show of abstract sculpture in a small downtown gallery.

It was not a formal "date" and Hillary arrived at the space alone. Joe greeted her at the door. They felt like two left shoes for a moment, and then Joe seemed to warm up. He asked Hillary about her taste in art.

"Well, I like that," Hillary said, pointing to a complex wooden architectural piece. "And that," she said, indicating a pair of interlocking stone carvings.

"As for that one," she said, nodding toward an assemblage of metal "found objects," "It reminds me of a car crash I had when I was seventeen. My parent's Buick took on a parking meter—and the parking meter won." Hillary looked at Joe and laughed heartily. Joe did not.

"Actually, that one's mine," he said, nearly inaudibly.

Hillary apologized but the damage was done. After that, when Hillary and Joe encountered each other in the halls, they moved past each other like wings on a Calder mobile—close, but silent and self-contained.

Of course, you are entitled to your opinion. But opinions should be shared with sensitivity. In a world where it seems that "everybody is a critic," the considerate, perceptive flirt should be the exception.

More than ten years ago, in my first book, *How to Attract Anyone, Anytime, Anyplace,* I introduced the concept of "social intercourse"—that exciting meeting of the minds that turns virtual strangers into friends or lovers in minutes flat. To many flirts, it is better than sex: You can do it anywhere and as many times a day as you want, provided you know how to make that initial encounter last.

Week 38

Let Absence Make the Heart Grow Fonder

Lorna, my hairstylist, was beside herself with excitement. She'd unexpectedly reconnected with her childhood friend Gary. There she was in the hardware store, a vision in paint—spattered sweats, shopping for spackle, when Gary popped out of the plumbing aisle. Although they had never dated, they had always traveled in the same circles. Lorna and Gary hastily exchanged stories at the checkout. She was reconstructing her life after a recent breakup; he was in from California to help his mother with some home repairs. Outside the store, they congratulated each other on not having "changed a bit" in the years since high school. Only something *had* changed. In a matter of minutes, somewhere between the shellac and the protective eyewear, Lorna and Gary had experienced a powerful mutual attraction. When Gary flew back to the west coast they began a torrid, electronic romance.

For the next two years, Lorna and Gary carried on a long-distance relationship that set their Internet circuits ablaze. There was little courtship. Who needed that? They'd been friends for years . . . they knew everything about each other! And their chemistry was undeniable. So instead of flirting, they went straight for each other's hot buttons. While other separated swains chatted and teased, they lusted and longed. They exchanged red-hot messages, suggestive photos and X-rated packages. And when they met for occasional visits or vacations together, the result was a chemical explosion more intense than anything you'd encounter on the New Jersey turnpike. Lorna was over the moon. I would have been excited about her "find" but for two small details: Lorna owned a shop on the New Jersey coast and Gary lived outside of L.A. . . . and she was burbling about it with my hair in one hand and a pair of shears in the other. Neither scenario was very encouraging.

When at last Gary announced that he would be moving permanently back east, Lorna was thrilled. She was anxious to begin their future together. When Gary finally came east, however, things want south. She was anxious to spend time together; he was asking for an afternoon, an evening and, finally, a weekend alone. By the time he had hung his last picture on the walls of his new apartment, the relationship that had been so spicy had gone down in flames.

What happened? Lorna was mystified. I was not. Because she and Gary had gone for the gusto they had skipped over the flirting stage. And while no one can know the inner workings of any relationship (let us all be grateful for that!), things may have gone better if they hadn't skimped on the preliminaries.

As I have said, flirting is playful—but that doesn't mean it isn't important. While chemistry is profound and immediate, flirting is definitely the long game. It is about beckoning a new friend forth and showing your interest in him so he will, in turn, show himself to you in a meaningful way. Lorna and Gary had shown each other plenty, believe me, but was it meaningful? Two years after their long-distance relationship had begun, they hardly knew each other. In their haste to fan the flames, they forgot the warmth and fun of flirting.

Over the years, I have interviewed many singles who have either enjoyed or endured long-distance relationships; some felt truly committed—others contend that they should be committed if they ever considered such a arrangement again. If you are one of those adventurous love-seekers whose romantic reach exceeds your grasp; if you are wondering whether a happy, healthy flirtation can really be sustained from a distance, I have news for you: It can! And in this electronic age, more than ever. Simply use the techniques in this book to bridge the gap, encourage closeness and allow the relationship to grow, and you'll beat the pressures of distance by more than a mile. How do I know? I've recently visited the online bridal registry of a former business contact, Lisa, who turned an intercontinental connection into a happy union—and she's not the only one. This is her story:

Lisa had married and divorced before she was twenty-two. By her thirty-fifth birthday, she felt that she had seen everything and everybody her home city of Houston had to offer. One day, having exhausted the entertainment potential of online shopping, she began to browse the profiles of men who lived beyond her geographic region. Since she had always been something of an Anglophile, she decided to take a chance and respond to some of the profiles posted by men in and around London.

At first she thought she wouldn't get much of a response. Most men were looking for someone they could physically see, then and there. She couldn't realistically promise she'd be making her way "across the pond" at all, but, she figured she'd give it a try. She replied to several profiles that caught her eye, trying to keep her prose as conversational as possible. Sure enough, she got a few answers—among them, a very expressive e-mail from a literary agent named Mitch.

The British are thought to be reserved but Mitch was not. He confided in her—his love of classical piano, memories of his father who'd died when he was three, the tribulations of being a single parent and, of course, the trials of being single. What began as an interesting diversion for Lisa quickly deepened into a very real partnership. Mitch was no longer a "pen pal" but a very real companion upon whom she relied for opinions, support or a good laugh. And the feeling was clearly mutual. The day he had to put his beloved English sheepdog to sleep, Lisa and he "chatted" for hours. Mitch's contact with Lisa may have started out as a lark, but she was now his girlfriend in every sense but one. Since Mitch traveled to the U.S. for book conventions and other business, they arranged to meet in person nearly a year from the day their correspondence had begun. It was as though they had known each other forever.

Now Lisa lives in a rowhouse with a lovely garden outside of London with Mitch, his two children and a young sheepdog named Camilla. Lisa admits that the relationship has recently jolted over some bumpy patches—she and the children are working through the rigors of forming a family—though the problems they've had are those caused by close quarters rather than distance.

We've all heard the caveats. "Long-distance relationships never work." "Out of sight, out of mind." I'm happy to say those admonitions no longer apply. In fact, there is a great deal to recommend long-distance flirtation. It eliminates the "cleverness" bonus. There isn't so much pressure to pull just the right zinger out of your repertoire at a moment's notice. You are free to consider your responses and think before sending a message. Much of the sexual pressure is also disbursed. With little chance of making physical togetherness a fait accompli, you are able to explore each other more fully as people. This doesn't mean the total absence of titillation—nothing of the sort! But the possibility of friendly, mischievous flirting is often cooked when a couple turns up the heat too soon. If absence makes the heart grow fonder, it's because heads stay cooler. And that's not all. Shy flirts benefit from long-distance love because they find it easier to express their feelings when they're not face to face. And of course, there is no chance of face-to-face rejection.

Of course, bad things can happen when lovers are apart. The long-distance relationships that used to happen over snail mail and the telephone are now an Internet phenomenon, and that doesn't put a "smiley" on everybody's face. E-mail and instant messages are easy to misinterpret—and that can cause plenty of disruption when clear communication is crucial. And, as in Lorna's case, long-distance liaisons can lack true intimacy. When that happens, the passion is easily snuffed, no matter how hot it has burned.

Long-distance flirtation can be whatever you choose to make it—a route to friendship, an inroad to an intimate friendship or the basis of a meaningful romance. To make a long-distance relationship work, you must make it *real.* Here are some ideas that will help you move your long-distance crush closer to where you want to be as a couple:

♡ *Make meaningful "I-contact."* How can you grant that special man or woman a glimpse into your soul when eye-contact is not an option? By using each exchange as an opportunity to paint a uniquely personal and, most of all, inviting picture of your life and your world.

Whether you're writing or chatting on the phone, remember: Depth is in the details! If you are mad for Volkswagen Beetles, have taught yourself to play Mozart on the harmonica, write a little, act a little, travel or dream about traveling, don't cover up your quirks as if they were an odd assortment of chocolates—pass them to someone who can appreciate their uniqueness! The idiosyncratic jumble of skills, interests and eccentricities you've accumulated sets you apart from more mundane flirts and will help to develop your new friend's real-world interest in you.

♡ *Use the three Rs.* Your special friend may live half a world apart, but you can still turn him or her into a close *confrère* by using the three Rs: Repeat, rephrase, reflect. Whether you're burning up the telephone lines or deep in online chat, just subtly repeat and rephrase any statement that catches your interest ("You say you're best friends with your ex-hubby/wife? Well, isn't that remarkable!) and keep reflecting the focus of the conversation back onto your partner. Your long-distance sweetie will feel validated, not judged. And you will have opened the door to a much deeper level of communication.

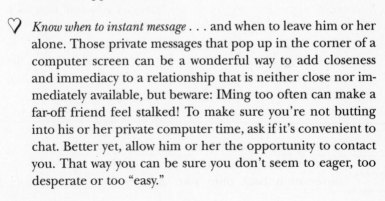 *Virtual date.* Chat rooms can be fun; e-mail can be erotic . . . but for two people who would like to know each other a little better, there may be no more nearly real way to do so than to go on a virtual date.

Just what is a virtual date? Simply, it is an agreement between two people to simultaneously visit the same website and, as they explore, to communicate their thoughts and impressions (and, of course, their silliest comments) via instant message—just as they would if they were meeting at a real-world hot spot.

Where can one go on a virtual date? Literally anywhere in the universe and beyond! Virtual dates quickly transport singles to far-flung places that would take a lifetime to visit in the physical world: from the Tower of London to the pyramids at Giza, from the Uffizi in Florence to the jungles of Sikkim, where wild orchids bloom and red pandas roam.

It's very easy to invite a friend on a virtual date—just send him or her a link related to a hobby or an interest the two of you share. Before you know it, you're off to explore whatever common ground lies between you—and a universe of amorous opportunities.

Know when to instant message . . . and when to leave him or her alone. Those private messages that pop up in the corner of a computer screen can be a wonderful way to add closeness and immediacy to a relationship that is neither close nor immediately available, but beware: IMing too often can make a far-off friend feel stalked! To make sure you're not butting into his or her private computer time, ask if it's convenient to chat. Better yet, allow him or her the opportunity to contact you. That way you can be sure you don't seem to eager, too desperate or too "easy."

♡ *Watch the "forwards."* Passing along the jokes we receive in
e-mail can be an easy (if superficial) way to keep in touch,
but be aware: Some of these jokes may be too "forward" to
pass as friendly flirtation. If you simply cannot resist sending
unsolicited jokes along, screen them carefully. It's difficult
enough to lose a hot prospect. To lose one over something
you didn't even create is just a waste.

♡ *Give him or her something to hang on to.* Send a small gift. A
nice photo. An expression of your ardor on tasteful sta-
tionery via snail mail. (Note: Real paper tributes have nearly
gone the way of the quill. Because they have become so
rare, they are especially romantic.) Or treat yourself—and
your companion—to a webcam so you can see each other as
you "converse." The images can be a little grainy and even
sort of creepy, like a police line-up, but if you've lost your
heart to someone who is far away, it can be the next best
thing to being there! Last but not least,

♡ *Don't let this friendship keep you from flirting with others.* A relationship isn't real until it exists in the real world. Unless one
of you is willing to relocate or you can visit often, exclusivity
should be out of the question.

   Of course, this tip sounds like the kiss of death—but it
needn't be. I know of one long-distance friendship that actually blossomed after he began to tell her the details of his
failed dates with other women! His candor prompted her to
take a risk and arrange a visit; her visit assured him that she
was the date he'd been looking for: a very sweet reward when
they finally met in the geographical middle.

How to Give Great Phone

*"I tell a story; he clams up. I ask questions; he grunts.
I try to pick up on a conversation we started at dinner
the night before; he can't wait to hang up. Calling a guy is like
making contact with an alien."*

—Janice, age twenty-six

*". . . It's my day off. The phone rings. The next thing I know,
she's yacking and yacking and I'm thinking, 'How much
more could she possibly have to say? I just saw her two days
ago!'"*

—Ross, age thirty-one

For her, the telephone is a social lifeline, a direct connection
to the friends and family members who encourage her dreams
and nourish her soul. For him, it's a way to get a pizza to arrive at
his door. For her, a telephone isn't just a necessity of life; it is a
means for her to "reach out and touch someone" she knows and
cares about. For him, the phone is the nuisance that can prevent
him from rejoining the real life he has in progress—especially if
he makes the mistake of picking it up when it rings. Is it any wonder then that wires can seem crossed when these two very different telephone users get on the line?

We all know men and women who don't fit the "she runs on,
he runs off" stereotype. Nevertheless, so many otherwise compatible men and women find themselves hung up on the issue of

what constitutes adequate communication on the telephone, that we could not leave this issue unaddressed.

Most relationship experts agree that poor communication is the number-one reason for failed relationships. Although it may seem like a minor issue, a poor connection on the phone can be a deal breaker, particularly if a relationship is relatively new.

The good news is that while men and women may have vastly different conversational styles, it's easy to send a seductive, satisfying message once you start pushing the right buttons! This week, give these gender-specific tips a trial before you dial. They may be just what you need to keep the lines of communication buzzing!

Five Ways to Show Her You've Got Her Number

♡ *Forget the "three-day rule."* Is it really necessary to schedule a three-day "cooling-off" period between meeting a woman you like and calling her on the phone? I can't think of a single woman I know who honestly believes that a prompt telephone call from an attractive man is anything but a delightful compliment! If you like her, why not show it? Believe me, if she's like most women, she's already spent so much time awash in some man's submerged feelings she may fear she's developing gills. An up-front man would be a breath of fresh air.

♡ *Put a smile in your voice.* A telephone manner as silky and smooth as satin sheets may fit your definition of cool, but it runs the risk of coming across as downright cold. Remember, she can't see you (that's why you are able to make those calls in a SpongeBob muscle tee and plaid boxers). There is no body language for her to search for clues about your feelings. Letting her hear the smile in your voice lets her know that you're glad she took the time to come to the phone. It may no longer matter how long the conversation continues. Just hearing your tone brighten at the sound of her voice may have communicated everything she wanted to know.

♡ *Try to make it "real."* If you're like many men, you want to transmit the necessary information, hang up the receiver and return to "real life" as quickly as possible. Hold the phone! Telephone conversations can be "real," too, if you make an effort to personalize the conversation.

Don't think of the receiver as a piece of plastic in your hand (much like the remote control or your video-game system controller). Think of it as your conduit to *her*. Imagine her holding the phone to her ear, listening to you. Picture her in her house or apartment, reacting to what you are saying. Try to imagine yourself face to face with this woman. We have come to associate the telephone with so many annoyances in our lives that we have perfected the art of the "psychological hang-up." After years of depersonalizing nuisance callers, it may help to remind yourself that this is a real conversation, the kind you might have if you were face to face. To make it last, make it personal.

♡ *Take control of the conversation.* "I have learned by experience that, when I call a woman, it's best to get off of the phone as soon as possible," said Steve, a divorced man of forty-four. "I don't know how or why it happens, but one minute I'm chatting sort of mindlessly, and the next minute, somehow I've said the wrong thing!"

Ah, yes—the conversational minefield! You just never know when you're going to wander into dangerous territory.

It's good to bear in mind that so-called "idle conversation" is never really idle; it is always being directed by one conversational partner or the other. Let someone else chart the course of the chat and you may arrive at a destination that would best be avoided.

To keep the conversation safe, be mindful of where it is going. If the questions get too personal, too probing or just too problematic, use the three Rs to redirect the focus back onto your conversational partner. Use silence to draw your partner out (and stay out of the hot seat yourself). Most of all, refuse to be "baited" or "worked." When a comment strikes a nerve, don't respond defensively. Simply assure your friend that you've heard her ("I know what you mean," or "Been there, done that!") and move on. There are those among us who crave drama. But just because you've shown up for tryouts, that doesn't mean you've agreed to join the cast.

♡ *Don't just say good-bye.* Tell her that it made you happy to hear her voice again. Say that, in your mind's eye, you can visualize her twirling her hair, the way she does when she's deep in thought. Divulge that her laugh never fails to bring a smile to your face. Whatever words you choose, let her know that the time you've shared has meant something to you. Convey the idea that, while you may have spent the last twenty minutes holding a piece of molded plastic, you are also holding tight to the memory of what makes her special to you. You don't have to be an "operator" to know that these are the kinds of sentiments she'll think about long after the connection has been severed.

And now, for the women on the wire,

Five Ways to Clear His Line for Romance

♡ *When you call, have something to say.* My female friends routinely leave me voicemail messages saying, "Don't call me back. I didn't really want anything," but that kind of aimless approach may not fly with a man. Men tend to think of the telephone in a utilitarian way, and the total lack of an agenda—or at least a focus—may make a man antsy! The reason for your call need not be earth-shaking. Asking about the status of an ongoing issue (perhaps his latest run-in with the boss from hell) or requesting additional information about something you've discussed previously ("Remember when we talked about how Skybars just disappeared from the market? Where did you say you could buy them by the case?") would be reason enough. Just bear in mind that a sounding board is an inanimate object. You want him to play a very real role in your everyday life.

♡ *Don't multitask.* Aren't cordless phones and supple shoulders wonderful? Put them together and voilá! Your hands are free to write holiday cards or scrub the bathtub while you chatter. But be warned: Multitasking spawns formless, rambling conversations. If the man on your speed dial is not prone to mindless chatter, these conversations may become a nuisance to him. Keep your mind on the conversation at hand, or you may have more than enough time to clean the oven while you're waiting for him to call you.

♡ *Casual questions or interrogation? He'll be the judge.* "What are you doing?" "Hey! Where ya been?" "When you didn't call yesterday, I got worried." "Oh, you're finally home." These are a representative sample of the kinds of misguided conversation openers that are more likely to open a can of worms than a satisfying dialogue. Some, however breezily delivered, smack of ownership. Others are just plain bossy. All of them, in all of their variations, are to be avoided.

Really, in most situations, "hello" will suffice. It will also keep your conversational partner from saying good-bye.

♡ *Don't be a voicemail harpy.* As the song goes, his "eyes are clear and bright, but he's not there." If you call and he doesn't answer, leave *one* message. That's it. That's your allotment. If he doesn't return your call in the next few hours, you are not to leave another. The voicemail harpy—the frantic redialer who leaves multiple messages of a badgering kind—invites only one kind of response: "Delete all." Your goal as a flirt is to work your way into that certain someone's memory, not out of it.

♡ *Leave him wanting more.* OK, so you haven't told him every detail about your latest tangle with your recalcitrant brother (he blew the cash on your joint Mother's Day gift on *what?*), and maybe you haven't regaled him with the most colorful stories from your checkered past, but isn't it possible that those tales are best shared with a girlfriend?

He may not have gotten all of the nuances that add up to the last ten years of your life—but provide them and I guarantee he will get this: bored. Don't let that happen! Leave him with a few questions and he'll have a reason to call you back.

A word about cell phones: Unless you are a high-ranking government official with access to "the button" or a medical professional or civil servant who is on call, active cell phones have no place on dates. Accepting a call while you are socializing is rude. Depending on who is making that call (your ex, your mother, an angry client, etc.), it can also be embarrassing. If you must carry a phone, turn the ringer off or set the phone on vibrate. If you absolutely must take a call, do it in private. And don't ever suggest that the caller is a rival for your affections (even if he or she is). Stirring up jealousy isn't fair flirting—and it could make a noncompetitive love interest flee.

Week 40

Bulk Up Your Online Address Book

"No wonder I can't connect with a woman in the real world . . . they're all hooking up with people they've met on the Internet," groused Michael, a burly high-school football coach and self-described "computer oaf."

"Of course, I'd like to get in on the action, but how? I don't like blind dates, so the personals are out. I'm not much of a typist, so I'm useless in a chat room." Michael waved his hands at me as if to prove he had ten left thumbs. Then he continued: "It's funny—face to face I feel like I'm on a level playing field but get me on a computer and suddenly I feel like I've been sidelined! What about the guys who don't have flying fingers? We want to be players, too!"

What's going on here?

Bzzzwerd: so I sd, u gotta give me some space and she sd consider it done and she must have meant it cs I haven't seen her since ☹

Rocknjamilla: age/sex/loc check k?

Hevyhittr364: 22/m/boston

Crzeefrharlees: 20/f/Central FL

Femmesferst: give u space? You were asking for it, bzzz! Wooda done the same!

Dianaramma: 2 2 bad, Bzzzz. Sorry.

Luvmegadeth: FL here too, Crzee. Could it be hotter? The filling in my Oreos melted in my hand!

MyLitleFrend: anybody see the new Ben Stiller flic? I heard it's
    a riot.

Crzeefrharlees Ha. Melts in yr hand not in yr mouth!

Rocknjamilla: Revere Beach here. Gotta pic, Hevy?

Bzzzwerd: I don't really miss her, Diana. Fillin the extra space
    now. U single?

No, it is not evidence that what the world really needs now is a
global spelling test. It is the script of a typical, fast-moving online
chat. It demonstrates what is best about chat rooms as well as what
is difficult for the online flirt.

First, a bit of background. Chat rooms come in several types:
public (general interest rooms that anyone can enter and exit at
will), special interest (chats that are geared toward a specific seg-
ment of the population, for instance "Twenty-somethings," "Single parents," "*Xena* fans," etc.) and private chat rooms (rooms to
which you and all the other participants must be electronically invited).

Although chats do provide singles with a casual place in cyber-
space where they can get to know each other, there are certain aspects that make them less appealing. The exchange is immediate,
but the conversations tend to go where the most dynamic personalities in the room steer them. Chatter flows freely, but several
conversations take place simultaneously. This can make it difficult to really to connect with a participant who really interests
you. Most of all, chat-room exchanges move along briskly. If you
are not dexterous, you may be left in the digital dust—and that
would certainly eliminate any possibility of keyboarding your way
into someone's heart.

Plenty of people are, like Michael, challenged typists. They
simply can't express themselves in Times New Roman 12-point
the way they do in person. Others require a bit of pleasant interaction with a prospect before any action—or even a date—can
commence. For them, placing a personals ad in an online singles'
site is also out of the question. Meeting a blind date is simply too
much of a turn-off. But that doesn't wipe Internet romance com-

pletely off the menu. Fortunately, there are kinder, gentler options for flirts who want to get to know somebody better without having to reduce their identities to a series of numbers and letters ("40+/m/Cacoast"), without having to pass a touch-typing test and without feeling as though their romantic possibilities are scrolling by.

Anyone who has attended my seminars knows that the question I am asked most frequently by singles from sixteen to sixty is, "Where is the best place to flirt?" My answer is always the same. The best place to flirt is wherever you happen to be. In my opinion, that advice holds true whether you are strolling through a local park or navigating the web. Of course, most of us don't gravitate to places that make us feel uncomfortable. We go where we feel welcomed and at home—and that holds true on the Internet, as well. That's why many flirts who are looking for a like-minded connection rather than a quickly formed one choose to "get a room"—that is, an ongoing message board, forum or auditorium where they can reveal their particular brand of charm in their own time.

There are several types of "rooms" for you to consider. Find one that complements your hobbies, preferences or personal style, and it will be easy to get your feet wet as an online flirt—and perhaps dive into a long-term relationship with an exciting 'net pal who shares your pastimes and passions. They are:

 Auditoriums. Want to add significantly to your knowledge about a hobby or interest while you hunt for that elusive significant other? Are you looking for a place where you can initiate conversation with witty, urbane men or women while you stimulate the perpetual student in you? If so, an online auditorium may be the place for you.

Set up like real-life seminar rooms, Internet auditoriums are forums where a variety of experts and authorities speak on an endless array of subjects, from installing a backyard gazebo to grand opera to weight training. Unlike real-life auditoriums, audience members are encouraged to chat among themselves, generally within smaller groupings, while the talk is proceeding. Since the chat groups are usually formed of people said to be seated within the same auditorium "row," they tend to be limited to a manageable number of people. Moreover, because there is no reserved seating at these events, you are free to "move" to another row if you aren't finding the kind of interaction you crave.

There are auditoriums in use all over the web. Many are sponsored by larger Internet servers. Others are sponsored by individual websites and held at specified times. Sports sites, for example, play host to an ever-changing lineup of celebrities, which is great to know if you are a fan—or someone who wants to throw a pass at one.

To find an auditorium that best suits you, just follow your interests. They will lead you to an event that is compatible with your favorite pastimes—and perhaps, to a new friend who is compatible with you.

♡ *Message boards.* Looking for love? Leave a message! Message boards, which you will find at nearly every special-interest or hobby site, make it simple to connect with a virtually limitless number of interesting new people. Designed to function much the same way a bulletin board might, message boards enable you to compose and "post" a message of your own creation on any subject pertinent to the board. (For example, if the board to which you wish to contribute is devoted to singles' travel, it is the perfect place for you to comment on the cultural richness of Berlin. It is not, however, the place to leave political commentary or, indeed, an opinion on any subject other than travel, whether you feel it is pertinent or not.) If you prefer not to introduce a subject, or "thread," you can also reply to someone else's posted question or comment, then wait for a reply yourself. If the site is a popular one, you won't have to wait long.

In order to make the best possible impression, you might want to visit several message boards that seem well-matched to your interests and read the messages there without posting. This is called "lurking." Reading the posts will give you a good idea of the mix of personalities involved. It will also enable you to zero in on any posters you might be especially keen to impress before making your presence known.

How can a message board help the online flirt? In several ways: Unlike chat rooms, message boards give you the freedom to interact without pressure. You have time to collect your thoughts before responding, thereby minimizing the possibility of saying something you might regret. And boards that focus on a specific subject also enable you to develop relationships with others while focusing your attention on a subject other than yourself. That can make flirting easier even if you are the shy or reticent type. Other options for standoffish flirts? I suggest:

 Friendship networks. The hottest trend in online relating, friendship networks offer the fledgling flirt the best of both worlds—cyber-socializing and real-life encounters. How do they work? On the "six degrees of separation" networking theory—and, to hear satisfied members tell it, beautifully! The typical experience goes like this: A member of a site like Friendster.com invites several of his nearest and dearest to join. (Yes, you can opt to be the founding member yourself and invite the buddies you choose.) Your friends can in turn invite interesting people they know. Before you know it, you are at the hub of a large assemblage of interesting, pre-screened people. From this pool, you can begin to choose new pals, colleagues, business connections, workout buddies and, yes, dates in your geographic region.

Of course, the best systems for dating and relating allow for the different strokes required by different folks. Friendship networks are no exception. Just type "friendship network" into your favorite search engine and look around. You'll find a number to choose from, including:

Meetup.com—an online place where offline groups can arrange outings. What kind of groups? Shi-tsu owners, bridge players, knitting clubs (Did you know that men are knitting now? I'm not just needling you!) . . . social groups of every stripe. Meetup will send you updates on upcoming meetings in your area, so if you find a gang you click with, you can commune at your leisure.

Friendster.com—Easy to use for even the clumsiest "newbie." Friendster offers a virtual network that connects you to thousands of potential contacts. You can even use the search tool to check out your options by interest, location and dating status.

Others, including Craigslist.org and Tribe.net, have their own distinctive personalities. Explore them as you would any new social group—that is, at a relaxed pace—and you'll find the place you fit in best.

Ready to "get a room" on the world wide web? You could be within a few keystrokes of the relationship of your dreams! I asked some of the singles (ages eighteen to sixty) who attended some of my recent School of Flirting seminars the best tips for encounters on the web. While my casual poll hardly constitutes a scientific sampling, certain answers came up over and over again. This is what they told me:

♡ *Choose a screen name that is as attractive as you are.* Consider one that alludes to your interests, hobbies or profession. That way those who share your pastime will recognize you as a kindred spirit. Or consider a name that describes you in some way. A moniker like Brneyz, Musclebeach or Lil1 can paint a picture for those visual types who have difficulty relating to others in a world without smiles, body language or other visual aids.

♡ *Netiquette: Be polite.* It is easy to overstep your bounds if you are unaware of the customs of a site. DON'T SHOUT. Typing even a friendly message in capital letters is tantamount to screaming. Go with the flow. Hijacking an ongoing conversation and attempting to take it to another destination is considered unspeakably rude. Keep it clean. Vulgarity is never impressive and may even earn you a public reprimand from a chat room host. How embarrassing is that?

♡ *Post a profile.* Major servers encourage their clients to fill out a brief questionnaire detailing their interests and marital status. Posting this kind of basic information can't harm you. Best of all, it allows those who may want to flirt with you to check you out further. Wouldn't it be nice to flirt back for a change?

♡ *Be honest.* The Internet flirts I know have their antennae out for less-than-sincere flirts. At the first sign of contradiction, they're gone. Smart people! It's wonderful to get taken out but not if it means getting taken.

♡ *Show an interest.* Although the singles I asked didn't phrase it exactly that way ("What am I looking for? Why, I'm looking for someone who is interested in me, naturally! Now, enough about the men and women I meet on the web. What do you think about *me*?"), they did describe an online friend as someone who was interested in their welfare, who cared enough to keep up the relationship and who e-mailed or met for web dates often.

♡ *Be interesting.* This may seem obvious, but think about it. The web is an amusement park for adults. From entertainment sites to virtual tours of foreign lands to information on any subject, the web's got it. Though you may not have to be a jewel to outsparkle the tired band in your local singles' hangout, it takes a truly multifaceted individual to shine brighter than other Internet diversions.

♡ *Establish a friendship first.*

♡ *Have an active and interesting real life beyond the computer monitor.*

♡ *Be clear about whether or not you want to move your flirtation off the Internet and into the real world.*

Week 41

Find Your Niche on the Internet

A "lucky in love" flirt like you now knows exactly where to go looking for love in your neighborhood or town, but where do you begin to find close encounters of the romantic kind on the world wide web if the sites from last week fail to spark your interest?

You can bypass the sprawling singles' sites and go for the "niche"—a more precisely targeted site.

Where do you look for companionship if cat-haters give you and your feline fits? Try www.datemypet.com and you'll find find a man or woman with a comfy lap for you and your pets! What if the someone you seek is buff and brainy? Check out a www.right stuffdating.com and you'll find a select group of men and women with smarts, sex appeal and a degree from an Ivy League college or university. In fact, where can the hikers, bikers, millionaires, spiritual seekers, raw foodists, former hippies, die-hard Republicans and singles of virtually every stripe go to find partners who share their interests, lifestyle choices, sexual options and even their attitudes about tattoos? I suggest that you start right here!

Flirting is a numbers game, but a smart flirt knows how to target his or her search to attract only the most compatible prospects. Although this list of chats, personals sites and just-for-fun spots for singles of all ages is by no means exhaustive, it should give you plenty of ideas for seeking out flirting forums that suit your style, your geographical realities and your unique personal preferences.

Children

www.singleparentsmeet.com
www.cfpersonals.com (for those who choose to be
child-free)

Ethnicity

www.blackpeoplemeet.com
www.iraniansingles.com
www.saltandpepperpersonals.com (ethnically diverse
singles who wish to date outside their race)

Lifestyle

www.animalpeople.com
www.bikerkiss.com (for singles into motorcycles)
www.countrymatch.com (country personals)
www.datealittle.com (matches for those affected by
dwarfism)
www.datemypet.com (for flirts who come with furry
"baggage")
www.datingforsmokers.com
www.deafmatch.com
www.disabilitydating.com
www.equestriansingles.com
www.recoveringmates.com
www.requestadate.com (gay dating by criteria: cowboys,
daddy types, pet owners, preppies, twinks, etc.)
www.sciconnect.com (for singles who are into science)
www.soberandsingle.com

www.veggiedate.com (matches for vegetarians, raw
    foodists, vegans, Adventists, Buddhists, macrobiotic,
    and more)

Mature Flirts

www.mature@matchopolis.com
www.seniordatefinder.com
www.seniorfriendfinder.com
www.silversingles.com

Political

www.actforlove.com
www.concernedsingles.com (an ethical, progressive
    dating service)
www.conservativematch.com
www.democraticsingles.net
www.greensingles.com
www.hippiepersonals.com ("peacenik, progressive
    personals portal")
www.singlerepublicans.com
www.unmarriedamerica.org (advocacy for single
    Americans of every lifestyle)
www.unionworkerssingles.com
www.usmilitarysingles.com

Sites for Active Singles

www.fitness_singles.com
www.mygolfdate.com
www.newfriends4u.com (check out the "sporty" category)
www.singleandactive.com
www.skierdating.com

Spirituality

www.adammeeteve.com (Christian personals)
www.avemariasingles.com ("orthodox" Catholic singles)
www.catholicsingles.com
www.christiancafe.com
www.episcopalsingles.org
www.jdate.com (Jewish singles)
www.jewishcafe.com
www.muslimmatrimonials.com
www.paganconnection.com
www.secularity.com
www.secularsingles.com
www.singlec.com (Christian singles)
www.singlechristian.net

Travel Aficionados

www.cruise-chat.com
www.cruisingforlove.com
www.fastdatertravel.com
www.meetmarketadventures.com
www.singlestravelintl.com
www.trekamerica.com (adventure tours and vacations for
   single travelers)

Upscale

www.executivesingleparentdating.com ("upscale personal
   matchmaking")
www.millionairematch.com (for flirts who earn more than
   $1 million per year)
www.rightstuffdating.com (matchmaking for holders of
   Ivy League diplomas)

Post a Provocative Profile on the Web

*Physically fit SWM seeks female partner/companion,
age 18–29. Love sunsets, sand between my toes,
holding hands and long, leisurely strolls on the beach. If you
want to join me for some special moments, shared pleasures
and old-fashioned romance, respond to box_____.*

This is the text of an actual personal ad written by a very handsome, accomplished and wickedly funny man I know. As an ex-
periment, I invited six of my wittiest, most perceptive women
friends to join me for a bit of lunch and a face-to-face chat
about online flirting. The tiramisu had just been spooned onto
the plates when I served up my male friend's personal, which
he had posted on a very popular Internet dating site with little
success. What follows is a smorgasbord of the women's comments:

"Oh, he's physically fit, is he? Well, these days 'physically fit'
means one of two things: Either he can still manage to bend
over and pick up the remote control when it falls on the floor, or
he's popping Viagara."

"He seeks female companionship between the ages of eighteen and twenty-nine? How old is this guy, anyway? Do women
go past their expiration date at thirty?"

"He loves sunsets and long strolls on the beach? Well, who
doesn't? Even Adolf Hitler loved mountain climbing. But that
didn't make him a sensitive, caring type, did it?"

"If he likes sand between his toes does that mean he has lint
in his belly button?"

"I have a bad feeling about these 'special moments' and 'shared pleasures.' What does that mean? Is he one of those 'best things in life are free' types? I want 'old-fashioned romance' but I could use a little dinner, too!"

Listening to a group of "been there done that" singles dissect a personal ad, particularly one you might have written yourself, can be a painful experience. But knowing what works and what doesn't when you're playing the Internet personals game can fill your online address book to the crashing point, so it's well worth your time and effort to compose an ad that is as intriguing as you are.

Are there any downsides to becoming a part of the personals phenomenon? As some of my poetically challenged friends will tell you, there is only one: Your ad can only begin to work for you after you compose it!

Whether you're a closet bard or prose comes hard, this week you'll write and post a successful Internet personal ad. Just clear out space in your inbox and use these simple guidelines:

♡ *Think about who you are and what you want.* Are your hobbies central to your life? Do you find it impossible to last a day without a workout, time to read or a megadose of Metallica? Anything really important to you is important enough to mention. Now consider your personality. Are you a quiet, bookish flirt searching for a blockbuster counterpart? Or are you the consummate football fan in search of a mate who can stir both your soul and your tailgate chili? Put your interests—and your eccentricities—front and center! These aren't just the quirks that make you you—they are also the details that will make your ad pop for the right reader.

♡ *To grab a browser's attention, think "headline."* Two tips: Be specific and think in images. Do you have a buttoned-down image and a wide-open mind? Why not describe yourself as a Connecticut-etiquette type with a California twist? Just began your career as a legal eagle? Say you're an Ally McBeal in search of an interesting case! Abbreviate what you are (SWM, DJF, etc.) and you become a demographic. Paint a picture and your profile will become unforgettable.

♡ *Dish up the facts—and just the facts.* Virtually every personal listing offered by a singles' site will suggest that you fill out a profile form. This condensed fact sheet ensures that subscribers will have easy access to such basics as age range, occupation, race, religion, smoking/drinking status, a general physical description and a brief description of the type of companion you are looking for. Be sure to include this information. It will eliminate people who are not looking for you.

♡ *Keep your profile brief!* A three-paragraph entry provides you with plenty of room to express your sparkling personality, detail your preferences and include a little wit. What it does not allow is enough space to spin such a lengthy yarn you will either bore the reader or hang yourself. Which reminds me . . .

♡ *Don't include things people don't want to know.* The details of your medical history can make you seem like a hypochondriac. The disappointments of your lifetime can make you sound bitter. Chronicling your pet peeves will only highlight your peevish side. And as for your sexual fantasies, well . . . put them in print and they are guaranteed to remain unfulfilled fantasies. Remember, your ad is an introduction. Your best foot should be forward; not in your mouth.

♡ *Promptly discourage those you do not want.* If I had a quarter for every profile I've pored over only to discover somewhere on the bottom of page four that the writer, who seemed like my soul mate, is only interested in a Houston-based, Protestant brunette who shares his penchant for naked polo, I'd be a millionaire several times over. If a person's preferences, location, size, habit or affiliation are a definite turn-off for you, say so as close to the beginning of your profile as possible.

♡ *Photo: To submit or not to submit?* While browsing online, I recently came across a photo of a man I've always considered very attractive. The man is a professional photographer. Yet in the artistically shot black-and-white he submitted, he looked gaunt, drawn, sickly and thin. You would think a photographer would know better the importance of image, but image is in the eye of the beholder. The photo remains on the website and the man remains unattached.

These days there is tremendous pressure to submit a photograph along with your profile. Among some browsers, there is even considerable suspicion about those who don't. If the idea of publishing a photo along with your ad compels you to search not for an available scanner but for an alternate face—and believe me, many swell-looking male and female flirts are photo-phobic—then my advice to you is don't do it. Tell anyone who is interested that you will be happy to trade photos once some degree of mutual interest has been established. That should be enough to satisfy anyone who is truly interested in more than your appearance.

If you feel that you must submit a likeness and you aren't the portrait type, consider a pose that reflects your lifestyle rather than just your appearance. If you are a mountain biker, why not peddle your devotion to the sport by submitting an action shot? If you are a female whose hobby is fly-fishing, how about posing mid-river in waders? These types of photos not only distinguish your image from the mind-numbing columns of headshots you find on these sites but they let the beauty of your spirit shine through. You may snag more admiring e-mail than you ever did fish!

What Does Your Reply Say About You?

I have a dear friend who makes a life's work of placing and answering ads on the web. She used to place her ads in newspapers and magazines, but has become a woman of the new century and wants a man equally savvy.

She is one of the best flirts I know, but can't seem to make her skills work online. She laughs at the winks and e-mails sent to her, but her sense of humor disappears in the ether.

She gave me permission to print some of her replies—the good, the bad and the ones in between—but before I do, let me make you privy to her profile, which she also uses to reply to messages, while protecting her privacy. She is what we call in the world of online communication a TMI—a Too Much Information gal. The profile below had one hundred eyes view it, but only two replies. See if you understand why.

"I am a COMPLETE WOMAN, upbeat, warm-hearted, stable, secure, educated, romantic lover, loyal friend, a gal who is not afraid to let you see her without makeup in the morning. When you click on my photo with the flowers on my robe, you will use words like classy, worldly, interesting, feminine. I certainly have a good sense of humor. Other words to describe me are optimistic, healthy, flexible, genuine, a good listener and fun to be with. I sing, studied voice, like to write. I was a decorator and had my own radio talk show. I lecture on design, love to garden, don't watch much TV, love classical music, make a great peach tart, listen to NPR, enjoy foreign films, hiking and bike riding. If the color is purple, I love it. I love to hug and cuddle and miss that in my life. My photos were taken this year and I answer all responses."

Are you asleep yet? Bored, overwhelmed, think this person is conceited? Ironically, my friend was annoyed when she received one of her two responses. It was a three-page description of him, covering his life from the time he was born, in a trunk in Brooklyn, to his recent prostate surgery and purchase of a condominium in a retirement community in North Carolina. Both profiles had a case of TMI; though you'd think they'd be made for each other, each thought the other ridiculous. The most successful ads are short, sweet, specific and to the point; the replies should be even more so.

Here are some other notable replies. Try to figure out which will lead to a future reply and which will lead to a sign-off.

"Hi there, I live in Palm Beach and on West Side of Manhattan. My fantasies take me to all the wonderful things we could do together in both places. How great would that be!"

"I am fantasizing about meeting you."

"I really enjoyed communicating with you, shall we e-mail or telephone? What is your preference?"

"I have the Sunday paper, the bagels and all that is missing is you."

"Hi there again, pretty lady."

"Each day, as I read the *Sun-Sentinel*, I see so many wonderful film festivals, concerts and plays; I would love to have that special someone by my side to enjoy them with."

"I'm Dr. Sam, and I want to be your man."

"You sound like a lot of fun. How about going to a comedy club with me?"

"I am passionate about jazz. Let's meet, and then, if there is any chemistry, we can go to a jazz club." (If he/she hates jazz that could terminate the e-mails.)

The best replies let people know who you are. If he abhors your beloved jazz and insists on classical or doo-wop music, hates to read subtitles when your favorite movie is *Das Boot*, and would rather watch TV than see a play when you have season tickets, you need to rethink further communication. But he's given you the opportunity to move on. There is no dearth of partners on the world wide web.

This Week

♡ *Write your reply and save it overnight.* You can read it again the next day with fresh eyes before you send it.

♡ *Make your pictures current and don't lie about your attributes.* What good relationship is founded on lies?

♡ *Avoid writing replies that are:*
   too wordy
   too serious
   too narrow
   too fussy
   too demanding
   too needy
   too aggressive
   too anxious
   lacking your sense of humor
   not mysterious enough (Leave something to the imagination!)

♡ *It's OK to:*
   send the wink, tease, reply to an invitation; but allow your partner space to take the lead.
   shave a few years off your age. But don't go nuts.

Learn to Flirt on the Fly

> *"After a while, the singles scene begins to feel in-bred. You start to feel like you've met every available person within a fifty-mile radius. That's why speed dating has been so much fun for me. In no time flat, you meet a group of totally new people and that gives you totally new options."*
>
> —Colleen, age thirty-two

> *"Speed dating? Yeah, I've tried it. It's quite the time saver. In a little over an hour, I met eight new people and didn't make a single match. That's the way I like my rejection. Immediate service. No waiting."*
>
> —Ben, age thirty-eight

You've heard me say it before—a quick rejection is a favor because it gives you a reason to use the flirts' favorite four-letter word: Next! Speed dating is an increasingly popular option for men and women who like their romance—and rejection—on a rapid-fire basis.

How does this quick-turnover dating work? An even number of male and female singles gathers at a club or restaurant. Each is given a name tag (first names only!) and a scorecard. Female flirts are then seated alone at tables for two. When a bell rings, each of the men moves to a chair opposite a waiting woman. The pair is then allowed four to seven minutes of one-on-one conversation to introduce themselves, make an impression and, one hopes, establish a connection. When the signal sounds again, they note their interest or lack of it on their scorecards and move on to their next "date."

At the end of the entire cycle, which seems very much like the flirt's version of musical chairs, each participant has "dated" and rated eight to ten new people. The participants are then allowed to mingle while their program hosts tabulate the scores. If a male and a female participant have noted a spark of interest in each other, a "match" is made. They are then provided with the contact information they'll need to arrange a traditional date. If a participant has no matches, like my friend Ben, he or she may be offered a complimentary follow-up session or, if the organizers are not that generous, he or she is simply released back into the wilds of singledom.

While the idea of flirtation on the fly strikes some as unromantic, there are good reasons why so many singles prefer to accelerate the dating process. There is no pretense in speed dating. There are no browsers or players in the room. Every man and woman there is looking for a compatible companionship. Period. And it's a venue that provides clubbed-out singles with a fun place to meet far from the madding bar crowds. (You won't hear any of these prospects slurring the details of their college days!) Speeddating also separates groups of friends who tend to travel in herds, making in-depth conversation more likely. It's also economical, available in almost every sizeable town and safe. Personal information is divulged only after a match has been made. But most of all, speed dating is hard to take too seriously. With bells ringing and partners switching, the event seems more like a game than a date. Participants are laid-back and at ease despite their streamlined approach to ardor.

Of course, not everybody thrives on an assembly line. If you are slow to warm up to strangers or if you feel that a few minutes is not enough time to decide whether someone is worth a whole evening, love in the fast lane may not be for you. No big loss! You can always return to traditional courting methods.

"That's all terrific information for the slim, the quick on the uptake and the instantaneous knockout. But I am none of those," scoffed Joan, a woman in my bridge group. "I can just see myself sitting there, trying my best to be charming. Meanwhile, the guy across the table is smiling at me, thinking 'Wrinkles, saddlebags? Sorry, lady, you're a definite no!'"

While it's true that split-second judgments can lend themselves to superficial decisions, an eight-minute date *can* lead to lasting love.

Adele Testani from Hurrydate and Julie Ferman, founder of the web-based matchmaking service Cupid's Coach, have been on the forefront of speed dating since it began. They agree that confidence, not appearance, is the key to success in brief encounters. As Julie puts it, "Dating is 90 percent attitude and 10 percent logistics. A woman may be gorgeous, but if she lacks confidence or is too full of herself, guys are turned off."

Both Adele and Julie cite numerous cases where a flirt who was not physically perfect won the day because of her self-assurance and enthusiasm. Julie describes the phenomenon as having "it." And what is the "it" people are looking for in speed-dating? Playfulness, charm, warmth and sensitivity are sexier than anything else. These qualities will get you much further than a great exterior.

Adele agrees. She remembers one devilishly handsome man who came in "like a stone," with a stiff, unfriendly, entitled manner. Although his looks were model perfect, Adele knew he had no chance. He felt he was too good for the crowd; the crowd had no choice but to let him know that kind of condescending attitude was, indeed, not good enough. He got one or two "give it a try" hits (what the heck—he was a looker!) but no real interest.

As for those of you who might be carrying a couple pounds of extra weight, Julie would like you to know that one of the most successful fast-and-furious flirts she has ever seen was a charming but definitely chunky woman at least forty pounds overweight. The other women may have looked her over and thought, "Well, no threat there!," but she was smiling, energetic and enthusiastic

234   *Lucky in Love*

in conversation. At the end of the night, she had racked up a number of matches and turned many men into admirers.

Speed dating is a great way to increase your odds of meeting someone special. But there are a few more tips that might make a difference in your romantic bottom line. Bear them in mind as you move from seat to seat:

♡ *People are interested in those who show interest in them.* To keep the focus on your partner and gently draw him or her out, remember the three Rs. Repeat and rephrase what they have told you; then reflect attention back onto them. You'll find out much more about your new friend, and he or she will come away thinking what a gifted conversationalist you are!

♡ *Smile when you say that.* You may be hinting at the fact that you've been unemployed for more than a year (Me? I'm at leisure!), or you may be avoiding the disclosure that you live with your parents (Roommates? Yes, I have roommates). Whatever you're saying, make your statement with a smile and you'll maintain an approachable, trustworthy demeanor.

♡ *The eyes have it.* You've heard it from me, now take it from Julie: The most successful speed dates are those who make good eye contact. Why? Eye contact shows that you are present in the few moments you have together. And it makes whomever you're speaking with feel as though he or she is the only person in the room.

♡ *If you're female, be cool.* Julie lays it on the line: If you're a woman, be the catch, not the predator who's looking to snag a man! People want to hook up but they don't want to feel as though they've *been* hooked or trapped.

♡ *Do ask! Do tell!* Showing interest in your conversational partner will take you a long way but if you don't reveal something of yourself, your dates will begin to suspect you're in the witness protection program. You have only a few minutes. Let your sparkling personality shine!

♡ *Use body language to your advantage.* Use gesture clusters to send the message that you are one date who deserves a second look! Cross your legs or lean in your partner's direction. Flip your hair, smooth your tie or demonstrate some other "preening" behavior. And no matter how nervous you may be, uncross those arms! Let him or her know that you are open and approachable.

♡ *Don't interrogate like the grand inquisitor.* This is not a job interview. Allow the conversation to flow at its own pace. You should be doing 50 percent of the talking and 50 percent of the listening.

♡ *Are you getting older? Or are you getting bitter?* The kiss of death is a bitter attitude. And never talk badly about your ex. Instead, present yourself as good-humored and positive.

Week 45

Rekindle an Old Flame

Nicole was a small-town girl from New England who had spent the twelve years since high school moving resolutely into a big-city future. An avid history student, Nicole threw herself into the subject in college and grad school, becoming something of a political firebrand on campus and the department's expert on the Vietnam era in America. After she received her master's degree, she moved to Chicago, a city she had always loved, to live out her metropolitan dreams. The pay at her new teaching job wasn't great, but it enabled her to leave her small town behind once and for all. To Nicole, that was priceless.

As the years went by, Nicole felt more and more a part of the "Windy City" and increasingly less like some outsider the bracing breeze blew in. She distinguished herself at work; she put a down payment on a small condo in funky Lincoln Park. On weekends, she cheered for the Cubs or ran along the lake or shared a few yuks with friends at a local comedy club. But her romantic life never quite came together. While she was in school, she'd had no time for dating—or so she told herself. After she had thrown herself into her work, dates were more plentiful, but unsatisfying. Most of the men she dated were guys she met at work. Most were intellectual enough, but not fun. Others were fun, but reluctant to commit to a more serious relationship.

Nicole was still wavering as to whether to continue seeing a man she referred to as "the divorced professor of the moment," when she received an unexpected telephone call from her father in Vermont. Nicole's mother had suffered a stroke. Although she was expected to recover fully, the process would take several months. Nicole's dad needed support. Could his daughter possibly arrange to come home for a few weeks? Nicole didn't think twice. She quickly arranged for a leave of absence, threw a few things in a bag and headed to O'Hare.

Every day for the next several weeks, Nicole worked tirelessly. When she wasn't caring for her mother, she was cleaning the house or cooking for the family. In fact, she stayed so busy, she didn't even think about calling any of her old friends from town. Most days, she left the house only briefly, usually to pick up supplies at the pharmacy or grocery store. Then, every evening, she would run a mile or two along the quiet, tree-lined streets, just to decompress. She was jogging home through the neighborhood one night, deep in thought, when she heard a familiar voice call her name.

"Nicole? Nic? Is that you?"

Nicole came to a stop and realized that she was standing in front of a large white house with an inviting wraparound porch. She smiled. She had sat whispering and giggling countless evenings on that porch as a teenager. This had been the home of her childhood friend Nora. There, leaning against a column looking waaaay more handsome than he ever did in school, was Rob, Nora's older brother.

Suddenly Nicole was wishing she weren't quite so sweaty. She made her way up the broad wooden steps and took a seat near Rob on the porch rail. She had always trusted Rob. Unlike most older brothers, he had been fiercely protective of Nora and her friends. Nearly a decade later, Nicole found Rob very easy to talk to. He was a teacher at the high school they both had attended, he told her. He was divorced from his high school girlfriend, and since his parents had retired to Florida, he was now the owner of this charming old house. It wasn't long before Nicole found herself pouring out the details of the last few arduous weeks—and of the last few lonely years.

In the weeks before her return to Chicago, Nicole found herself running past Rob's house every day the unpredictable New England weather permitted. Their conversations were always easy and refreshing, like the local birch beer they sipped together. Still, when it was time for Nicole to return to Chicago, she was almost relieved to go. She was feeling so comfortable in this small-town scenario it was actually making her uncomfortable! It was time to take a little of the heat out of this relationship—and there was no place better suited for that than the home of the bone-chilling "lake effect."

When she returned to Chicago, she found herself lonelier than ever—for the easy familiarity she had felt with Rob. Apparently, he was, too. One night, he instant messaged to say that he had just agreed to chaperone this year's prom. Would Nicole be his date? He promised to buy her a corsage for her wrist and to get her home by midnight. She flew home and they danced the night away in a room decorated with tissue-paper flowers and had their photo taken under a banner that read "Believe," after Cher's 1999 megahit. Two years later, they have made a long-distance relationship work.

There was a time when Nicole was in a hurry to leave her small town behind; now she isn't so sure. A man from her past has become central to her future happiness. She feels like she's traveled through time to meet her match. Under those circumstances, she isn't likely to let a few hundred miles stand in her way.

Still doubt that the people who were significant in your past can also figure prominently in your future? Don't! "Rekindling"—stoking the sparks of affection we have always felt for our first loves—is a real phenomenon, and one of its most recent success stories is none other than Donna Hanover, former wife of ex–New York City Mayor Rudolph Giuliani. As she explains in her recently published book, *My Boyfriend's Back,* her romance with college sweetheart Ed Oster was, thirty years earlier, a victim of the couple's youth and changing plans. Then one day, as a newly divorced adult, she picked up the telephone to find none other than Oster on the line. They arranged to meet—and when they did, it was as though the two interlocking pieces of some cosmic puzzle had at last fallen into place. Although it seemed as though their relationship had taken place in another lifetime, their connection was stronger than ever. Hanover and Oster married in 2004.

Cynics may scoff that the loves of our youth are little more than the party favors one might pick up at a reunion, but the connections we make as young adults run much deeper than that. Rekindled romances are not only more intense than newly forged relationships, they are also strong, passionate and remarkably long-lived. According to Dr. Nancy Kalish, author of the landmark book *Lost and Found Lovers,* revived romances are more than just "good" relationships; they are the red-hot romances people describe as "soul-mate reunions." Indeed, of the 2,000 "reunitees" between the ages of eighteen and ninety-five interviewed by Kalish, 63 percent reported that these relationships offered them the best sex they'd ever had in their lives. But don't be misled: These relationships aren't all heat and no enduring warmth. Kalish found that first loves not only fall back in love with each other faster, but stay in love longer. If that isn't a very good reason to start paging through your high-school yearbook, I don't know what is!

When I tell the single-and-looking men and women I know to take another look at the people in their past, some are skeptical. As my friend Jody put it, "My first love ran over my father's fence while dropping me off after the prom, regifted me with a chintzy box of Valentine's chocolates he had gotten from another girl, then dumped me for a color guard in the marching band. I'm not so sure he's a better catch today." No doubt about it, passing along secondhand chocolates is difficult to defend. Still, few of us show the same insensitivity that we did when we were sixteen. And, symptoms of immaturity aside, the fact is that there is a great deal to recommend those relationships the "old dogs" around us refer to as "puppy love."

What makes our first love especially worthy of a second look? We tend to have a great deal in common. We grew up in the same town or region, attended the same schools, ran with the same circle of friends and shared formative experiences. We knew each other's families. We shared roots and values and, consequently, understand each other in a way no "outsider" possibly could. To see what that can come to mean over time, you need only ask my collaborator, who grew up in a very small, very ethnic mill town. She and her first love attended a grammar school where they were taught in Polish. They belonged to a church where they sang in Polish. And every day after school, they stopped for something sweet at a bakery where the clerks, bakers and customers did business in Polish. So when she received a surprise gift of a freshly baked babka via FedEx last April, what did that mean to her? Two things: that her first love didn't care if he sabotaged her low-carb lifestyle, and that, even after all these years, they still "speak the same language." What could another man give her that would mean so much?

But that's not the only reason those first tugs on our heartstrings grow into ties that bind. Young love begins with friendship, not lust. We come to know each other deeply and joyfully. And because we do not enter these relationships scarred and cynical, we offer our affection with abandon—in a way many of us never do again. These are the relationships, then, that become the "standard" for all the romances that follow. To one extent or another, each date thereafter becomes a part of our ongoing search for a love we may have lost when we were seventeen.

How do most people locate a lost love? Many people find their former dates on the Internet. Most Internet services have directories that allow members to search for people by name and location. High schools and universities often maintain message boards where alumni maintain contact, and an accomplished former friend can always be "googled" (google.com). And almost anyone can be contacted the old-fashioned way: tracing them through friends in common, sending a letter to his or her old home address or just looking them up in the phone book. Considering how popular Internet searches have become, it is interesting to note that most of the "rekindlers" who responded to Nancy Kalish's request for information found their lost loves through personal contacts or mail rather than on the world wide web.

There are a few good reasons for not reestablishing contact with a former flame. Emotions forged in youth die hard and that warm glow of memory can turn into a powerful reaction if the chemistry between you and your first love is right. So it is probably best to forgo reunification if either of you is married. But even if you are both available, I would suggest that you look very carefully at your motives for wanting to get together. Any feeling that you are "getting a redo" or—ack!—"getting even" should send up a red flag. Vengeance has no place in flirtation. And redos can be tricky. You may share a history but you have undoubtedly changed in significant ways. The relationship may not unfold the way you think it will. Besides, flirting with an agenda is simply not good flirting.

As a reality check, it may help to explore the reason why the relationship didn't last in the first place. Most of the couples who successfully reunited were simply too young to sustain the pressures of going off to college, parental interference, etc. For couples who were pulled apart by situational factors rather than personality issues, reunification is a relatively simple thing. They are not impeded by hard feelings, a tortured past or residual guilt. Pairings that fell victim to more serious issues, however, should be looked at with a more critical eye. Abusive relationships certainly do exist in very young couples. If your former flame had a hot temper or tended toward verbal or physical abuse, I would urge you to move on in your search for love. The best match for you may be a thrill you haven't experienced yet, rather than a blast from the past.

Whatever happened to that special guy/girl who still fits so comfortably in your "soft spot"? This week, why not look back at your romantic future and find out? Here are some tips that may help:

 Aim for Mr./Ms. Right. People don't reunite successfully with just any former love; most click best with someone they fell in love with when they were seventeen or younger. Why? Because our earliest *amours* are without reservation, ulterior motive or guile. It is this kind of love we continue to miss as we move into adulthood. And remember, when you're thinking back on the former dates who were most significant to you, friends count! Many of Kalish's most successful couples weren't really romantically involved back in the day. They were buddies! Admit it—haven't you always wondered what would have happened between you if things had taken a turn away from the platonic? Now may be the time to find out!

♡ *Don't rush.* He has always been able to make you laugh. She finishes your sentences. Make no mistake, this is heady stuff—and heady stuff can affect your common sense. If you didn't have time to allow your relationship to fully develop before, take the time now. If your sweet feelings have lingered all these years, they will still be there for you when you are sure the time, place and person are right.

♡ *Meet on neutral territory.* A candlelit picnic near the stream where you skinny-dipped or a slow dance on the terrace of the faux-Tudor "manor" where you had your prom may bring back memories, but it may not be the place you want to go to reunite. Romance is not a Disney product; it cannot be "re-created." Instead, arrange a first meeting on neutral territory, preferably in the light of day. That way, if there is no "love connection," you can smile, shake hands and relegate your used-to-be to a dusty corner of your heart for another thirty years. And if your heart is set aflutter? Then wherever you happen to be is a special place, and nothing you plan or do or contrive could possibly make it more so! The sepia-toned past may have brought you together but now is the time for making new memories. Celebrate where you've been but be open to where you might go!

Find a Relationship That Works!

"I had just returned to work after a long lunch with a college friend. We had spent the entire hour scarfing down Mrs. Field's White Chocolate Macadamia cookies and complaining about how we never meet anyone. The next thing I knew, I was in the conference room taking notes in an R and D meeting and suddenly, it just hit me: Here I was, an entry-level assistant surrounded by engineers, computer whizzes and young software designers. I didn't have to hit the streets to meet smart, fascinating men—I was knee-deep in them every day! It was a revelation—like I'd died and gone to singles' heaven."

—Emily, age twenty-seven

"Do I date people I meet on the job? I work seventy hours a week! For me, it's a matter of either finding someone at work or not finding anyone at all."

—Sam, age thirty-one

Efficient flirts know: One of the best places to date, relate and meet your mate is on the job! Where else would you find so many available, attractive go-getters who are all interested in the same thing? And where else could you possibly find a more level field of play than the carpeted hallways of any large corporation?

But wait a minute. Isn't finding love, like or lust over the fax machine somehow taboo? Dick, a VP at a commercial bank, spoke up as soon as I brought up the possibility of on-the-job flirting at a recent flirting lecture. "The bank president has made it very clear that as far as interoffice romance is concerned, there's a hands-off policy in effect. Whether we fall in love or play with the money, he's made his position clear: We're out the door."

There are, of course, some sound reasons for not wanting the personnel to get too personal. If attraction leads to dating and dating leads to disagreements, the resulting in-fighting could undermine corporate teamwork. If, on the other hand, colleagues get hot and heavy, their romance can impose a burden of a different sort. While they carry on like a house afire, the suspicion of favoritism may give coworkers the feeling that they've been left in the cold. Finally, there is the issue of sexual harassment, which is always a danger when the flirtation is one-sided or when it crosses hierarchical or departmental lines.

Still, most bosses will admit that nature does take its course—and very often that course meanders from the boardroom to the bedroom. A recent poll revealed that more than 50 percent of all employees have been involved in a romantic relationship with a coworker—and that 30 percent of those liaisons ended in marriage!

Can a relationship with a professional colleague make your heart hum like the copy machine? It almost certainly can if you follow these simple rules for protecting both your paycheck and your recent merger:

♡ *Be subtle with body language.* Body language can speak louder than the interoffice public address system. You wouldn't be willing to announce your attraction for the entire staff to hear, would you? Then make sure you don't telegraph it with your posture, gestures or movements.

Ideally, your body language should be like your office door—half-open so that others can approach you, and half-closed to maintain your privacy. To that end, keep your eye contact light, playful and, most of all, respectful. And while you're thinking about it, spread the glances around. Of course, you may meet the gaze of someone you like when you're chatting at the water cooler, but as in any flirtation, don't exclude others. People in the office are especially sensitive to slights, real or imagined; in the workplace their paychecks may depend on being included.

♡ *Send mixed messages.* If there's a man or woman in your workplace who interests you, you can show your interest by leaning in slightly as you converse, but then limit the flirt by turning your shoulders slightly away. Or you may keep an arm's-length distance while collaborating on an important project but then extend an open palm when making a point. (A palms-up gesture signals that you are open for friendship.) Kinetic messages are powerful attention getters. Use them with subtlety and you'll become a pleasant part of that special coworker's day. Use them overtly and you'll become fodder for the office rumor mill.

♡ *Don't mix business with pleasure.* It doesn't matter if you're meeting and greeting on a sandy beach or strolling the halls of academe, one important edict remains the same: Good flirting is always free of serious intention.

It doesn't matter if you are thinking of ambushing the department chair or chatting up the resident mailroom cutie, the reasons for your interest should have nothing to do with your professional agenda. Before you act, think: Do you really find the district manager appealing, or are you mainly attracted to what he might do for your sales career? Would the personnel director qualify as the woman of your dreams if she weren't interviewing candidates for the job you've always coveted?

Relationships aren't mergers; they're partnerships. It is neither wise nor fair to put the moves on anybody if those moves happen to be a boon to your career. Besides, if the object of your flirtation has what it takes to get to the top, doesn't he also have what it takes to see through your shady intentions? Once that happens, you won't have to worry about how you'll be spending your downtime: You'll be too busy writing up your resume.

♡ *No personal compliments.* Although Stephanie described herself as "just an accountant," Warren knew she was much more than that. A financial planner at a major brokerage firm, Warren had worked closely with Stephanie on many occasions. He knew she was not only bright and capable, but tenacious. She would work long and hard to get the job done. Warren decided he would work long and hard, too, if that's what it took to get Stephanie to join him for dinner.

One night, while working late, Warren lifted his head from the columns of revenue he'd been checking and caught sight of Stephanie in her cubicle. He hadn't eaten. Neither, he supposed, had she. This was the opportunity he had been waiting for.

Without thinking the plan through further, Warren got up from his desk, perched himself in her doorway and said the first thing that came to mind: "How can you work so hard, yet look so gorgeous?"

Warren had expected Stephanie to smile. Instead, she seemed flustered. She began to gather up her belongings, looking around the office frantically as if to see whether anyone else had heard. "You're right, Warren. I do work too hard," she answered finally. "It's time for me to go. See you tomorrow."

If Stephanie's reaction seems a little extreme to you, consider this: Personal compliments—particularly those that focus on appearance—are about as indigenous to an office setting as pink elephants are to a mailroom. You simply don't expect to encounter them there. To maintain a professional environment while scoring a few personality points, keep the compliments respectful. Comment on a coworker's skill, productivity, creativity or wits. You may find yourself sharing a leisurely dinner with your peer instead of eating your own words.

One last thing: Women have fought long and hard to be

considered more than the sum of their physical attributes. Male flirts take heed! Unless you're attracted to what's between a coworker's ears, she may be less than receptive to your thoughts on any of her other attributes.

♡ *Be careful crossing hierarchical lines.* If you know anything about business, you know that a lateral move is the exchange of one job on a particular level for another position on a similar level. You also know that kind of a job change is a safe way to round out your resume. In my business, which is flirting, a lateral move is a flirtation with a professional peer. It, too, can be a safe and pleasant experience. But when your romantic interests lie beyond your strata on the corporate ladder, your reach can exceed your grasp of the situation—and the repercussions.

To sum up, hell hath no fury like a superior scorned. So if you're thinking of hitting on the boss, you may want to think again.

And if you are the manager? You no doubt know that any flirtations you initiate with subordinates can be risky business. They can stir up animosities that can bring down a department, and they can end your career.

Of course, not all underlings become fair-weather lovers. And not all inter-hierarchical romances end badly. Still, such liaisons can have consequences that can reach deep into both your wallet and your heart. I suggest that before you ask that attractive employee for a date, you ask yourself the following questions: Is the employee someone who reports directly to you? If so, he or she may not feel free to spurn your advances; this kind of proposal can create an environment for harassment. Are all of the possible outcomes of the relationship acceptable to you? What do you see up the road? If you can't bear the thought of risking your job for this romance or confronting an angry-ex every morning at the coffee wagon, this flirtation should not be on your agenda. Can the object of your flirtation be discreet?

Can you? If not, give it up. If not for your sake, then for your paramour's.

Judging from the statistics, flirting on the job really works. (The 30 percent marriage rate offers you a better shot at success than a lot of matchmaking services!) Just approach the men and women you meet with manners, sensitivity, respect and good taste and and you're sure to be a success—in the office and out.

Week 47

How to Work a Meeting

Sally had worked as a trainer in corporate communications for eleven years. As do most of us, she had hoped to "have it all" by now—an interesting career and a relationship. But somehow her plan was not falling into place. "I feel at my best at work. Confident . . . capable. That's why I always thought I'd find a man I could love through the job I love," Sally told me. "But somehow all I'm getting is a paycheck."

I truly believe that we get from people pretty much what we give them. So if you are like Sally, and not finding close companions among your colleagues, you need to ask yourself: What are you bringing to work besides that beaten-up briefcase and the same old lunch?

For many of us there is little connection between our professional and personal lives. But whether we want to admit it or not, friendships lay the foundation for much of what happens to us at work. People are promoted not just because they are capable, but also because they've connected with the people around them.

Others are fired not because their output lags, but because they don't put out the right vibes. Wherever we work, whatever we do, we get by with help from our friends. We find new jobs, improve our productivity, think of new approaches, share successes and bear up under failures with the collaboration of the hardworking men and women around us. Acknowledging that our coworkers are people and connecting with them on a personal level enhances not just the quality of our day-to-day lives, but also our long-term prospects for ongoing success.

So what does that mean to the diligent flirt? It means that it pays to connect with the able, attractive men and women you work with—and the best place to connect is at a meeting.

Think about it: Meetings are all about creating an easy atmosphere. Indeed, they cannot function optimally if those involved don't feel free to contribute, brainstorm, share their thoughts and interact. Flirting can make that happen! After all, what is this skill about if not forging links, encouraging cooperation, enhancing comfort and opening avenues of communication? Flirting, on the professional level, is the basis of being one of those "people persons" we've heard so much about! Why not schmooze and be schmoozed?

Connecting over a table can, of course, lead to deeper feelings. How can the office flirt use the meeting to improve a career and/or a romantic life? Here are a few thoughts:

♡   *Make a boffo first impression.* Hallelujah, angel—the halo effect is real! What is the "halo effect"? It is the tendency we mortals have to judge certain new acquaintances as capable, special and "worthy"—then provide ourselves with evidence that our first split-second judgment was accurate.

What should you do to make sure your first impression shines? According to the experts, you have ten to twenty seconds to imprint a favorable image. After that, you have approximately five minutes to affirm that impression in the mind of a new associate. How can you earn your wings? Arrive at the meeting early and make personal contact with as many of your colleagues as possible. This shows them that you feel they are "worth" your time. Speak clearly—this denotes confidence. And dress professionally. Everybody at the meeting may get lunch—but you've got to be a "winner" to make it to dinner.

♡ *Say my name.* We learn how sweet our names can sound when they are crooned to us as babies—and that warm and fuzzy association does not change as we age. Make it a point to memorize the moniker of anyone who captivates you at a meeting and use it several times in conversation. It's a simple technique, but it always scores points.

♡ *Say "eye."* In a business setting, eye contact always needs to be subtle. In a conference room, where every nuance of behavior is subject to the scrutiny of others, that is especially true. Shared glances, frequent gazes, winks, twinkles and other gestures may seem harmless to you but they can appear conspiratorial to any envious or threatened types at the table. Meet his or her glance once or twice, then give it a rest. Further eye contact may raise eyebrows—and professional suspicions.

♡ *Give a new relationship a fair shake.* A firm, assured handshake conveys the message, "I'm as solid as a rock. You can trust me." This type of shake assures you he's interested in the deal . . . but is he personally involved as well? Check for a cluster of nonverbal signs to be sure.

If you're on the receiving end of a bone-crushing clasp, you have just been given this message: "I can't bowl you over with my electrifying personality or daunting intelligence, so I'll overpower you with my grip." The crusher desperately wants to impress you but his low self-esteem may be more than you can handle.

As for the stiff, postured shake, it communicates the following message: "I'll meet you, but I won't meet you halfway."

You'll find a more flexible partner if you look for someone who's leaning in your direction.

If you want to send a message of interest to a certain someone without seeming obvious or unprofessional, try what I call a "flirting handshake." Grasp your acquaintance's hand; hold the handshake a moment longer than necessary, and make eye contact (smiling eyes, please!). Or, if you really want to shake up the encounter, use a hand-over-hand clasp. Countless men have told me that when a woman offers her hand, then covers the grip with her other hand or strokes it lightly, it makes them feel important, enticed and especially well liked. It's a clever way to signal your feelings without telegraphing them to the entire room.

♡ *Join the team.* Is she looking for volunteers to help with that new project she's working on? Is he looking for out-of-the-box-thinkers to brainstorm the launch of that product? Put yourself on that attractive person's team! You'll get a chance to reveal yourself at your creative, cooperative best—and, who knows? It could get you a promotion, too!

♡ *Follow up.* The meeting may have ended, but the flirting should not! A follow-up phone call or post-powwow e-mail not only reiterates what went on at the conference, it reestablishes your link with that hardworking coworker! To move the relationship forward, loosen your buttoned-down professional demeanor a little bit. Make the tone of your communication friendly and collegial rather than distant and professional.

Of course, it wouldn't do to send a love letter—or even a like letter. Nevertheless, there are many acceptable ways to confess your admiration. Many, many personal relationships have begun with professional compliments. So, if it's appropriate, please do congratulate that attractive colleague on a job well done. And if your joint project is a team or departmental effort, remember to copy everyone from the brass to the mailroom sorters. You'll make the object of your flirtation look good to his coworkers—and that will make you look good to him.

♡ *If it's an ongoing project, you might also suggest getting together for lunch once a month "to make sure everybody's on the same page."* (You might fill a few pages in your date book while you're at it.) And don't worry about having to invite the whole gang. Use the tips for flirting in a group setting you'll find in week 17, and you'll be in business.

♡ *Make the most of joint contacts.* Business may be global but the corporate world can seem like a very small, inbred circle. If you've been outstanding in your field for some time, you may have friends and colleagues in common with the man or woman who interests you. Make the most of them! Mention the connection in passing. This will make you seem more familiar to a new friend, even if you barely know each other. You might also use the connection to move your professional liaison into the personal sphere. Very often, just seeing someone in street clothes and out from behind their desk can shine a new light on their image. Do what you can to turn it on!

♡ *As the relationship deepens . . . be respectful of your own position— and his/hers.* Don't drag your colleague into any of your workplace dramas. Don't use him or her as a sounding board for your gripes, complaints or vendettas. This relationship will work as long as it works for everyone: you, your friend and your employer. So keep it positive. Edit the interdepartmental information you share. Separate business and pleasure. A deepening, developing relationship has its own risks; there's no need to jeopardize anyone's income. Remember: Flirting is always a playful, affirmative pastime; being with an affable, upbeat flirt like you should never seem like work!

Lose Love and Like It

I was having a chat about lost loves with a pair of thirty-ish women, Barbara and Sindee, before my workshop. Barbara asked me what a person could do to get over the loss of a long-time boyfriend. I told her that sometimes losing a love is the best thing that could possibly happen to you.

"It is very hard at first, but when you are able to think about the relationship in a realistic way, you'll see that it was wrong for you or incomplete in some way. When you realize that, it's easier to move on."

"Oh, so every relationship is somehow bad? Every boyfriend is at his best when he's gone?" Barbara countered with an annoyed look. "That's ridiculous."

I smiled. "What I'm saying is that the pain is only temporary. Once you are free of the relationship and the negative emotions, you are better off."

Now Sindee was indignant. "How can you say that? My ex was the best thing that ever happened to me, and now he is gone! Tell her, Barbara!"

Barbara looked at me, as if for guidance. I began to feel that I was defending myself against a tag team with an agenda I wasn't privy to. As for Sindee, she was on a roll, and there was nothing anyone could do to cut her short.

"Honestly, Susan, how can you say breaking up was for the best? You don't even know me! And you certainly didn't know Hal."

"Sindee," I said gently. "Let me talk with you privately after the workshop." By now, the other workshop participants were beginning to take their seats. Meanwhile, Sindee was fighting back the tears. It was not the ideal way to kick off a talk on a subject as fun as flirting.

"I don't want to trivialize your relationship, Sindee, and I am truly sorry for your loss. I know it hurts. But it has been my experience that if you lose love, it was probably not yours to begin with. It wasn't right for you even if, right now, it seems like it was." I tried to make eye contact with Sindee but she stared resolutely at the floor. She didn't want to let me—or my message—in. I tried to draw her out. "How long were you and your boyfriend together?" I asked gently.

"Eleven months. We would have had our one-year anniversary if we had stayed together another two weeks." The tears welled up in Sindee's eyes. "But you don't know anything about us! We were so right for each other. He was smart . . . a lawyer . . . We were together constantly! He took me to the Bahamas for our six-month anniversary! I felt so secure with him. He even reminded me of my father."

Now Sindee was openly sobbing. Barbara walked her slowly to the back of the room as the last of the workshop participants straggled in. It was time for me to begin the class.

I started the workshop in the usual way. I smiled at the crowd and said, "I'm a flirt and proud of it. What does the word 'flirt' mean to you?" but my words fell on preoccupied ears. Sindee and Barbara were talking loudly. The other attendees were too busy trying to overhear their conversation to tune in on mine. I had no choice but to address the situation.

"Sindee, do you want to share this with the class? Maybe others feel the way you do." My question was direct but my tone was soft.

"Yes, I do," Sindee sniffled. "Barbara dragged me to this seminar. She thought it would help me get over my breakup with Hal. But I don't think I belong here. I don't want to flirt. I don't want anyone else. I want my boyfriend back."

"Maybe what Barbara was trying to show you was that being

out with people and communicating with others can help," I re-minded Sindee, "especially if you feel a little lost and lonely."

Sindee brushed away her tears and blew her nose. I looked around the room. It seemed to me that there were a few other people here who might be feeling a little lost and lonely as well . . . my clients! This was a seminar on flirting, after all. Most of them were here to attract the love of their lives. Even Sindee, who had allowed herself to be "dragged" to my talk by Barbara, was here for the right reasons: to meet someone new and per-haps forget someone whose memory had overstayed its welcome.

The class was obviously distracted by what was taking place. I decided to divert the discussion from the subject of flirting and address the issue at hand.

"How many of us here have had broken relationships and have felt it was the end of the world?" Three quarters of the at-tendees raised their hands.

"How many have felt that the end of a relationship is so painful that it makes us feel awful, hopeless, inadequate, alone, desperate, lost and lonely?" The hands flew up, higher than before. I wasn't surprised. Who among us has been spared that experience?

Now I had their attention. "Part of being a good flirt means identifying the myths that keep us from relating to others. Some of those myths have to do with rejection. Maybe tonight we will focus on those myths—and how, by changing our be-liefs, we can keep life's disappointments out of our heads . . . and our social interactions."

Barbara spoke up. "Sounds good to me! Sindee can't spend her life grieving! She cries every night! She never wants to go out anymore . . . not to dinner, not to the movies. And the worst part is, he was no good for her anyway! All of her friends told her that, but somehow, she thought he was perfect. And all the time he was a garden-variety creep!"

"How can you say that?" Sindee was visibly peeved at her best friend.

"Susan was talking about myths," Barbara said. "I think your relationship with Hal was a myth. It wasn't real! It was a story you created and bought into."

"I think romance in general is a myth," offered William, a man in the front of the class.

I nodded. "I'm afraid you're right, William."

Romantic love is a myth and the plot goes something like this: He sees her across a crowded room and he is smitten. She chats a little and somehow, he feels he knows her. He helps her on with her coat and she attributes to him all the kindness, gentleness and thoughtfulness only an ideal lover can possess.

Of course, we don't construct these castles in the clouds by ourselves. We get plenty of help. Hollywood serves up a brand of romantic love that's as lite and fluffy as popcorn—and we ingest it compulsively. Magazines and book jackets reassure us that love can be forever once we fork over the purchase price on the cover. Even the songs we unconsciously hum as we go about our mundane tasks reinforce the importance and magic of love. Heck, Jerome Kerns wrote songs that guaranteed it:

"I Can't Help Loving That Man of Mine"

(Is that a good thing?)

"So in Love with You Am I"

(This week . . .)

"All the Things You Are"

That one always makes me smile. All the things you are? Even the lousy things? Why do those so rarely count?

We spend a good deal of time with the men and women in our lives. Sometimes we share a passion, a toothbrush, a life or a child. Yet, when this relationship composed of two imperfect people suddenly goes awry, when it reveals itself as something less than ideal, it somehow takes us entirely by surprise. So it was with Sindee. As it turned out, the breakup between her and Hal came about not because of some unfortunate misunderstanding, but because he was cheating on her! He went to a reunion, reconnected with a former sweetheart and poof, he was gone. Unfortunately, the mythology Sindee had created about Hal, and love, lingered on. And what makes me so sure it was a myth that Sindee was clinging to? Because no right-minded individual would mourn the loss of a duplicitous louse! Sindee wasn't lonely without Hal. Not really. She never really had him in the first place. But she did have her dreams, until Hal proved them to be as empty as his promises.

What are some myths we commonly hold about love? I asked the men and women in my workshop to suggest a few. We ended up filling a white board! Here is a sample:

- ♥ I am nothing without love.
- ♥ A person cannot live without love.
- ♥ People in love have an innate understanding of each other.
- ♥ There is only one soul mate who is perfectly right for you.
- ♥ True love lasts forever.
- ♥ Being in love makes you a better person than you otherwise would be.
- ♥ If you lose your one true love, you will never be happy.

Listed as they were on the white board, it was easy for the group to see the fallacy of some of these beliefs. However, discerning the truth is not always so simple. The myths we live with are repeated to us over and over again, by our parents, our peers, the media. Then, one day, we have memorized the myths like a script, and that's when we begin to play them out.

According to Dr. Albert Ellis, president of the Institute for Rational-Emotive Therapy, myths are irrational thoughts. They are the comfortable untruths we create to keep us from the temporarily uncomfortable effects of living honestly. When we undergo a trauma, like a breakup, we wrap our irrational thoughts around us like armor. "He may be gone . . . but he'll be back!" "She said it's over . . . true love lasts forever! I'll show her!" Even when they aren't particularly comforting in themselves ("I am nothing without love!"), our irrational thoughts comfort us. Lovers may leave, but our myths never change. On this we can rely.

Every one of us has loved and lost. It takes time to recover. Some are consumed by romantic grief while others gradually begin to view these upheavals as opportunities to change their lives for the better. How do they manage to swing the latter? By rewriting the script, debunking the myths and banishing the irrational beliefs that keep them from healing.

You can lose love and like it! Start this week with these simple strategies:

♡ *Get rational about myths.* Without love, I'm nothing. One is the loneliest number. Love is blind. These aphorisms sound right . . . they must be right! Right? Wrong! How do I know? Because without love, I'm still hot stuff. Numbers are never lonely because they can multiply! And believing that love is blind is just dumb! So isn't it time you gave your irrational beliefs a reality check?

Research has shown that, above all, it's what you think that determines how you feel. And the way you feel—about yourself, your worth, your prospects—determines your potential for success as a flirt.

As Shakespeare said, "There is nothing either good or bad, but thinking makes it so." This week, make a list of the irrational beliefs about life and love that may be keeping you stuck in a hopeless relationship or a social holding pattern. Take a good, hard look. Then jot a rational belief next to the obsolete, irrational one. This list will serve as a reminder that by changing your thinking, you are changing your life. Best of all, it will have you feeling better about losing love (is love really what you lost after all?) and moving on!

Your list should look something like this:

Irrational Belief	Rational Belief
I am nothing without love.	Single or attached, I'm quite something! I'm a strong, resilient person, a trusted friend, and I'm a heck of a storyteller at the local pub, too.
I cannot live without love.	Many people live quite well until they find another love. Ask Donald Trump.
People in love have an innate understanding of one another.	That must be why I hear so many couples arguing in restaurants.
There is only one soul mate who is perfectly right for me.	There are any number of people who are "right" for me. All I have to do is find one! I think I'll start right now.
True love lasts forever.	True love lasts as long as it lasts.
Being in love makes me a better person than I otherwise would be.	Sometimes being in love made me behave like an idiot!
If you lose your one true love, you will never be happy.	My love is gone. That means I can start dancing/listening to punk music/going to museums, and all those other activities he/she never liked.

(Hint: Having trouble zeroing in on your irrational beliefs? Take a look at the maxims your parents lived by. They don't just model irrational beliefs—they install them!)

Write an epitaph to your lost love. We have wonderful, memorable rituals for falling in love but few for falling out. Writing an epitaph to your lost love is a great addendum to the exercise above because it enables you to take a written inventory of a former flame's less-than-lovely characteristics and lay them to rest forever.

The epitaph Sindee wrote for Hal went something like this:

> Here lies Hal. At first, he seemed like a catch—smart, funny, an attorney's income—but then he seemed like an illness I caught. He didn't like my friends. He didn't like my family. And, judging by the cheating, he never really liked himself, or me, either.
>
> The nicest thing he did for me was to get his smelly sneakers out of my foyer.
>
> May he rest in pieces.

Writing things down makes them real. It also makes them easier to remember. Have fun with this exercise! Sindee did. A month later, she was free of her myths—and Hal—forever.

Week 49

Getting Over the One You Loved: More Practical Solutions

As the song goes: "Got along without him before I met him, gonna get along without him now." I used to chant that refrain in school or camp, after someone dumped me. Why do I take it so seriously when the one I loved doesn't love me, now that I'm an adult?

Though our hearts may be shattered, we're scared to death to love again, and are convinced that true love will never happen to us. This is just not true. Love will happen again.

We all heal in our own time and our own way, but I would like to give you some suggestions that may speed up the process:

♡ *Stay away from romantic novels, movies and songs that proclaim, "I can't live without you."* Instead, read murder mysteries or comedies, or tune into hip-hop or punk rock, but do not, I repeat, do not listen to love songs.

♡ *Women,* take a cooking class, cut a rug, join a museum, sign up for a lecture series, set sail, take fencing lessons, take a ride down the Amazon River, fish for salmon in Alaska or at least watch the Discovery channel. Start a book club; wine and dine with your best friend; buy those beautiful shoes you can't afford; have a makeover, a facial, a massage.

♡ *Men,* take a cooking class, cut a rug, join a museum, sign up for a lecture series, set sail, take a ride down the Amazon River, fish for salmon in Alaska or watch the Discovery channel. Buy *GQ*; go to Saks and let the salesman talk you into that too expensive suit, tie and thirty-dollar socks.

♡ *Pick one or two social events, like outdoor-bound adventure trips.* You may encounter the opposite sex. Who knows, he/she may have a similar break-up story, and you might soon be paddling the same canoe.

♡ *Make a list of pros and cons* about your ex and make sure the cons outweigh the pros.

♡ *Have a pity party* with all your best friends, *but* limit it to one hour. Then bring in a pepperoni pizza and "death by chocolate" dessert.

♡ *Talk about your past lover to your best friend,* but make sure he or she wears a stopwatch. Ask your friend to give you ten minutes before you move on to another subject.

♡ *I have one friend who was so distraught over the loss or her boyfriend that she watched football day and night to zone out.* Guess what? She became a devotee of the sport and an expert on Monday night football. She found lots of guys who wanted to score a touchdown with her.

♡ *Conversely, a guy I know tuned into the cooking channel.* He said it was soothing and he didn't have to think. As the weeks went on, he began to try out the recipes and met his new girlfriend in the cookbook section of Borders.

♡ *One of my favorite behavioral techniques to get over a lost love is the STOP technique.* Think of two fantasies that exclude your past love. Then, every time you think of him, scream "STOP," and replace those thoughts with one of your fantasies. Who wouldn't rather sip that piña colada in Barbados? Soon you'll be fantasizing more and despairing less.

♡ *Last but not least, every time you look at a whole loaf of bread, think of my "half a loaf" theory.* All relationships start out as a whole loaf. As they progress, if they are not working, the loaf gets cut in half. Then you have slices. Week after week, the slices get smaller and smaller until you are reaching for crumbs. Who wants a crummy relationship, anyway?

Ageism

It is a funny thing about age. When you're young you want to be older. When you're old you pine for the days of your youth. Single-digit persons want to reach their teens. Being a college coed is very exciting to a high-school senior. It seems those who are between twenty-five and thirty-five have the least complaints, and then comes the big 4-0. Some singles live in fear of their fortieth birthday. Others embrace forty and say they feel more comfortable in their skins than they did when they were young. Of course, some choose to remain thirty-nine for at least another five years.

The dating game is harder after fifty, but aren't we mature adults up for a challenge? We may not have as many options as our younger counterparts, but who cares that the odds are against us? We are secure and terrific people. Sure, the numbers dwindle and older women seem to lose their edge in our society, but one can be a magic number, not a lonely number. We only need one special person, and we can find that person if we are active and out there.

I urge you to disregard that ridiculous joke, circulated years ago, that went, "A woman over forty has as much chance of meeting a man as getting run over by a Mack truck." Nonsense. Many mature adults marry, date, have companions or live with a significant other.

The best news about getting older is that you know who you are, and are realistic about your companions. You know that the white knight doesn't exist, and that we all have our warts and imperfections. We aren't impressed by Personal ads that promise to sweep you away with "Beautiful sunsets, dining out and good times." Is there anyone who doesn't like those things? Who would place an ad promising stormy days, dinner at McDonald's and difficult times?

Let's look at another ad that was bombarded with answers: "I am an average nice guy. Not handsome, but presentable, looking for a regular woman who knows herself, can laugh at herself and is ready to love." Humble is refreshing. That is not to say we don't yearn for romance and enjoy that tingle of physical attraction, but we know there is more to life once the honeymoon period fades. In fact, the reality of getting older can be a blessing. Anxiety and unrealistic expectations fade, and we tend to throw out our superficial top-ten list in favor of the the five top traits we truly need.

That said, when we mature men and women venture out to seek a companion, we face a changed and unfamiliar world. Romance can seem confusing and elusive, but it need not be. Yes, the rules have changed, but you're likely to share the old cues with people your age.

What does it take to meet a companion, lover, mate in the later stages of life? Here are a few hints:

♡ Ask a friend to fix you up.

♡ Attend (and throw!) dinner parties regularly.

♡ Join a newly divorced, widowed, bereavement or compassionate-companion group.

♡ Ask your friends to tell you the ten most wonderful things about you, and write them down to help you rebuild your confidence and believe that romance is possible.

♡ Be open to new experiences. Be flexible and able to face rejection as part of life.

♡ Make a list of activities that you enjoy and that give you the opportunity to socialize with the opposite sex.

♡ Go back to school. The Institute for Retired Professionals exists in many cities, and there are many courses at adult-education centers that can open new possibilities.

♡ Take up a new hobby or sport. (Older people can ski in the over-seventy ski clubs for free.)

♡ Start your own club. I know a woman who started a classical music club for singles over forty. She started with ten people and, at last count, the membership had grown to forty-five.

♡ Attend your local religious organization regularly.

♡ Do volunteer work.

♡ Enlist dating services.

♡ Join a golf club. It's always a party on the eighteenth hole.

♡ Join book clubs and attend lectures at bookstores.

♡ Try bridge clubs, reunions and AARP conferences.

♡ Go on cruises. Or, when you travel, travel with Elderhostels with other adventurous singles.

♡ Log on to Classmates.com, friendfinder.com or senior friends.com

♡ This one embarrasses me, but it works. I call it "the casserole brigade." Read the obituaries and bring a casserole with condolences to the grieving widow or widower.

♡ If you're still looking for ways to increase your odds, look beyond your age group.

♡ As is true for all singles but even more vital for the mature set: Always keep hope alive and trust that love can happen to you!

Week 51

Now That You've Opened the Door, Be Sure to Close!

Rob met Sherry at the annual fund-raising auction at his young son's school. Sherry was eyeing the "Italian Cooking" basket. Rob stood nearby, transfixed by an item in the middle of the basket that was labeled simply "pasta fork." He peered into the cellophane-wrapped basket curiously.

"'Pasta fork'? What do you suppose that might be?" he muttered. Then he turned to Sherry and grinned. "I admit I'm not much of a cook but I have to say, I'm perplexed. What could possibly make one fork more suitable for pasta than another?"

Sherry leaned in to examine the package more closely. "Actually, it looks like it might be battery operated," she observed. "See the compartment in the handle?" She turned to Rob and giggled. "Pretty strange, isn't it? My grandmother was Italian and a fabulous cook and I can tell you, you wouldn't find one of these gadgets in *her* kitchen!"

Now Sherry and Rob were really intrigued. They searched the package for clues, pressing their faces close to the cellophane.

"Aha—instructions!" Sherry cried, finally. "And now I am convinced that truth really is stranger than fiction. This pasta fork is battery operated so the tines can rotate." She stood upright and shot Rob a mischievous glance. "In other words, this fork doesn't just transport pasta to your mouth. It actually twirls it for you."

"Well, that's great if you're eating linguine but what if tortellini is on the menu?" Rob teased.

"It will twirl that, too. And penne. There's nothing like twirled penne!"

Sherry and Rob laughed and slipped a few of their raffle tickets into the pot for the prize. They joked a bit about which of them deserved to win it. ("I hope *you* win this." "No, no, I insist—this item should definitely go home with *you*.") Then they smiled at each other one last time and wandered off to browse the remaining displays.

As it turned out, neither Rob nor Sherry went home with the pasta basket that night. It went to an older woman who seemed as bewildered by the fork as Rob had been. But Rob did win something: a gift certificate for a home-cooked dinner for two, catered by one of the finest chefs in town. He scanned the room for Sherry. It would be wonderful to share the prize with her! But Sherry was nowhere to be found. She'd gone.

Rob went home sure he'd lost the biggest prize of the evening.

What happened here? Simple! They got scared. They connected, then went their separate ways, each hoping the other would take a risk and express interest.

It isn't easy letting someone know you better. As a fledgling flirt, you are paralyzed by the prospect of what seems to be a fifty-fifty chance of rejection. What you need to understand is that the rejection rate climbs to 100 percent when you let a promising prospect walk out the door.

Appealing singles are like tempting appetizers. You have got to make your move before they're gone, as I learned from experience just a few months ago.

I was asked to do a lecture at a resort in Boca Raton, Florida.

These are always wonderful opportunities for me. First of all, this speaking engagement was getting me out of New York in the middle of the winter—and anything that enabled me to miss part of dirty-snow season was worth its weight in mukluks. But most of all, it was getting me into some conditions suitable for flirting—and that is always worth packing a bag for.

Now, I will admit that I am used to New York demographics. My talks in the city tend to draw an equal ratio of men and women. But in Florida, the ratio is skewed, and definitely not in favor of the female contingent. When I walked into the lecture room, I faced an audience made up of thirty-five women and three men.

That's when I saw him—a man with thick, beautiful, silvery hair (why is this hair color unavailable to women?) and startlingly bright-blue eyes. Despite the lousy male-to-female proportion, I thought I might get lucky. The man seemed to be drawn to me. He scanned the room, caught my eye and walked straight to the corner where I was chatting with a woman. Polite flirt that I am, I introduced him to my acquaintance. Big mistake! The next thing I knew, the woman I'd been chatting with was chatting up my prospect! By the time I took the stage, she had taken him to the far corner of the room, where she whispered and tittered into his ear for the next hour.

Things didn't improve after the talk, either. The woman had found her prize and now she had him cornered on the opposite side of the room and was warding off all comers. So when I caught his eye from across the room, I knew it was now or never. I took my shot. "Do you live in Florida year round?" I called across the room. "You have such healthy color!"

He smiled and replied that he was a "snowbird." He flew south for the winter only. The rest of the time he was based in New York.

Bingo! This dazzlingly handsome man might not be within my reach tonight but, eight months of the year, he was certainly within my grasp! I just needed to let him know where to find me. I reached into my pocket for a card. Pen, reading glasses, lecture notes . . . it couldn't be! Here I was, the paradigm of romantic readiness, and I was cardless! Across the room, I saw the woman moving toward the door, my prospect in tow. Once again, I had no choice but to shout across the room: "When you get to New York, call me! My business number is on my website! It was nice to meet you!"

The man smiled and nodded, but I knew he wouldn't call. The woman who snatched him up had all winter to work on him. Time was on her side. As for him searching out my website, I suspected there was little chance of that. Older men can be as intimidated by professional women as they are leery of computers. I missed a fabulous opportunity. All I could do was give myself an "F" for the evening. I had failed to close.

Ending a flirting encounter with a proposition can seem like risky business to a fledgling flirt. But what are you risking, really? Isn't flirting the art of relating without serious intent? If you expect nothing from an encounter and get nothing, you've lost nothing! And if your respectful come-on wins you a positive come-back, you have everything to gain!

Now for a few "closing thoughts."

Closing is not the same as ending. In fact, a properly "closed" flirtation opens the door for further social intercourse . . . and how can that be a bad thing? Unsure what to say when you've got to go but want to leave a good impression behind? Here are some great ways to say "see you later" rather than "good-bye":

♡ "I love running/walking/Rollerblading, too, but I've gotten bored with my old route. Where do you go? Would you mind showing me?"

♡ "Your ideas on _____ were so fascinating. I'd love to hear more. Would you mind if we exchanged cards?"

♡ "Thanks for the laugh! I needed that! I'd love to return the favor."

♡ "I've got to be going, but I'd love to continue this conversation another time. Are you free for a quick lunch? Is Thursday good for you?"

♡ "What an interesting ammonite you have set in your necklace! Have you seen the fossil exhibit at the Museum of Natural History? I was thinking of going on Saturday and would love some company!"

♡ "If you really want to learn how pasta should be eaten, maybe you'd like to meet for dinner at an authentic Sicilian restaurant I know. I'll bring a bottle of red. You bring the pasta fork!"

Week 52   Your Story

I hope the stories in this book have given you ideas and inspiration. I would love to hear your story. E-mail it to SRabin7128@aol.com and title it "Lucky in Love," so it will make it through the spam protector, or send it snail mail to P.O. Box 37, New York, New York 10128.

Good Luck and Happy Flirting!

Susan